Between Europe and the Mediterranean

Between Europe and the Mediterranean

The Challenges and the Fears

Edited by

Thierry Fabre
University of Provence, Aix-Marseille 1, France

and

Paul Sant-Cassia
Reader in the Department of Anthropology
University of Durham, UK

First published 2007 by
PALGRAVE MACMILLAN
Houndmills, Basingstoke, Hampshire RG21 6XS and
175 Fifth Avenue, New York, N.Y. 10010
Companies and representatives throughout the world

PALGRAVE MACMILLAN is the global academic imprint of the Palgrave
Macmillan division of St. Martin's Press, LLC and of Palgrave Macmillan Ltd.
Macmillan® is a registered trademark in the United States, United Kingdom
and other countries. Palgrave is a registered trademark in the European
Union and other countries.

ISBN-13: 978–0–230–00223–4   hardback
ISBN-10: 0–230–00223–4   hardback

This book is printed on paper suitable for recycling and made from fully
managed and sustained forest sources.

A catalogue record for this book is available from the British Library.

Library of Congress Cataloging-in-Publication Data

Between Europe and the Mediterranean : the challenges and the fears /
    edited by Thierry Fabre and Paul Sant-Cassia.
        p. cm.
    Includes bibliographical references and index.
    ISBN 0-230-00223-4 (cloth)
        1. Europe—Emigration and immigration.   2. Europe—Relations—
Mediterranean Region.   3. Mediterranean Region—Relations—Europe.
I. Sant Cassia, Paul.   II. Fabre, Thierry.

JV7590.B48 2007

304.8'401822—dc22

                                                                2006049432

10   9   8   7   6   5   4   3   2   1
16   15   14   13   12   11   10   9   8   7

Printed and bound in Great Britain by
Antony Rowe Ltd, Chippenham and Eastbourne

Contents

List of Figures   vii

List of Tables   viii

Preface   ix

Notes on Contributors   x

Introduction: Between Europe and the Mediterranean: the
     Challenges and the Fears   1
     Thierry Fabre and Paul Sant-Cassia

Part I   The Challenges of Demography and Migration   9

1   Demographic Transition in Europe and Around the
     Mediterranean   11
     Chris Wilson

2   Does Europe Need New Immigration?   28
     Catherine Wihtol de Wenden

3   Putting Asylum to the Test: Between Immigration Policy
     and Co-Development   41
     Sylvie Mazzella

4   The Mediterranean Divide and its Echo in the Sahara:
     New Migratory Routes and New Barriers on the Path to
     the Mediterranean   51
     Ali Bensaad

Part II   The Challenges of Identities and Cultures   71

5   Identity, Nationalism and Anthropologists   73
     Maria Couroucli

6   Altering the Perspective   88
     Dionigi Albera

7   Identity Crises and Value Conflicts   113
     Abdou Filali-Ansary

  8 The Face of the Foreigner: Reflections on the Case of
    Lebanon's Palestinians   124
    Daniel Meier

Part III   Political Challenges   135

  9 Turkish Conservatism and the Idea of Europe   137
    Hakan Yilmaz

 10 Europe in the Mirror of the Mediterranean   162
    Kalypso Nicolaïdis and Dimitri Nicolaïdis

Part IV   Geopolitical Fears and Institutional Responses   195

 11 Europe, America and the 'Greater' Middle East   197
    Martyn Bond

 12 Expansion towards the South: an Alternative Scenario
    for a Partnership in Crisis   207
    Jean-Robert Henry

 13 The Euro-Mediterranean Partnership: Reformulating
    a Process   219
    Thierry Fabre

Index   226

List of Figures

1. Total fertility rate in EU-25 and Med-10 countries — 14
2. Age-sex structure of Med-10 countries, 2004 — 16
3. Age-sex structure for EU-25, 2004 — 17
4. Age-sex structure of EU-25 (shaded) & Med-10, 2004 — 18
5. Age-sex structure of Northern-7 countries, 2004 — 19
6. Age-sex structure of Southern-4 countries, 2004 — 19
7. Age-sex structure of Med-10, 2030 — 24
8. Age-sex structure of EU-25, 2030 — 24
9. Age-sex structure of EU-25 (shaded) & Med-10, 2030 — 25
10. Dilemmas and tensions in the EMP — 167

List of Tables

9.1   Indicators of the Tanzimat syndrome in Turkish public opinion: public attitudes towards basic rights and freedoms   148

9.2   Indicators of the Tanzimat syndrome in Turkish public opinion: public attitudes towards basic rights and freedoms   148

9.3   Indicators of the Sèvres syndrome in Turkish public opinion: Europe's historical intentions towards Turkey   153

9.4   Indicators of the Sèvres syndrome in Turkish public opinion: public beliefs on the Crusades, capitulations and the Sèvres Treaty   154

9.5   Indicators of the Sèvres syndrome in Turkish public opinion: public attitudes towards the idea of 'Westernisation without the West'   154

Preface

This edited volume has emerged out of a collaborative interdisciplinary research network on the Mediterranean region, supported by the 5th Framework Programme of the EU until 2005. The Research Network, called REMSH, was ably coordinated by the Maison Méditerranéenne des Sciences de l'Homme (MMSH) at the University of Aix-Marseilles. A series of international specifically focused seminars were held in Alicante, Durham and Genoa, on various aspects of Mediterranean societies and cultures, grouping together anthropologists, historians, political scientists, policy-makers, and specialists on the Middle East and North Africa, amongst others. The various essays are now published in English as part of a series entitled 'Mediterranean Studies'. The aim of this series will be to provide original, well-edited material of high quality that will act as a catalyst for further research within a sound framework of academic excellence.

The editors would like to thank the following who generously assisted in the preparation of this volume for publication: Mrs P. Craven, Dr D. Middleton, Mrs J. Starkey and Dr R. A. Wilson. They would also like to thank Penny Allen for translating a number of the contributions from the original French.

Notes on Contributors

Dionigi Albera is an anthropologist affiliated to the CNRS (Idemec, MMSH, Aix-en-Provence). His most recent work is *La Méditerranée des anthropologues: fractures, filiations, contiguïtés* (edited with Mohamed Tozy), Paris, Maisonneuve et Larosse 2005.

Ali Bensaad is a geographer and Maître de Conférence at the University of Provence, Aix-Marseille 1.

Martyn Bond's career has spanned academia, journalism and the European civil service. Among his various roles, he was Director of the UK Office of the European Parliament, and Director of the Federal Trust for Education and Research. He is also visiting professor of European Politics and Policy at Royal Holloway, London.

Maria Couroucli is an anthropologist and Chargée de recherche, CNRS (University of Paris X, Nanterre). She has worked extensively on Greece and the Greek world.

Thierry Fabre is a researcher, essayist, and a Mediterranean specialist, based at the Maison Méditerranéenne des Sciences de l'Homme, University of Provence, Aix-Marseille 1. He is the author of *Le Noir et le Bleu* (Librio, 1998), *Traversées* (Actes Sud, 2001, Grand Prix littéraire de Provence) and *Les Représentations de la Méditerranée* (Maisonneuve et Larosse, 2000) and other works.

Abdou Filali-Ansary is Director of the King Abdulaziz al-Saoud Foundation for Islamic Studies and Human Sciences in Casablanca, Morocco, and editor of the journal *Prologues*.

Jean-Robert Henry is Director of Research at the CNRS, IREMAM-Aix-en-Provence.

Sylvie Mazzella is Charge de Recherche in Sociology at the CNRS (Institut de Recherche sur le Maghreb Contemporain, Tunis). Her most recent work focuses on the right of asylum in France and the recent immigration of sub-Saharan graduates to North Africa.

Daniel Meier is a sociologist and teaches at the Graduate Institute of Development Studies (Geneva). He has conducted extensive research in Lebanon.

Dimitri Nicolaïdis is a researcher on the European Union.

Kalypso Nicolaïdis is University Lecturer in International Relations, European Studies Centre, University of Oxford, UK. She is a specialist on the EU.

Paul Sant-Cassia is Reader in Anthropology at the University of Durham, UK. His most recent work is *Bodies of Evidence. Burial, Memory and the Recovery of Missing Persons in Cyprus* (Oxford: Berghahn, 2005).

Catherine Wihtol de Wenden is a sociologist and Director of Research at the CNRS (CERI), Paris.

Chris Wilson is a demographer at the International Institute for Applied Systems Analysis (IIASA), Austria.

Hakan Yilmaz is Associate Professor at the Department of Political Science and International Relations, Bogazici University, Istanbul. His most recent work has concentrated on the attitudes of the Turkish elites and masses towards Europe and the European Union.

Introduction: Between Europe and the Mediterranean: the Challenges and the Fears

Thierry Fabre and Paul Sant-Cassia

The world after 11 September 2001 in New York and 11 March 2005 in Madrid appears to have been profoundly transformed. A climate of war, tension, menace and fear has progressively insinuated itself into the public consciousness. This atmosphere contrasts singularly with the climate of confidence, peace and hope for a new international order that emerged after the fall of the Berlin Wall in 1989. Does this change in the international climate signify a corresponding change of era? What exactly is happening before our very eyes? It is sometimes difficult to understand the world around us.

We witness differences in reactions between the United States after 11 September 2001, which chose to intervene militarily in Afghanistan and in Iraq, and the reactions of Spain, which on the contrary chose to recall its troops from Iraq and to promote, in line with the United Nations, an initiative based on an 'Alliance of Civilisations', as witness to another type of relationship with the rest of the world. On the one side is an American perspective: fear, menace, insecurity, and war against terrorism; and on the other is that of Spain with a completely different experience of, and relation to, internal violence which has led it to respond differently to military and security issues.

This book explores these issues by taking its inspiration from the position adopted by Spain, that is to say, a somewhat different approach to one which assumes a 'clash of civilizations'. It aims to identify the principal challenges that characterise the relations between Europe and the Mediterranean. The Mediterranean is an important region of the world, in the process of development in its own right, but whose political evolution the United States, ardent defenders of a 'Greater Middle East', would, it sometimes appears, prefer not to see developing.

Initiated at a meeting that was held in Durham in July 2004 that gathered together a number of specialists on the Mediterranean region, this book explores broad perspectives and enables us to form a more precise and effective understanding of the challenges and fears that can be perceived on the horizon of relationships between Europe and the Mediterranean.

The challenges of demography and migration, analysed in Chapter 1, are without doubt those that disturb societies the most and can readily and easily mobilise popular and sometimes graceless public debate. It is necessary to look at the issues of demography and migration with some dispassion and precision to learn about European demographic scenarios in the next twenty years. This is indeed the route taken by the demographer Chris Wilson who presents us, by means of some very clear tables, flow diagrams and graphs, with some very critical choices. His aim is to indicate broad tendencies, notably taking as his starting point a comparative analysis of the age population pyramids of the populations of the EU, and those of the ten countries on the southern and eastern littorals of the Mediterranean. His conclusions are straightforward, if bracing: by the middle of the twenty-first century Europe will exhibit an inverted age pyramid in the form of a 'super ageing' population. Political leaders throughout Europe have already begun addressing one aspect of this worrying problem in terms of the pensions and social security deficits, often proposing scenarios that do little to allay popular public disquiet. The navigation of Europe is set between the Scylla of advanced retirement ages together with the privatisation of pensions (a profoundly unappealing personal prospect to many), and the Charybidis of a popular (but generalised and transcendable) disquiet at illegal migration, often whipped up by xenophobic extremist politicians particularly appealing to those social strata threatened by increasing economic globalisation. Wilson's conclusions are clear: there is no doubt that Europe needs to address the structural problem of its ageing population, quite irrespective of the challenges posed by migration: 'demographic forces strongly suggest that migratory movements towards the twenty-five countries of the EU will constitute an important and growing phenomenon. Given our shared history and geography, it appears certain that a considerable proportion of these migrants will be provided by the ten Mediterranean countries that have association agreements with the EU. This migration will have a massive impact on the development and cooperation of the EU and will profoundly effect relationships between Europe and the Mediterranean.'

Demographic data cannot be gainsaid. They reveal the differences between populations on one side of the Mediterranean and the other. Under these conditions, Catherine Wihtol de Wenden (Chapter 2), does not hesitate to question European policies 'which concentrate on the controlling of frontiers and the fight against illegal immigration, rather than responding to the more fundamental issue which is whether Europe needs to open its frontiers to immigration'. Posing the question in terms of migration *needs* from a European perspective (even if instrumentally posed), rather than in terms of increasingly dysfunctional national state ideologies of closure, control and legal taxonomies of 'the other', profoundly changes our analytical starting point. At the very least, it can help contribute towards modifying actual perceptions of migration that are often negative. And it points to the necessity for policy-makers to contemplate more seriously the various available avenues to address Europe's 'population melt-down' and its implications for taxation burdens. The original vision of a European 'social model' as distinct from a US 'market model' is probably not realisable without a radical rethinking of the ideological categories inherited from the nation-state that hold that the political unit and cultural unit should be identical. Such perceptions continue to infect and hold back not just European integration and cooperation at the supranational (political) level, but also can tend to subvert the very efforts by politicians and policy-makers to tackle these demographic-economic conundrums when the spectre of social disharmony is raised either for sub-national political strategies, or is enmeshed in national political debates. It is paradoxical that the route towards materially sustaining the European social model may only be achievable by an *openness* to immigration, a feature that characterised much of the US's history, now repudiated in its homeland in the name of 'national security'. It is clear that the relationship between *immigration* and (social) *imagination* needs to be radically reconfigured in order to think through, and realise, future scenarios. If the European social imagination is partly, but not exclusively, given a lead by politics, and politics is the art of the possible, perhaps the possible may be reconfigured.

We are, however, rather distant from realising this scenario, especially with regard to the issue of asylum rights in Europe, a topic investigated by Sylvie Mazzella (Chapter 3). She underlines how 'asylum policies can be seen as a sign of the evolving (and at times logically inconsistent) relationship between the North and the South. Whilst the southern countries of the Mediterranean are clearly considered as unequal economic partners of the North, they are also (paradoxically) considered fully equal (and now conveniently autonomous) political partners, to a large extent accountable for the emigrants who depart from their shores.' Europe also demands that its southern partners exercise increasingly repressive controls on the migrant, transient, populations that regularly cross their territories, and progressively install themselves there.

As Ali Bensaad points out in Chapter 4, what is actually happening is that we are beginning to witness the displacement of the southern Europe frontier as far as the Sahara. The geography of human relationships between the shores of the Mediterranean is in effect leading to profound transformations: 'If the Mediterranean can be seen as a fault line between Europe and its southern shores, the Sahara is beginning to function as a displaced fracture, a replica of that fault line, reflected in the interior of southern Europe itself. In effect, the exacerbation of tensions along the Mediterranean fault line generates a further transposed fracture line along the Sahara.' A series of complex and extremely preoccupying social developments have been developing along the Saharan frontier, which Europe has 'delegated' to its southern Maghrebi 'partners' to 'resolve', including the control and repression of migrants from (sub-Saharan) Africa. This has sometimes led to calls for the establishment of detention camps in the desert, which should at the very least call into question the notion of a 'democratic Europe'. Here is a challenge that has not yet become fully appreciated or addressed in European capitals. We augue that this book can contribute towards highlighting such a challenge.

Challenges to culture and identity, studied in the Part II of this volume, have loomed large in contemporary international relations. But they are often approached emotionally and apprehended largely through the media which can vitiate our understanding. A number of chapters by anthropologists in this volume enable us to adopt a more dispassionate and nuanced understanding of the challenges facing the relationship between Europe and the Mediterranean. In the case of nationalism, in particular starting from the Greek case, Maria Couroucli (Chapter 5) traces how certain nationalist-influenced suppositions evolved across time to bias even – at times – field research. The representations of 'the other' are never given, and it is important to establish a perspective from a certain distance to contextualise them, with the aim of understanding how such representations are manufactured by different social actors.

Dionigi Albera (Chapter 6) proposes to 'alter the perspective' with reference to Islam, notably taking into account the immense body of literature that tends to stigmatise and essentialise Islam as a religion and as a threatening, 'terrorist-producing', culture. Dominant social explanations have represented Islam as the primary explanatory cause of difference. The time has come to overcome these culturalist perspectives and 'this uneasy discomfort experienced in proximity with Islam', as Claude Lévi-Strauss indicated (and who did not escape from formulating certain caricatures himself, like some other anthropologists). Other routes towards understanding can be pursued, whether from ' "a macro-analysis which obliges us to escape from an endemic eurocentrism", or from a perspective which "takes the local as its starting point and which aims to deny the presuppositions of homogeneity, of coherence, and of fixity which characterise the culturalist position" '. In other words, Albera invites us, shrewdly, to *dis-cover* Islam.

Taking his starting point from this suggestion, Abdou Filali Ansary (Chapter 7) explores 'the serpentine history of identities and value conflicts', proposing another reading of history, particularly departing from the humanist tradition in the Muslim world. This tradition, born in the 1920s was, 'it is necessary to remember, rapidly submerged by nationalist and fundamentalist movements, closely resembling absolutist socialism'. Could it be that an escape from the infernal coupling polarities of Islam/the West, or Islam/Modernity, might enable us re-engage with a socially informed humanist universalism that escapes from the pernicious effects of narrow, politically divisive culturalisms?

An even more acute case of dislocation and its attendant problems than Cyprus is the case of Palestinians in Lebanon. Daniel Meier (Chapter 8) explores the legal and political aspects of identity. Beginning with the 'figure of the stranger' he uses the example of Palestinians in Lebanon to try to understand how the 'Palestinian Brother' is relegated to the margins of society without effective rights. He suggests that by using this particular case study, interesting light can be shed on the position of strangers in Europe more generally. One anticipates further courageous attempts at analysis of reciprocal perspectives and views.

Political challenges to the relationships between Europe and the Mediterranean, analysed in the Part III, touch specifically on the cases of Turkey and the Maghreb. But rather than the habitual (and now well-rehearsed) reformulations of the positions of the members of the European Union towards Turkey, it seemed to us more interesting to invert perspectives and explore how Turks perceive Europe from the perspective of their beliefs and conservative attitudes. This is pursued by Hakan Yilmaz in Chapter 9. There is no doubt that the relation of Europe towards Turkey, and of Turkey towards Europe, poses major challenges for the future. 'The most optimistic scenario for resolving the ideological problems in (and of) Turkey as regards democracy and liberty would be the opening and the development of negotiations for membership in the European Union', asserts Yilmaz. 'If one were to take the most pessimistic scenario, an indefinite suspension or halting of negotiations would re-enforce conservative nationalism and isolationism.' Taking into account the current political crises in Europe, it would appear that this would rather be a pessimistic scenario that only an optimist would take.

Kalypso and Dimitri Nicolaïdis, in their in-depth analysis of 'Europe in the Mirror of the Mediterranean' (Chapter 10) aim to disentangle its political challenges. Beginning with a critical analysis of the Euro-Mediterranean partnership as a 'Eurocentric process', they attempt to envisage a regional Euro-Mediterranean, 'beyond civilisations', and one that goes beyond the supposed clash between Islam and the West. They note the need for a political agenda that is truly post-colonial for the idea of a EuroMed project to develop effectively. Significantly they note the need to put the Mediterranean back in the centre of the Euro-Mediterranean partnership, not as some hyphenated entity, and to discover a 'vocabulary of shared culture', along the lines suggested by the new Anna Lindh Foundation for dialogue between civilisations and cultures.

Geopolitical challenges call for a variety of institutional responses in accordance with the actors, like those analysed in Part IV on 'Geopolitical Fears and Institutional Responses'. The notable case of the United States, analysed here by Martyn Bond (Chapter 11), is built upon the notion of a 'Greater Middle East', a geopolitical framework and strategic representation that corresponds closely to their interests in the region. Europeans have to situate themselves for better or for worse within a framework that is not their own and they propose diverging definitions to that proposed by the United States.

Could a redefined Euro-Mediterranean partnership without its hyphenated implications offer a suitable answer? This is the implicit question posed by Jean-Robert Henry (Chapter 12) who asks whether enlargement towards the South could not be an alternative scenario for a partnership in crisis? He explores the possibilities of Europe's expansion towards the South to provide an alternative scenario for its management of a partnership in crisis. Rather than allowing himself to 'be imprisoned by the false new approach of neighbourliness, indicatively rhetorical of an unitary ethno-cultural view of Europe', it is important to build a genuinely human, political reality, because 'the societies on the other side of the Mediterranean, notably in the Maghreb, are present in our history and our debates (as in the case of veiling in France), and inhabit "our" simultaneous time'. Poetically using metaphors of the house, he sees the Maghreb as looking in through Europe's windows, at times participating in exchanges, but clearly disadvantaged as long as Europe's door remains closed. How long will Europe resist and at what cost?

Thierry Fabre reflects further on the concept of the Euro-Mediterranean partnership in Chapter 13. He notes that the partnership has long been viewed as characterised by dissymmetry and subordination. Ten years after its launch it could be considered to have reached an impasse. The Euro-Arab dialogue has been buried out of sight, and the Euro-Mediterranean partnership, contested both within and outside Europe, does not appear to be a suitable medium and instrument to enable us to understand, anticipate and meet the challenges posed by our times. A radical reinstrumentalisation is thus necessary because 'the greatest challenge facing our political generation is no longer to make a Europe *without* the Mediterranean, but *with* it'. Faced with reciprocal fears, that invariably re-enforce themselves through that mutual facing, would it not be wiser to rise to the challenges that are presented and to strive towards the creation of a common future, shared between Europe and the Mediterranean?

Part I
The Challenges of Demography and Migration

1
Demographic Transition in Europe and Around the Mediterranean

Chris Wilson

Introduction

Demographic trends underlie a great many economic and social processes. However, because populations tend to change relatively slowly, demography is often taken for granted and its impact under-appreciated. Rather like some slow geological process that is imperceptible in the short run, demographic change often has an ineluctable force, and ends up changing the whole social and economic landscape. When trying to understand the relationship between the European Union and its neighbours to the South and East of the Mediterranean, an understanding of the demographic forces at work is essential. In this chapter I will present an outline of the main demographic trends in Europe and the Mediterranean over the last half century, and will look forward to sketch the most likely developments for the coming decades. The EU and its neighbours do not only share the Mediterranean, we also share a common future and demographic trends will play a crucial role in determining the nature of that future.

For simplicity, I will mostly refer in this chapter to two geographically defined entities. One group is the 25 members of the European Union from 1 May 2004 (EU-25), which I shall also refer to as simply as Europe. The other is a group of ten countries running in an arc from Turkey to Morocco (Med-10). The latter set excludes Israel, since that country has a very distinctive demographic profile, clearly different from Europe's other Mediterranean neighbours.

Of all demographic phenomena, immigration attracts by far the most attention in the media, and is addressed in detail in other chapters. However, it is easy to overlook the fact that international migration, in fact, has been a rather modest factor when compared to fertility and mortality.

Over the last half century the net inflow of migrants from the rest of the world into the 25 countries that now comprise the EU has probably been between 10 and 15 million people. Over the same period, more than 300 million babies have been born in the EU-25. Even now, with net migration into Europe close to its historic high, and with fertility lower than ever before, the annual total of births in the EU is over four times the annual number of immigrants. The relative importance of migration may well increase in the future, but it is likely to remain a substantially smaller-scale process than fertility and mortality. In this chapter, therefore, I will mostly focus on trends in these more fundamental processes, and their role in determining the age structure. In doing so, I hope to provide a basis for seeing migration in its proper context.

Demographic transition and population growth

When demographers try to make sense of the complexities of the world around us, they make use of one of social science's great generalising models: the demographic transition. In association with many other aspects of modernisation, every population in the world undergoes a set of inter-connected changes that is termed the demographic transition. As Paul Demeny (1972) has succinctly put it, 'In traditional societies, fertility and mortality are high. In modern societies, fertility and mortality are low. In between there is the demographic transition.' As a description of long-run trends, the demographic transition can be seen to be a universally applicable generalisation. At some point in the past, every population had high fertility (mostly between four and six children per woman) and high mortality (life expectancy varied between 20 and 40 years). With the spread of modern medicine and public health, mortality has improved; as family planning and contraceptive use became the norm, fertility has fallen. Usually mortality fell first, with a delay before fertility decline. This difference in timing leads to substantial population growth before the two processes come back into balance. The process of transition began in the late eighteenth and nineteenth centuries in Europe and the neo-Europes overseas; it became a global phenomenon after World War Two. Today, more than half the world's people live in places where fertility is at or below the level needed for long-run intergenerational replacement (about 2.1 children per woman). Similarly, global life expectancy is approaching 70 years.

The differences in the timing and duration of the demographic transition have played the main role in determining the differences in population growth between Europe and the Med-10 countries. Europe's population grew substantially during the nineteenth and early twentieth centuries, so that by 1950 populations of European origin around the world accounted for a larger fraction of the global population than ever before. In contrast, population growth in North Africa and the Eastern Mediterranean was much more modest. In 1950 the total population of what are now the 25 members of the EU was 350 million, while the Med-10 countries had around 70 million inhabitants. Since 1950 the relative trends have reversed; Europe's population has grown only modestly, to 455 million today, whereas the population has increased enormously in the Med-10, to 250 million in 2004. Although there is inevitably a degree of uncertainty about the future, it is virtually certain that there will be substantial further population growth in the Med-10 countries, but little or no growth, or even a decline, in the population of the EU-25. By 2050 the United Nations forecasts that the two groups of countries will both have the same population: 400 million. The importance of this change in the relative sizes of the populations of the EU-25 and the Med-10 can scarcely be exaggerated. In 1950, when the EU-25's population was almost five times as large, few people (the world's best demographers included) could have imagined that 100 years later the Med-10 countries and Europe would have similar populations. Quite simply, the scale of population growth in the Med-10 since 1950, and its further growth in the decades ahead, are changing the whole basis of the trans-Mediterranean relationship. What has powered this fundamental change and why can we be virtually certain that the future will continue to see markedly different population growth in the two groups of countries? To answer these questions we must examine the main components of population change: fertility and mortality.

Fertility

There is one overwhelming reason for the different histories of population growth since 1950: fertility. As Figure 1 shows very clearly, fertility has throughout this period been much higher in the Med-10 than in the EU-25. Fertility in Europe over this period never reached as high as three children per woman, whilst in the Med-10 it was almost seven in the 1950s. It began to fall in the mid-1960s, but even today fertility is higher in the Med-10 than it was in Europe half a century ago. The measure of childbearing plotted in Figure 1, and which I will use throughout this chapter, is termed by demographers the total fertility rate (TFR). This is a measure that indicates how many children would be born on average to a cohort of women over their lifetime if current rates continued to apply.

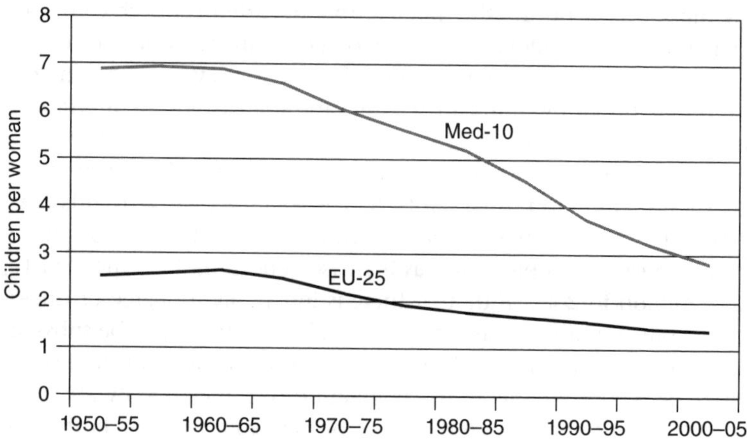

Figure 1:   Total fertility rate in EU-25 and Med-10 countries (children per woman)

In order to gain an intuitive sense of how fertility levels, defined in terms of children born per woman, translate into population growth it is convenient to make use of the concept of intergenerational replacement. A total fertility rate of 2.1 children per woman is conventionally regarded as indicating the replacement level. In order to ensure exact replacement, and ensure that each woman of one generation has precisely one daughter in the next, women must on average give birth to somewhat more than two children each. The sex ratio at birth is generally about 105 males to 100 females, and if all children born grew up to reach adult life, then 2.05 would be replacement level. However, even in the most favoured populations, there is still some infant and child mortality; specifying the level as 2.1 takes this mortality into account. Strictly speaking, a precise measure of replacement would use the exact mortality level and sex ratio at birth for each country to calculate replacement level. However, 2.1 is a convenient overall estimate.

Relating current fertility to this benchmark of 2.1 indicates how far above or below replacement fertility is. For example, in the EU-25 in 2003 the total fertility rate was 1.4. This implies that fertility is only about two-thirds of the level needed for the current generation of mothers to replace themselves. Fertility in Europe has been below the replacement level since the mid-1970s. In contrast, in the Med-10, during the 1950s the number of births was such that each woman was being replaced by more than three daughters. Since that time fertility has fallen substantially, and is in fact now probably below the replacement level in at least two countries: Lebanon and Tunisia, and possibly also in Turkey. However, all other countries in the region have fertility close to or above three children per woman, and taking the Med-10 as a whole, the TFR is 2.6, i.e. about 25 per cent more than needed for replacement. Fertility is still very high in Jordan and Syria (about four) and, especially, in Palestine (almost six). The detailed figures are given in Figure 1.

Assuming a continuation of the trends evident in Figure 1, it seems likely that fertility for the Med-10 as a whole will fall below replacement within the next ten years. Indeed, Figure 1, which is based on estimates made by the United Nations, may somewhat understate the speed of recent fertility decline. The UN's demographic experts have a track record of tending to overstate current fertility levels, especially for countries whose fertility is close to the replacement level. Thus, the apparent levelling off of the downward trend for the Med-10 since the mid-1990s might, in fact, be spurious, suggesting an earlier rendezvous with replacement level fertility.

Fertility trends in Europe present a very different picture. Figure 2 gives the total fertility rate over the last 50 years in three groups of European countries: a Northern-7 (France, UK, Netherlands, Sweden, Finland, Denmark and Ireland), an Eastern-8 (Poland, Hungary, the Czech Republic, Slovakia, Slovenia, Latvia, Lithuania and Estonia) and a Southern-4 (Italy, Spain, Portugal and Greece). Fertility in the 1950s and early 1960s was somewhat above the replacement level in all three regions, mostly between 2.5 and 3 children. For many European countries this was a marked increase on the values seen during the 1930s, when fertility fell close to or even below replacement. The increased fertility of the first twenty post-war years produced the famous 'baby boom', a phenomenon that peaked in most countries around 1965. The then Communist states of Eastern Europe, however, had a more immediate post-war baby boom, with fertility above three in the early-1950s. As is well known, the baby boom was followed by a 'baby bust', with fertility falling below replacement everywhere in Europe. However, the timing and extent of this recent fertility decline has differed substantially across Europe. Looking at the three groups of countries in Figure 2, fertility fell first in the Northern-7, but stabilised not far below replacement at around 1.7, a level it has held for the last quarter of a century. Fertility fell later in Southern Europe, but fell further, reaching as low as 1.2, and holding at roughly this level since 1990. The fall below two children per woman in Eastern Europe came only after the demise of Communism, but there too fertility has fallen to extremely low levels and is now virtually indistinguishable from that in Southern Europe. As we shall see below, these differences in the

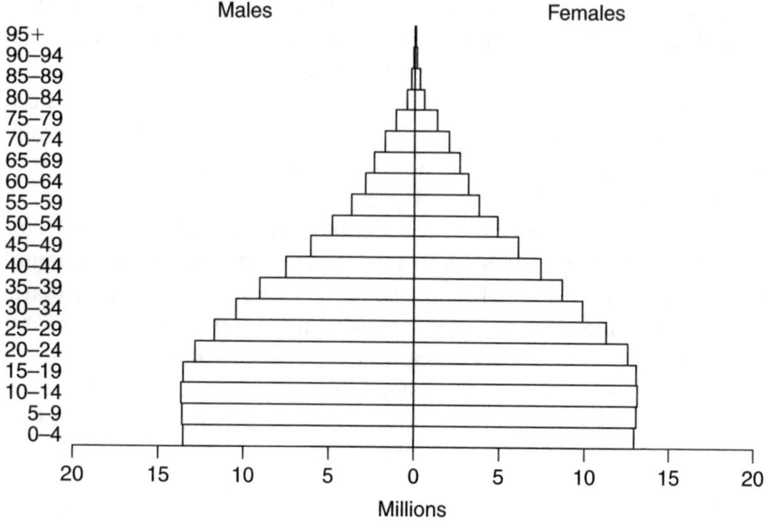

Figure 2:   Age-sex structure of Med-10 countries, 2004

timing and extent of fertility fall in the different parts of Europe have left their mark in very different age structures.

Mortality

Trends in mortality have, generally speaking, been more regular than those in fertility. Figure 3 shows that there has been a steady improvement in life expectancy in the EU-25 and rapid gains in the Med-10. The experience of the different Med-10 countries has been remarkably similar, and life expectancy has reached 70 years for the group as a whole. In the 1950s Lebanon held a clear health advantage, with a life expectancy of 56, compared with the 43–46 in the rest of the Med-10. Today this advantage has greatly diminished; life expectancy is 74 in Lebanon and 68–73 in the other nine countries. In Europe the principal contrast in the mortality trends has been an East–West division. Under Communism, life expectancy improved rapidly for the first 20 years after 1945, almost catching up with Western Europe. Whilst steady progress continued in Western Europe, life expectancy in the East stagnated after 1965; in the Soviet Union (including in the Baltic States) it actually worsened. By the late 1980s the Eastern-8 countries had life expectancy that was six years less than in the West. The gap was especially large for males. Since the early 1990s the eight post-Communist countries that joined the EU in May 2004 have

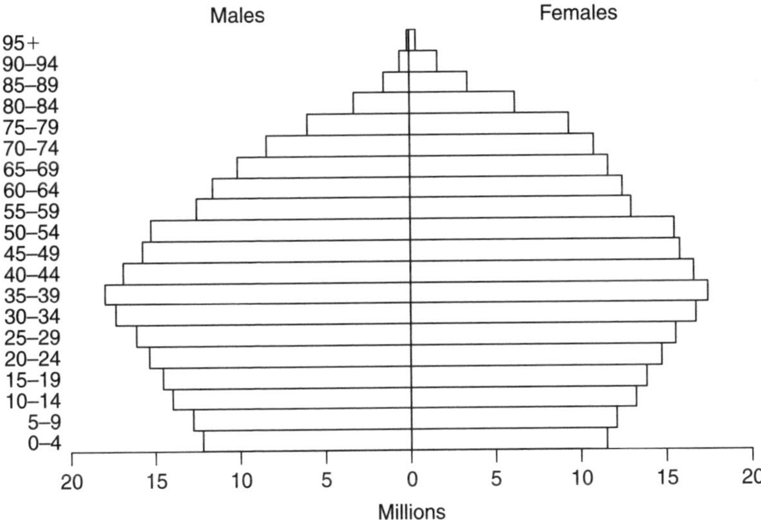

Figure 3:   Age-sex structure for EU-25, 2004

seen fairly rapid convergence towards the levels seen in the West, but there is still a gap of about four years in life expectancy. In this respect, trends in the Eastern-8 countries are, however, more promising than in Russia and the other post-Soviet states, where life expectancy fell further in the 1990s and has not yet recovered to its 1965 level.

Age structure

A country's past experience of mortality, migration and fertility is written into its age structure. Of these three processes, fertility is especially important. The high (if falling) fertility of the past 50 years in the Med-10 countries has given them all young age structures. In contrast, the lower and fluctuating fertility seen in Europe has left the EU-25 with a very different age profile. Demographers conventionally call their favourite graphs of age structure 'population pyramids', a pair of horizontal bar charts with the youngest ages at the bottom and the oldest at the top, and males and females on either side of the central axis. However, as is clear in Figures 2 and 3, neither the graph for the Med-10 nor that for the EU-25 looks very pyramidal. The high fertility seen in the Med-10 before the 1980s produced very rapid population growth. Above age 20, every older age group is clearly smaller than the cohort five years younger. Below

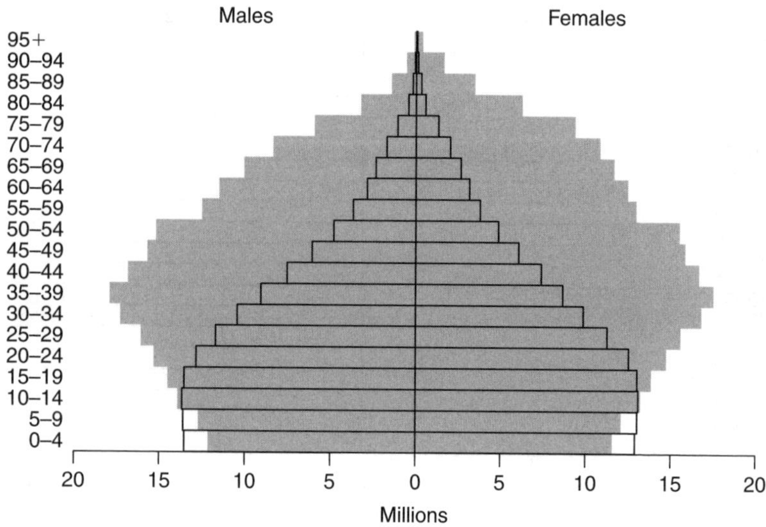

Figure 4:   Age-sex structure of EU-25 (shaded) & Med-10, 2004

age 20 the sides of the pyramid become flattened, indicating that since the mid-1980s, the number of births in each year has stabilised. Although not shown here, the equivalent pyramids for the Med-10 countries with lowest fertility, e.g. Tunisia, already have an 'under-cut' appearance, with the youngest birth cohorts actually smaller than those born ten or fifteen years ago. In contrast, the European age structure is shaped like a pentagon, with a peak in cohort size at about age 40 (the baby boom generation) and steadily declining numbers in each younger age group. In the mid-1960s almost 7 million babies were born each year in the EU-25; in 2003 it was less than 5 million. Figure 4 directly compares the EU-25 and Med-10 age structures. There are more than twice as many people in the EU as in the Med-10, but over the last ten years more babies have been born in the Med-10, and the youngest two age groups are larger there.

The different histories of fertility in the different regions of Europe are also reflected in their age structures. Figures 5 and 6 show the current pyramids for the Northern-7 and Southern-4, as specified in the fertility section. The more radical nature of fertility decline in Southern Europe has left them with a far more constricted base to the age pyramid than is true for countries such as France or the UK. In the seven Northern countries, the first years of the baby bust in the 1970s saw the number of births

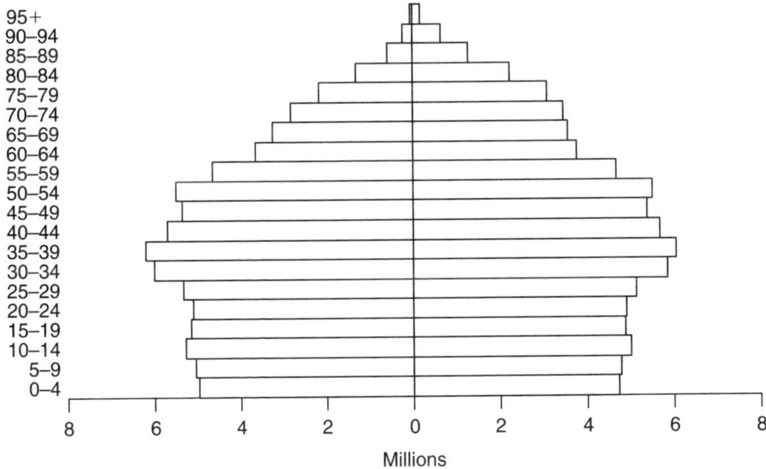

Figure 5: Age-sex structure of Northern-7 countries, 2004 (F, UK, NL, IRL, DK, FIN, SW)

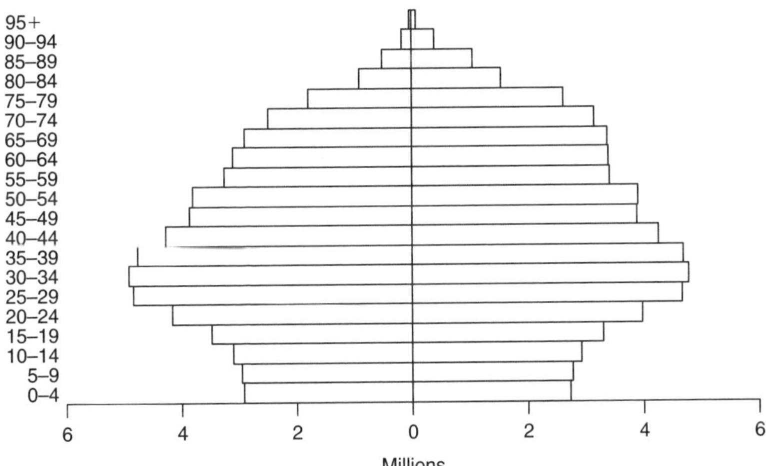

Figure 6: Age-sex structure of Southern-4 countries, 2004 (Italy, Spain, Greece, Portugal)

fall (the number of 20–29-year-olds is clearly less than of those aged 30–39). However, fertility has roughly stabilised since then, producing a broadly flat-side base to the pyramid in Figure 5, in marked contrast with the very narrow base in Southern Europe (Figure 6). Comparing the size of the age groups 0–9 with those aged 30–39 provides an approximate indication of intergenerational replacement in recent years, since the mean age at which women give birth to their children is about 30. In the Northern-7, 11.7 million women aged 30–39 have produced 9.5 million daughters now aged 0–9 (i.e. 80 per cent replacement). In the Southern-4, a slightly smaller number of women aged 30–39 (9.5 million) have produced far fewer daughters (5.5 million), or less than 60 per cent replacement. A further point is evident in Figure 6: to some extent the very low fertility of Southern Europe has been disguised so far because the baby boom cohorts were moving through the childbearing ages. The largest age groups at present are those aged 25–39. In the coming decades, however, the much smaller cohorts born since the mid-1980s will be in the reproductive ages. Unless these cohorts (currently aged 0–19) have much higher fertility than their parents, the number of births in countries such as Italy and Spain will shrink even more rapidly in the future than it has so far. In sum, while there are some broad similarities to age-structural changes across Europe, the differing fertility histories of the various regions means that the future impact will be much greater in Southern Europe than in France, the British Isles or Scandinavia.

Ageing, fertility and migration

From a reading of discussions of demographic issues in the media, including those in many generally serious publications, one could easily get the impression that the future ageing of European society is an impending disaster of almost apocalyptic proportions. Amidst the hyperbole, it is easy to lose sight of the fact that ageing is both inevitable and, in certain respects, desirable. All populations that have long life expectancy and low long-run rates of population growth will experience ageing. The only ways to avoid ageing are either greatly to worsen health conditions or to have substantial and continuing population growth. Given that most Europeans prefer long lives to short, mostly want few children, and do not wish there to be endless population increase, demographic ageing can be seen as a logical consequence of these preferences. Indeed, it could even be judged a measure of our achievement in extending life. However, whilst ageing is an inevitable and global phenomenon, Europe will experience a form of 'super-ageing' in the middle decades of this century; the baby boom cohorts are very large, and when they get old this will greatly exacerbate any problems that ageing generates. What should be the response of European societies in view of these changes? The most sensible goal is to attempt to stabilise the base of Europe's population pyramid. If each birth cohort is substantially smaller than the one before, as has been the case for the last 40 years, then it will be very hard in the long run to sustain the economic bases of our present social systems. However, this policy goal is more easily stated than realised.

To some extent, immigrants can fill gaps in the age-structure caused by low fertility. A shortfall in births in 1980 can in principle be made up for by recruiting migrants aged 25 in 2005. (And most migrants are young adults, generally aged 15–35.) The number of migrants needed for such a balancing trick to work can roughly be gauged with reference to the replacement level of 2.1 children per woman. In the EU over the last ten years, fertility has been about 1.4, or only two-thirds replacement level. In order for the cohorts born 1995–2005 to be as large as the cohorts of their parents, one migrant would need to be recruited for every two births. This is a much higher ratio of migrants to hosts than has ever been observed for a sustained period in any large country, let alone for an entity of 450 million people. In countries such as Italy, Spain or the Czech Republic, where fertility is 1.2 or less, the need for migrants to 'top up' the deficient cohorts would be even greater. Coping with migration on such a scale may be possible, but it will require a radical change in policies and attitudes.

Moreover, the long-run effect of this alternative depends not just on the scale of the immigration but also on how many children the migrants have. The logic of intergenerational replacement applies to migrants just as much as to the native born. Since migrants grow old too, unless they replace themselves more effectively than the native-born population, they do not 'solve' the problems of ageing. Only if migrants have higher fertility than their hosts will they help alleviate the consequences of ageing. From this point of view, it is clear, more or less everywhere, that the fertility of migrants tends to converge with that of the host population. The speed of convergence varies between migrant groups and cultural settings, but assimilation occurs sooner or later. In addition, low fertility is becoming a global phenomenon, so that even migrants from 'high fertility' countries may soon have fertility well below the replacement level. In short, migration cannot be regarded as a 'one-off' solution to the problems caused by ageing. In so far as it can help matters, it can only do so if there is a continuing large stream of immigrants. In order to get a better grasp of how these issues will play out over the coming decades, it is worth looking at what the populations of Europe and its Mediterranean neighbours will look like 25 years from now. To do so I will present some results of population projections made by the United States Census Bureau (USCB).

Future population trends

Any aspect of the future is to some degree unknown. However, when trends have been regular for long periods they provide a strong basis for forecasting what lies ahead. Just as past trends in fertility and mortality have shaped our current age structure, so future population growth is constrained by the age structure. This is the phenomenon known as demographic momentum. A population that, like the Med-10 countries, has been growing, will tend to keep on growing for some decades, even if fertility falls below the replacement level. This is because its present population has a large number of children and young adults (over 40 per cent of the population is under age 20). As these young people grow up and reach the childbearing ages, these large cohorts will inevitably produce a large number of babies. In contrast, a small cohort, such as those born in Southern Europe over the last 20 years, cannot produce a baby boom of comparable scale to that of the 1950s and 1960s, simply because there will be far fewer potential mothers in, say, 2030 than there are today. In consequence, while the Med-10's population is sure to keep on growing, that of the EU, and especially its Southern members, will almost certainly not produce a new surge in births, even if fertility per woman rises considerably.

Population projections need to be made according to certain assumptions. For both Europe and the Mediterranean, the assumptions used in forecasting mortality are straightforward, implying continuing steady gains in life expectancy. Trends in life expectancy have mostly been very regular for many decades, so they provide a solid basis for future extrapolation. Fertility and migration assumptions are more open to debate. In the projection results shown here, the USCB assumes that fertility will continue to fall in the Med-10, levelling off at 1.9 children per woman. In contrast, fertility in Europe is projected to rise from its current 1.4 to about 1.7. A continuing decline in fertility in the Med-10 countries seems entirely likely, given the experience of other parts of the world. The only doubt is whether it will stop at so high a level as 1.9. Fertility is much lower than this already in many parts of East Asia, for example.

The assumed increase in childbearing in Europe is probably more dubious. The logic behind this assumption (and similar ideas are used by the United Nations and many national forecasters) is that one factor in fertility decline in Europe since 1970 has been the delay of childbearing. For 35 years, Europeans have been having their babies at progressively older ages. This feature, known as the 'tempo effect', tends to cause fertility to fall more than if the age pattern was not changing. At some point, however, this delay can go no further before biological sterility sets in. Forecasters presume that the ending of this postponement will cause average fertility to rise by about 0.2 or 0.3 children per woman. Unfortunately for this argument, the underlying cohort fertility has also been declining in many countries (people really are having fewer children, not just delaying the births), and there is no reason to suppose that this decline will stop. Thus, even with an end to the tempo effect, fertility might fall further in Europe. However, few forecasters can bear to calculate what the European age structure would look like if fertility did continue to fall yet further to even lower levels.

Finally, what of migration? The USCB projection assumes relatively modest net migration into Europe (about half the level of the last five years). It also assumes modest outflows from the Med-10. In this respect, the American forecasters are following the line taken by most European national statistical offices and by Eurostat, whose forecasts mostly assume low to very low net immigration, even though migration is clearly a large and generally increasing phenomenon. Since migration has been a sensitive political topic in most of Europe in recent years, *de jure* policy is often to allow only relatively few migrants to enter a country. National forecasters are usually obliged to build in such low assumptions about migration flows, even if the *de facto* situation is quite different. This is just one example of the widespread policy of 'turning a blind eye' to migration. Italy is a classic case. Over the last decade the net inflow into Italy has probably been at least 150 000 people per year. However, Italian law supposedly limits the flow to a much lower figure, and a great show is made of apparent determination to prevent clandestine entry into the country. However, at periodic intervals the government acknowledges that a substantial undocumented population of migrants exists and offers an amnesty, allowing migrants to regularise their situation. The most recent such amnesty allowed 700 000 migrants to become legal residents of Italy. This style of policy implementation has long been used in the United States, where it has been disparaged by America's leading demographer of migration as 'smoke and mirrors'. In any event, for present purposes what matters is that the graphs shown here for the population in 2030 assume relatively little migration, certainly less than has been seen over the past decade.

Figures 7, 8 and 9 are analogous to Figures 2, 3 and 4; they present the USCB's estimates of the age structures of the EU-25 and the Med-10 in 2030, with Figure 9 making a direct comparison. The graph for the Med-10 shows that in 2030 the region's population will be substantially older than it is today. The projection indicates that the annual flow of births will

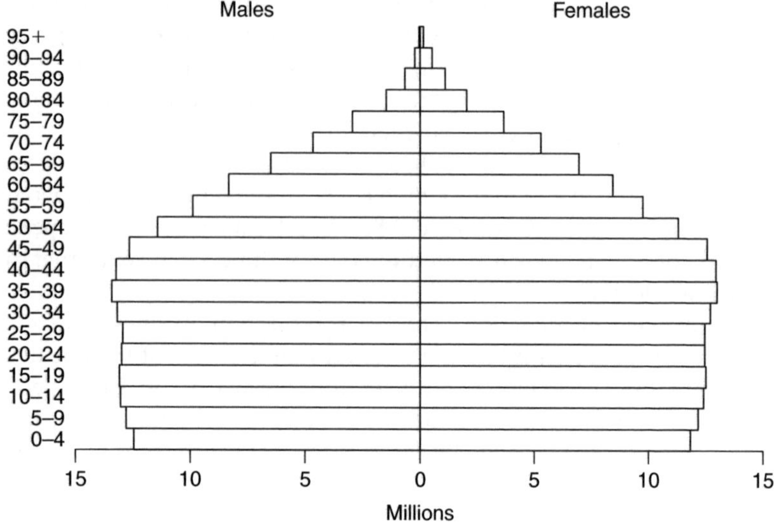

Figure 7:   Age-sex structure of Med-10, 2030

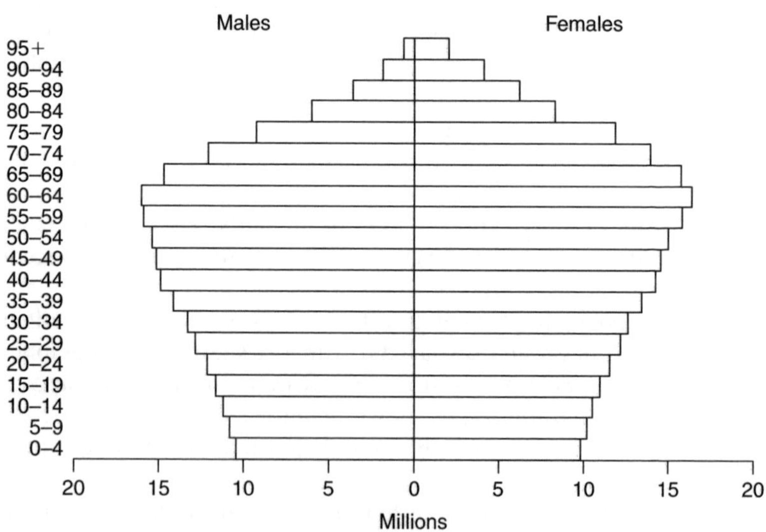

Figure 8:   Age-sex structure of EU-25, 2030

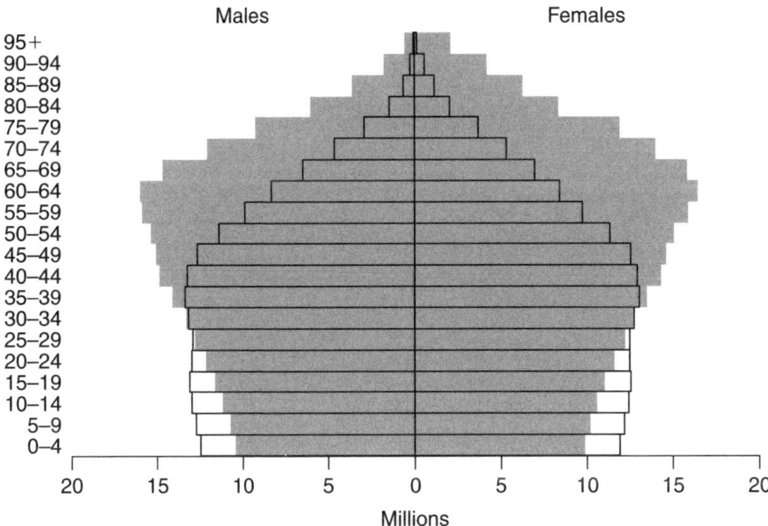

Figure 9:   Age-sex structure of EU-25 (shaded) & Med-10, 2030

broadly stabilise, producing a flat-sided population pyramid all the way up to age 50. In contrast, the births each year in Europe are expected to decline steadily, producing a pyramid that looks more and more top-heavy as time goes on. The comparison of the two age structures in 2030 in Figure 9 makes the divergence of experience all the more apparent. It is worth recalling that even this view of Europe's future is based on an assumption that fertility will increase. If the birth rate falls further, an even greater tapering at the base of the pyramid will occur.

Ageing and the economy

Not surprisingly, changes to the age structure on the scale that will be seen in Europe and the Mediterranean over the coming decades will have large economic effects. It is important to realise, however, that ageing *per se* is not necessarily a problem. The difficulty arises because Europe's social and economic institutions are not well set up for coping with it. Particular attention has been focused in recent years on the issue of pensions and other age-related welfare benefits; a consideration of these institutions gives a good example of the ways in which society is likely to need to adapt to cope with ageing. Europe's welfare state regimes were mostly created in their present form in the 25 or so years between the end of World War Two and the first oil shock, and the institutions put in place reflected the character of the economy and society at that time. However, taking a long-term view, we can see that this was a most unusual period. The baby boom led to substantial population growth, and economic growth was at record levels. Between 1948 and 1973 the GDP per head in continental Western Europe grew by more than 5 per cent a year. This was far higher than ever seen before or since for a sustained period. The long-run trend is about 2 per cent a year. The pensions and welfare state systems that we have today were based on assumptions that both the population and the economy would continue to grow rapidly. Only now, fully 30 years after these assumptions ceased to be true, are governments slowly coming to terms with the changes needed to make Europe's welfare state systems sustainable when neither of these two factors is growing rapidly.

While attention to the impact of ageing has tended to focus on the costs involved, especially pensions, in a more general sense what matters is the size of the labour force. Pensions and other welfare benefits represent a form of claim on the stream of wealth being created by the people who are at work. Thus, it is the relative size of the working and non-working populations that is most relevant. All other things being held constant, the low fertility of recent decades implies a marked shrinking of the working population over the next 25 years. The impact will, of course, be greatest in the countries where fertility has fallen most. Barring some miraculous discovery of how to return to rapid productivity gains, there are essentially only two ways in which the impact of this shortfall of workers can be mitigated. Firstly, the proportion of the population who are actually engaged in paid employment (and thus are paying taxes) can increase. Second, more workers can be imported by immigration. Neither of these two policy choices is universally popular. The former option involves persuading more women to work (especially in Southern Europe) and delaying retirement for both sexes. Such changes may be just as controversial as advocating large-scale immigration.

For the Med-10 countries the form of ageing that is to be expected over the coming quarter century is far more advantageous to the economy. Even by 2030 there will still be relatively few old people in these countries. However, fertility decline will mean that the proportion of the population made up by children will diminish. Thus, the relative size of the working-age population will increase substantially. This form of age-structural boost to the economy is termed the 'demographic dividend' by economists, and is regarded as having played a large role in the rapid growth of East Asian economies in recent decades. The first half of this century will be an era when the Med-10 countries will receive their dividend from the demographic transition.

Conclusion: shared demographic futures

The contrasting demographic futures of Europe and its Southern and Eastern neighbours provide the context within which other aspects of their interrelationship will be worked out. The underlying demographic forces at work strongly suggest that migration into the EU-25 will be a large and increasing phenomenon. Given our shared geography and history, it seems certain that much of this migration will come from the Med-10 countries. The way in which this takes place will play a pivotal role in shaping the nature of relationships around the Mediterranean.

Auguste Comte famously observed that, 'Demography is destiny.' He was wrong. To a substantial degree we can still choose our future. However, demography does impose strong constraints on the range of feasible options. Taking these constraints into account is the basis for all sound planning for our shared futures.

Reference

Demeny, Paul (1972) 'Early Fertility Decline in Austria-Hungary: a Lesson in Demographic Transition; in D. V. Glass and R. Revelle (eds), *Population and Social Change* (London: Edward Arnold).

2
Does Europe Need New Immigration?[1]

Catherine Wihtol de Wenden

At the beginning of the twentieth century, Europe had become one of the primary immigration regions in the world, with 1.4 million annual entries, ahead of the United States, Canada and Australia combined. However, since 1974, the policy has become one of exception, and the influx of salaried labourers has been suspended. This change occurred after the oil crisis of 1973 and was justified by a series of scenarios that did not in effect occur: the return of foreign workers to their own countries, the substitution of unemployed national labourers for departing foreign workers, the mobility of Europeans within Europe, and co-development as an alternative to immigration, etc. This closing of national borders provoked, or accelerated, a number of undesirable results: illegal entries and stays, a modification in the profiles of asylum-seekers, a settling in of illegal immigrants who could be neither regularised nor assimilated, and modern slavery in certain kinds of employment.

Beginning in the years 1985–90, European immigration and asylum policies, inspired by the need for security and lacking flexibility regarding sector- and structure-based demand for workers, did not match the reality of the migrant influx, with its obvious desire to immigrate to Europe. Unlike in other large zones of immigration in the world, immigration in Europe is not part of the constituent identity of nations nor of the Europe being created, and it is seen thus to be intrusive and illegitimate. Foreigners compose only 5.1 per cent of the population and, if citizens of other European nations are subtracted, they are only 3.5 per cent.

For twenty years, events have profoundly transformed international migrations, particularly within a changing Europe: the opening of the East and the enlargement of the Union to 25 nations, the boom and crisis in requests for asylum, globalisation and diversification of the influx, and countries of emigration to the South and East of Europe having become countries of immigration – to the point where it is now one of the strategic issues of the region. The rise in importance of the migration theme, once considered only a social issue and rarely taken seriously by the powers that be, is now seen to entail ethical questions: the assimilation of population movements into the security challenge, which brings up all the demographic, religious, cultural and social threats of a slow and continuous process that is neither a conquest nor an invasion; the contrasted vision of a bipolar but unbalanced world in which Islam has become a major issue; the disarray of nation-states and of even broader regions faced with what they consider a danger to their sovereignty, their identity and their well-being.

However, an ageing Europe structurally lacks workers in certain skilled and unskilled sectors and, looking ahead to 2020 or to 2050, is going to experience a lack of actively employed people. Nevertheless, it continues to choose to close its borders to all those who cannot claim the protections it offers (the Geneva Convention for the right to asylum, the right to live as families protected by national constitutions), and it lacks a proactive immigration policy. Despite the closure, migratory pressure on the borders persists to the point where Europe is becoming a continent of immigration in spite of itself.

The security goal itself has considerable political, economic, social, cultural and human costs: it transforms foreigners entering and residing in Europe into suspects, and it encourages the development of transnational networks, which use closed borders as a new way to make money. Figures on replacement migrations – furnished by a 2000 United Nations report that caused much talk – describe the extent of the phenomenon: 175 million people, or 3 per cent of the world's population, live in a country other than the one in which they were born. The number of immigrants has more than doubled since 1975, and almost one person in ten in the developed nations is an immigrant. In the European Union, 7 per cent of the total population, or 26 million people, are immigrants (but not all are foreigners), as compared to 14 million in 1970, and they are unequally distributed depending on the country.

Among world demographical trends in the next fifty years, the decline and ageing of national populations are most significant in Europe and in Japan. Several scenarios are projected by the United Nations regarding the number of immigrants necessary to rebalance the age pyramid or the proportion of those actively employed, even if immigration can provide only a partial answer and can do nothing in regard to the ageing of the population.

Do the southern shores of the Mediterranean offer a complementary vision? There, the economic and demographic context creates favourable conditions for more intense migratory movements within the Euro-Mediterranean space. The new younger generation has significantly fewer demographic responsibilities; it is producing fewer children as fertility levels are declining, and it can count on many brothers and sisters to take care of parents thanks to the higher fertility of the preceding generation.

This is a phenomenon that will last only for one generation. This freed-up human resource is characterised by an increasing 'desire for Europe' – nourished by transnational networks, where imaginary notions some-times are more important in the tentative Euro-Mediterranean dialogue than the social phenomena that gave birth to them. In reality though, far from being a place of mobility, the southern Mediterranean countries are left wanting, as European decision-makers vacillate between the temptation to close the gates and the dream of a Europe without borders.

The results of this non-synchronisation of realities and policies and non-decisions – described as improvisation – are legion: Sangatte, a bone of contention between France and the United Kingdom due to a lack of confidence in increased European harmonisation; the situation at entry points to Europe in Ceuta, in Melilla, and in the Sicilian islands; the semi-militarised borders with 2500 annual deaths; the illegals; the traffic in human beings; the sex trade; the growing interdependence engendered by globalisation of influxes; and the suspicion regarding potential immigrants – all these elements point to the need for a more enlightened immigration policy.

In Eastern Europe, the globalisation of influxes has greatly evolved, mak-ing the region including Central and Eastern European countries and their neighbours to the East a new area for movements. Was the enlar-ging of Europe in 2004 destined to bring a new chapter, wreaking havoc with pre-existing intense mobility between countries now candidates for European Union membership and their neighbours to the East, with whom the Schengen accords threaten to create a divide similar to what exists between the two shores of the Mediterranean? This will become clear only in the future.

In the sub-Sahara, will not globalisation merely be a change in perspec-tive? Sub-Saharan migrations have taken on a political dimension by default (via requests for asylum), and the positive effects of returning migrations remain limited in regard to development issues, because dias-poras resulting from precariousness are rarely development vectors.

On the European side, decisions made at the Seville (2002) and Thessalonica (2003) summits were only weak responses to the issues the European Union is now confronting, as they focused on border control and on the struggle against clandestine immigration rather than answering the fundamental question, which is to decide if Europe needs to open its borders to immigration.

Exclusion as the rule for thirty years: the discrepancy

Globalisation

The globalisation of migratory fluxes, which is in conflict with closing borders to immigration for the purposes of work, has been acknowledged only tardily by Europeans, who are often reluctant to recognise immigration as part of their history and identity. Immigration has long been seen as a last-minute response to labour shortages or to temporary political crises for refugees. Now, an increasingly rapid immigration in the East and the South is taking place along with the more well-established immigration, in some cases already a century old, into certain European countries, such as France.

The globalisation of migratory movements that Europe is experiencing today is the fruit of the confluence of several factors:

- countries of emigration turning into countries of immigration in the East and the South of Europe (Poland, Ukraine, Romania, Italy, Spain, Portugal, Greece), certain countries being both, or else transit countries (Eastern Europe);
- passports having become progressively commonplace starting only twenty years ago, perhaps even less, which has brought about a kind of generalised right to exit, although the right to enter has become more and more controlled by a system of visas and computerisation at borders (SIS: Schengen Information System; Eurodac: the computerised examination of digital fingerprints for those requesting asylum);
- acceleration of requests for asylum on a worldwide basis is no longer confined to pressure points: the Great Lakes region of Africa, South-East Asia, the Balkans, Near and Middle East, Central America and the Caribbean;
- the development of transnational networks, which create a border-crossing economy related to the difficulty of such crossings, encouraging migrations that start in exit regions and terminate in clandestine labour, which serves to reimburse, over the course of years, the cost of passage;
- the development of back-and-forth migrations, in which a person leaves in order to eventually return home to better conditions once he/she makes sufficient money abroad (Eastern Europe in particular);

- finally, the geographical proximity between exit regions (where economic and social disruption is severe) and Eastern Europe, the lowering of airplane fares, the access by ground transport to numerous destinations, the attractiveness of European lifestyles (publicised by radio and television, by local markets featuring manufactured products, and by funds transferred by emigrants) all arouse a 'desire for Europe' in backward areas.

Despite all these facts, Europe continues to be wary of migrations, often under pressure from public opinion, whereas it ought to address the challenges of an ageing population and of labour shortages.

The European position

The closing of borders has led to an acceleration of families brought to join immigrants and to the permanent settling in of foreign workers. Clandestine migration has developed, particularly in European countries without immigration policies (Southern and Eastern Europe), along with asylum migration. The fluxes of immigrants have diversified; unlike in the past, migrants now are less often manual labourers than educated middle-class urban dwellers. Of the 450 million people in Europe, there are 20 million foreigners, 5 million of whom are from other European Community countries. These foreigners are unevenly distributed: thus Germany, with 7.5 million foreigners, is the principal country of immigration in Europe, followed by France (3.5 million) and the United Kingdom (2.5 million); the nationalities represented vary according to neighbouring countries, colonial history, the existence of 'migratory couples' brought about by mass immigration in the 1960s (Germany/Turkey), and migratory networks.

Familial and matrimonial migration is the source of most entries, followed by asylum, for which demand has seriously increased in recent years. In Eastern Europe, ethnic migrations, the fruit of Europe's debalkanisation, have occurred since 1989 and 2000 (2 million *Aussiedler*, ethnic Germans, have come to live in Germany), whereas others have adopted mobility as a lifestyle. But the great migratory wave has come neither in the East nor the South, contrary to alarmist thinking. In any case, despite the closing of borders, migration continues, slowly but surely. In many exit countries, there is no hope of changing one's life in the short term apart from migration.

Admission and asylum policies, formerly national, are now European-wide but on the defensive: control of external borders (the Schengen accords), more restrictive harmonisation of the right to asylum (Dublin accords I and II), passage from the third intergovernmental pillar to the first Community pillar (determined by the Amsterdam Treaty and in effect since 1 May 2004), with priority given to the struggle against clandestine immigration and to dissuasion (re-entry accords signed with exit countries, the return of potential asylum-seekers to borders and to camps located at points of immigration in countries bordering the EU). Although the European Union abandoned the goal of 'zero immigration' after the Tampere summit in 1999, seeking instead to define a common immigration policy based on its economic and demographic needs, obstacles remain, such as the 'priority for Europeans in employment', which largely closes off employment to non-European Community members; and wariness is the rule in regard to quotas of skilled and unskilled labourers.

Individually and often unacknowledged, several European countries have nevertheless surmounted the closures – and many of the administration constraints – via bilateral labour accords with their neighbours (Italy/Albania), by policy calls for skilled immigrants (computer technicians), or by new immigration policies (such as in Germany, with its new law in effect since 1 January 2005) inspired by the Canadian model. On the European level, recent directives have moved towards harmonisation of policies related to entry, asylum, reuniting families, and the status of non-European Community citizens in relation to foreigners. Mutual trust is beginning to manifest itself as solidarity between European countries in questions of border controls, control of illegal immigrants, and the handling of asylum, even if from time to time there is unpredictable behaviour as a consequence of decisions made by certain countries to remain outside of adopted norms (United Kingdom, Ireland, Denmark).

At the national level, despite the diversity of migratory situations, there is consensus regarding opposition to employment for non-Europeans who seek to enter the labour market, with the emphasis on making illegal immigration a crime and on restrictive asylum policies – even as more positive trends are developing for those already in place, such as the extension of citizenship based on residency. In the very failures of national policies, convergences exist, such as successive regularisations of those without papers, the creation of a category of asylum-seekers who can be neither regularised nor deported, the tolerance of black-market labour, or the lack of solutions for worker shortages other than illegality. The lack of long- and medium-term policies dominates, along with the refusal to see in co-development something other than a disguised policy of deportation. A glimmering of the right to mobility is beginning to turn up here and there, but it carries little weight in decision-making by national and international institutions.

In the East and South: risks of fractures

An opening in the East

On 1 May 2004, ten new countries became part of the European Union, eight of them from Eastern and Central Europe. These countries, with the exception of Poland (38.6 million inhabitants), do not pose a large migration potential, especially since their demographic growth is weak and their population ageing (the record being held by Germany and the Czech Republic). Since the fall of the Berlin Wall, migrants from the East have been mobile (back-and-forth migrations) rather than settling in the West. These new countries were required to furnish guarantees of good behaviour by adopting European Community regulations, that is, promising to control their external borders, to apply Schengen procedures, and to accept re-entry agreements with their neighbours to the West as regards illegals who transit their territory. Entry into the European Union, for those whom some already call half-citizens, looks like a temporary closure behind which the original fifteen shelter themselves, despite the new European discourse about being open to legal immigration for purposes of work. While benefiting – since 1991 for certain Eastern countries (Poland, Czech Republic, Hungary), since 2001 for the last two (Bulgaria, Romania) – from freedom to circulate, migrants from the East will not immediately be joining the European job market, because the fifteen original members of the Union sheltered themselves behind protective measures just before the ten new members entered. Even if workers from the East are often appreciated for their readiness to work, their education level, and their ability to adapt, they are submitted to a specific procedure. Geometrically variable periods of transition have been established to protect against new arrivals. The fifteen established a transition period of a maximum of seven years before freedom to work and to circulate (fundamental principles of the European Union) become operational.

However, the details are different in each of the fifteen original countries, in each of the ten new countries joining the Union, and in different work sectors. Each country can define its position regarding new member nations, whether by delaying access for two years with a possible extension to three years, then for two additional years (but only if it can be justified by serious disruption of the job market). The period of transition thus operates according to a '2 + 3 + 2' calendar. Bilateral accords can also be made between an old and a new member country according to work sector. A flexibility clause permits a new member to ask an old one to re-examine the operational period of transition. The EU-member preferential treatment for employment is operational during the transition period, and it is national law regarding non-EU citizens that prevails during the transition period. A special situation applies to service providers and to those who were already regularly employed inside the EU. This institutional mosaic continues even though the East was required to adopt all EU procedures regarding border controls. It is astonishing to see so many protective measures put in place even though new member countries present a weak potential for immigration, and a deregulation of the job market involving *de facto* precarious status occurs, given the choice of working illegally.

In the South: closure

Since 1995, the immigrant question has become a completely separate element of the Euro-Mediterranean dialogue: the Barcelona accords, inspired by the North American Free Trade Agreements (NAFTA) established the liberalising of trade as an alternative to free circulation of people and immigration where co-development is concerned. For its part, the visa system, imposed on Southern countries since 1986, blocks freedom of movement between populations on the two shores, while encouraging random settling in by those who have succeeded in entering Europe. At the same time, current events are catching up with decision-makers: in Gibraltar, in Vlores in Albania, and in Brindisi, illegal immigrants have been making the front page news for several years. In many regards, the Mediterranean is one of the great divides in the world, because its north shore and its south shore represent demographic, economic, religious, social and political disparities despite historical (the shared Mediterranean of the ancient world) and geocultural similarities (some attribute the latter to the shared cultivation of olive trees). A comparison with the Rio Grande between Mexico and the United States, another great dividing line, is often made, but this does not take into account the diversity of migrations in the Mediterranean region (South–North migrations but also South–South and East–West). Transnational networks are developing between the north shore and the south shore, between the East and the West throughout the region.

While the population in countries on the north shore grew by about one-third between 1950 and 2000, from 158 million to 212 million, countries in the East and the South of the Mediterranean saw theirs multiply by three, going from 73 million in 1950 to 244 million in 2000, an evolution depending on the country of 32 per cent to 53 per cent in a half century. During the 1990s, the rate of natural growth (the difference between the birth rate and the death rate) was 1.5 per cent on the north shore, as opposed to 20.3 per cent on the south shore – despite the demographic drop seen in the eastern and southern countries of the Mediterranean during the same period (a sharp drop in both fecundity and mortality since 1950). As a consequence, in countries south of the Mediterranean, 50 per cent of the population is today less than 25 years old, while the North shows stagnation or decline in its population depending on the country. Between 1950 and 2000, the North-West of the Mediterranean grew from 128.6 million inhabitants to 167 million, while the East grew from 28.9 million to 101.2 million and the South from 44 million to 142.8 million. The rate of fertility – with the exception of Tunisia, where it is 2.3 children per female – is nearly 3 children per female in the countries in this region – even if all, with the exception of Palestine, have shown a demographic decline for several years. Egypt, Turkey, Algeria and Morocco have a large potential for migration for the next twenty years and will equal the population of France, Italy and Spain, where ageing is already occurring. Urbanisation is advancing: in 2000, with the exception of Albania, Bosnia and Egypt, the urban population was above 50 per cent; taking note of the fact that megalopolises are the waiting rooms of illegal immigrants, this fact is alarming. Between now and 2025, the population of the Maghreb could grow 48 per cent, as opposed to 3 per cent in the European Union.

Employment is another dividing line: for the year 2000, the GIP by inhabitant in the European Union was 14 times higher than in the countries of North Africa. It was 20 times higher in Germany, 19 times higher in France, and 12 times higher in Spain. Transfers of funds related to emigration are also a significant resource for exit countries: they represent 6.3 per cent of the GIP in Morocco, 2.3 per cent in Algeria, and 4.1 per cent in Tunisia. But these countries are themselves becoming transit countries for populations coming from further south with hopes of crossing the Mediterranean. This is already the case in Turkey, Morocco and Algeria. The Mediterranean, the divide, is also a passageway for urban educated migrants; and the border traffic becomes, for certain people, a way of making money – in the Canary Islands and the Balearic Islands, on the Italian and Greek coasts and islands, or even further in the East, between Romania and Moldavia. Closed borders are the source of Mafia-controlled traffic, employment and housing. Closure also causes those without papers to settle there since they cannot go back and forth, as opposed to those who are not required to have visas (experts, merchants), who sometimes create businesses or traffic (*trabendo*) around the border crossings. Borders, dividing lines, thus become a source of income. Networks and businesses flourish in the crevices, interstices and crannies of larger systems: businesses to get people across, counterfeiting, prostitution, contraband, but also 'ethnic' occupations continue to function outside of Euro-Mediterranean institutions.

All countries on the southern shore of the Mediterranean seek the liberalisation of borders, the loosening of visa rules established in 1986, and the structuring of their economies around the labour needs of northern countries. For them, migration is an economic (transfer of funds) and social (exportation of unemployment) resource and a factor in modernisation (political and cultural). Talk of a brain drain is beginning, because these countries, in their incapacity to employ everyone, understand the benefits to be gained from exporting their managers. On the European side, all European Union countries are not equally engaged in the dialogue: their interest in the Euro-Mediterranean process is often linked to geographical proximity, to real or imagined risk of immigration, or to the existence of historic, colonial, linguistic or cultural ties. Confidence in northern European countries in the way southern European countries control their borders is not absolute, despite the principles of solidarity written into European treaties. Only the countries of southern Europe seem to show a sustained interest, because they are directly affected by illegal migrations, illegal workers, competition and free-trade in markets (fishing, agriculture, textiles), the political situation on southern shores, and the potential increase of demand for asylum in case of serious crisis. Radical Islamism contributes to reinforce the security aspects of immigration.

Non-respect of human rights: contradictions

In favour of open borders

Discussions about opening borders, among both decision-makers and academics, have taken place since the 1990s, with, on the one hand, a vision of a sovereign and secure Europe, and, on the other, a nationless world of transnational networks. In this context, many have argued in favour of the universal right to migrate: according to the 1948 Universal Declaration of Human Rights, everyone has the right to leave a country, including his own. The situation has evolved since this text was written in the context of the pre-Cold War, and the call for the right to migrate has grown stronger, based on the idea of a world citizen as elaborated by Immanuel Kant. Another argument calls for the democratisation of borders, because the reality is that those with money or contacts always succeed in crossing. Still another emphasises the contradiction between the free circulation of ideas and merchandise and the restriction of free circulation for human beings, because the circulation of goods means that human resources will follow.

A further conjecture is that closed borders encourage inequality in development and block dialogue between the different regions of the world. Finally, experience with freedom of circulation refutes the efficiency of border controls: for example, until the closing of Algerian borders in 1973, many people went back and forth between France and Algeria in an endless procession. They settled in, for the most part, after the borders were closed. The same thing is happening in Mexico. Having crossed the border between Mexico and the United States people regret not being able to return to their country owing to their irregular status. The eastern countries are another example: after the fall of the Berlin Wall, many claimed that immigrants from the East would flood into Western Europe. Nothing of the kind occurred. When these countries first asked to join the European Union, the Union cancelled Schengen tourist visas. This move encouraged back-and-forth migrations: people didn't settle in, because they knew they could return home and then come back.

This is why open borders ought to be a medium-term goal for countries receiving immigrants. The visa system at present is very rigid regarding the diversity of potential immigrants. Europe, like its neighbours to the East and the South, would gain by receiving immigrants who are not the poorest, who seek to be able to come and go freely, and who will not settle in precisely because they can come and go freely. Examples of failure of the closed border policy offer food for thought. First, the development of illegal immigration, which is marked by daily deaths at the gates of Europe, is an undesirable occurrence in relation to principles of human rights so favoured by the European Union. Second, the high number of regularisations, after years of chaos, is an admission of failure, since this is an attempt to patch the holes in failing controls. Finally, economic needs ought to be taken into account. If a job offer exists, skilled or unskilled, which attracts new immigrants who are from outside, the priority is given to European Union citizens; this is, therefore, an obstacle for sectors needing workers. The status quo is sold to the public via symbolic controls, with managed media attention for deportations to borders and for sanctions against irregular employers. The practice is to give the public the illusion that immigration is being controlled, while everyone knows illegal immigration is useful for the job market. The phenomenon is not new: in the past, politicians such as Georges Pompidou, Jean-Marcel Jeanneney and Michel Massenet made statements along these lines. However, with regard to the elite, policy is more flexible, because the idea is to attract highly qualified immigrants in the fields of medicine or computers, who are drawn at present to the United States and Canada.

Against open borders

The essential argument against open borders is tied to the idea of social welfare, to the system of social protection. In European countries border controls are increasingly based on the idea of social protection (Thomas Marshall's notion of social citizenship). A minimum solidarity exists among residents around social rights: people pay taxes and contribute in order to meet the needs of those who are in their country legally. This is a strong argument for maintaining closed borders. The social bond today is defined by the performance and rights of those who are legally in a territory. Internal solidarity arises from this phenomenon. It is equally true at the European level since today France, for example, participates as much in the development of northern Portugal as it does in the development of a region of Crete, unknown to most people – and, starting this year, in a region in the East. The notion of social welfare, of the common social good, demands that solidarity exists within a territory, but that it goes no further. Today, borders are mainly based on the social state, that is, solidarity – which is not without limit – between residents, natives or legal foreigners, of a given territory. This idea is often used to legitimise the closing of borders. Border controls are associated with the preservation of well-being in both the country of final destination as well as the country of origin.

This notion implies political pressure in favour of closures because of immigration's social costs and budget items corresponding to assimilation of newcomers. The issue of insecurity comes on top of costs. Today, in European countries, border control is dictated by the security issue and by the power of the extreme right. The extreme right exercises a strong pressure in favour of border controls, states being torn between national electoral sanctions against open borders, mechanisms of European Community and security decisions, and a consciousness of demographics, of shortages of workers in the labour market, of needs of employers and certain public services (education, hospitals), and of human rights.

In a recent speech before the European Parliament in January 2004, Kofi Annan encouraged European countries to open themselves more to legal immigration of skilled and unskilled workers, families and technicians, temporary and permanent immigrants, and he pointed to the crisis in Europe concerning the right to asylum: 'The majority of migrants are an opportunity for Europe . . . migrants need Europe and Europe needs migrants. A closed Europe will be a weaker, poorer, older Europe. An open Europe will be richer, stronger, younger . . . Migrants are part of the solution, not part of the problem.'[2] Others besides Annan have spoken out along these lines, such as Zigmunt Bauman,[3] who recalled, on the subject of asylum, the idea of a world citizen as defined in 1784 by Immanuel Kant.

Notes

1. Translated by Penny Allen.
2. Kofi Annan, Speech to the European Parliament, 29 January 2004.
3. Zigmunt Bauman, 'Vivre ensemble dans un monde plein', *Le Monde*, 3 February 2002.

References

Annan, Kofi (2004) Speech to the European Parliament, 29 January 2004.
Association marocaine d'Etudes et de Recherches sur la migration (2000) *La Migration clandestine* (Morocco: Rabat).
Bade, Klaus (2002) *L'Europe en mouvement* (Paris: Seuil).
Balibar, Etienne (2004) *We, the People of Europe?* (Princeton: Princeton University Press).
Bauman, Zigmunt (2002) 'Vivre ensemble dans un monde plein', *Le Monde*, 3 February 2002.
Bribosia, Emmanuelle and Rea, Andrea (eds) (2002) *Les Nouvelles Migrations* (Bruxelles: Complexe).
Chemillier-Gendreau, Monique (1999) 'Droit international ignoré, relations internationales de la France compromises', in *Sans-Papiers: l'archaïsme fatal* (coll.) (Paris: La Découverte).
Gotman, Anne (1998–2004) 'Tendances des migrations internationales', OCDE, SOPEMI: Annual Reports, 1998–2004.
Gotman, Anne (2002) 'Les frontières du droit d'asile', *Hommes et Migrations*, no. 1238, July–August.
Gotman, Anne (ed.) (2004) *Villes et hospitalité: les municipalités et leurs 'étrangers'* (Paris: Maison des Sciences de l'Homme).
Pratt, Sandra (2004) 'Immigration: a Stumbling Block in Europe's Foreign Policy', paper presented at the Wilton Park Conference, London (Foreign Office) (27 February).
Tinguy, Anne de (2004) *La Grande Migration* (Paris: Plon).
Wihtol de Wenden, Catherine (1999) *Faut-il ouvrir les frontières?* (Paris: Presses de Sciences Po).
Wihtol de Wenden, Catherine (2001) *L'Europe des migrations: La Documentation française* (Paris: CNRS).
Wihtol de Wenden, Catherine (2003) 'L'Union européenne face aux migrations', in *Les grandes tendances du monde, RAMSÈS*, 2004 (Paris: Dunod).

3

Putting Asylum to the Test: Between Immigration Policy and Co-Development[1]

Sylvie Mazzella

> Alas! Remembering his sweet adventures,
> Looking, without entering, through the barricades,
> Like a pariah,
> He wandered all day long, toward nightfall,
> His heart as sad as a tomb.[2]

Many experts today believe that asylum policy is in crisis, in Europe and everywhere in the world. In Europe, this crisis must be understood first as the result of tension between a region-wide impulse (particularly the desire for an EU Community-wide right to asylum, which could result eventually in the creation of a single European entry point) and the establishment of partnerships with former colonies who are now economic partners, in the context of a new Euro-Mediterranean free-trade zone to be created between now and 2010.

This political-economic tension – closing to people versus opening of markets – is not without effect on the asylum policy conducted in Europe in recent years. A certain number of writers have analysed the shifts in European asylum policy, which tends to be confused with immigration policy. We shall discuss here the results of this research. We shall put the questioning of asylum back into the context of strengthening co-development policies: certain experts see this as an assault on the Geneva Convention, the international treatment of asylum, and its universal status through the creation of regional rules, of 'local universalisms', as is the case in South America or the African continent. At the very least, experts are signalling with alarm the exportation of the handling of refugees, a kind of outsourcing of the asylum problem by European governments.

Europe seems in effect to be heading towards the creation of a Euro-Mediterranean asylum right, whose form would be more contractual than universal, more economic than political, with bilateral accords and re-entry accords signed between European and non-European nations. One of the European Union's great challenges is unquestionably to succeed in negotiating terms for these accords, without neglecting the clear ethical question asked of France by the historian Gérard Noiriel: to whom does Europe wish to grant asylum?

Right to asylum and immigration control

In 2000, the United Kingdom attracted the largest number of asylum requests (98 000), moving ahead of Germany, which was long the leading country for asylum in Western Europe. France saw the number of requests for asylum progressively increase during the 1990s. This increase continued into 2000 (25 per cent) and 2001 (22 per cent). However, a slow down began in 2002, with an increase of only 9 per cent, and by 2003 asylum-seekers had slowed down to 2 per cent. Despite less of a slow-down than in Germany or in the United Kingdom (−41 per cent as compared to 2002), within the context of an overall drop in requests for asylum in Europe (−1.7 per cent), France is now part of the group of European countries receiving the most requests for asylum.[3] The rate of requests granted is not, however, proportional to the number of requests. On the European Union level, only 10 per cent acquire the status of refugee. We are thus seeing a growing number of asylum requests without then seeing more refugees in host countries.

Following the objective of Community-wide policy initiated at the beginning of the 1990s, the European Union seeks to adopt common norms regulating the acceptance of those seeking asylum, procedures to be followed, and conditions for obtaining refugee status, with the likelihood of only minimal harmonisation following already restrictive policies of member nations. The absolute respect of the right to seek asylum was reaffirmed by the European Council in Tampere on 15–16 October 1999, which determined the main themes of European political asylum. Their objective is the establishment of a common European asylum policy beyond the minimal norms set forth by article 63 of the European Union Treaty: this implies that authority will no longer reside with individual countries but with the European Community, according to decisions made by a majority of the Council of Ministers of Justice and Internal Affairs, in co-decision with the European Parliament. The European Councils of Laeken (December 2001) and of Seville (June 2002) sought to accelerate the work and to set a schedule for harmonisation, but the Thessalonica summit in June 2003 showed once again the disagreements between various countries regarding the definition of refugee status.

The European Union, despite its heterogeneous legislations, globally recognises the crisis in asylum, resulting mainly from the massive increase in requests and from their redefinition as economic migrations. The idea of a crisis in immigration control, linked more and more to asylum policies, is developing in Europe (but also in North America and in Australia). Asylum is becoming a vector of irregular immigration. The disparities within the European Union has led to a 'goose chase' for those requesting asylum and the practice of 'asylum shopping' (the choice of destination based on the states offering the best treatment). The European Union takes a dim view of its own accumulation of a 'multi-procedural' international population sent on a chase around Europe, leaving behind them the negative of a photograph yet to be printed. Countries such as Italy established only tardily an asylum policy (the Bossi-Fini law on immigration and asylum came into effect in 2002). Italy is one of the rare countries in the European Union not to have a specific law on asylum, separate from the judicial status of immigration. The right to asylum is strongly criticised in the Italian press, which accuses migrants of being for the most part clandestines seeking to profit from an asylum system.

However, this politically omnipresent notion of the false asylum-seeker masks other realities. Aristide Zolberg recalls in his article 'Chemins de la faim, chemins de la peur' ('Paths of Hunger, Paths of Fear') that the main reasons for flight remain war, totalitarianism and violence – and the resulting poverty.[4] D. Perrin[5] recalls that most often it is countries neighbouring a crisis zone that are the most concerned by the question of refuge: the three main host countries in 2001 and 2002 were thus Pakistan, as a result of war in Afghanistan, Iran, as a result of the Iraqi situation, and Germany, as a result of refugees from ex-Yugoslavia. For his part, Rémy Bazenguissa reaffirms that refugees are not on a goose chase or 'in a world apart', as they are often described, but completely present and in relationships with populations of countries that do not recognise them.[6] Inversely, there is a risk of opening the way to a sort of 'internal asylum',[7] keeping refugees in place. Catherine Wihtol de Wenden points out that the High Commission on Refugees tends increasingly to take action at the source of conflicts, encouraging the return of displaced persons, establishing temporary protections in the countries of origin.[8] She states that the 'duty to remain in place', in 'human sanctuaries' situated in the middle of conflict zones, is now replacing the 'right to leave one's country' and the right of refuge as enunciated in the Universal Declaration of Human Rights.

From legal clandestine to false asylum-seeker

According to Godfried Engbersen,[9] and borrowing Michel Foucault's expression, we have changed in the 1990s from a fortress Europe to a panoptic Europe, because those without papers are marginalised – or criminalised – and the procedure of asylum-seeking pushes immigrants into a 'passive clandestine state', as Didier Fassin calls it,[10] an irregularity *because of* the law. Short of having asked for and obtained some kind of legal papers after the expiration of his tourist or other visa, a foreigner becomes irregular. National policies regarding asylum can even create legal clandestines. They would be those seeking the right to asylum, not refugees, not clandestines, not deportable, not regularisable, who are temporarily tolerated in a host country for the duration of a procedure which might last several years.

Should we attribute this invention to a deliberate strategy to cheaply manufacture excluded persons,[11] to a 'criminalisation of immigration'?[12] This is the thesis defended by Loïc Wacquant.[13] For him, 'panoptic Europe' is not a 'producer of reform': it does not propose to correct or to punish clandestines. It creates exclusion, and individuals adapted to their status as outsiders – a 'handy enemy', to use Zygmunt Bauman's expression.[14] It gives rise to many undesirable effects, itself creating infractions that must then be combated by means of complex mechanisms of identity control.

If one follows the reasoning of Loïc Wacquant, legal clandestine asylum-seekers would join the cohort of heavily over-represented foreigners in Europe's prisons or in retention centres for migrants in irregular situations, justifying the redefinition of immigration as a security problem. In fact, simple political indecision can explain the institutional manufacturing of clandestines. This indecision can, in the short term, lead to dysfunction in administrative services that are ill-prepared materially and humanly for the boom in requests and for the painful accounts of exile.

A management drift has been observed in the prefect services that receive asylum-seekers in France and that are directly confronted, like any other public administration, with the management of quantities of files, the restructuring of reception services internally and for the public, increased automation of processes, and pressure for productivity – rapid processing and backlog of completed files in the ministries – which has become the priority in services affected by the recent LOLF (new law organising the financing of public administrations).[15] However, if the evolution in managing public administrations, today a well-studied process, is ordinarily accompanied by individualisation in treating social problems, by specialisation of clerks, by multiplication of increasingly refined categories, here we see the reverse. The desire for improved treatment of asylum-seekers leads to simplification of criteria, collectivisation of cases, standardisation of clerks, and uniformity of attitude (a belief in false asylum-seekers). For Albert Ogien, if management thinking is taking over the realm of policy decisions, it is because it provides a scientific legitimacy that short-circuits the debate.[16] For Gérard Noiriel,[17] inversely, the depoliticising of the policy field has locked the question of asylum within largely unsolvable bureaucratic considerations.

Will we thus live to see the end of the right to asylum in Europe? François Julien-Laferrière[18] – following the example of Catherine Wihtol de Wenden,[19] Daphné Douteillet-Paquet[20] or Alain Morice[21] – reflects on this end of the right to asylum: the danger would be to construct European identity in the confusion between the policy of controlling migratory fluxes and the policy of asylum and not to construct the asylum policy independent from the control of fluxes and the need for security (though the absorption of asylum rights into immigration policy might be one of the symptoms of European construction, as Gérard Noiriel has analysed it for the nineteenth century). In any case, belonging to a country which, in the past, meant belonging to Europe, is being clearly re-established by homogenising the European territory via a hardening of border controls.

European-Mediterranean co-development: solution or externalising asylum?

While the Geneva Convention addresses only host countries, the current trend is to make countries of origin responsible and to identity them as 'safe non-member countries'. Judged responsible for provoking the flux, for failures in security and human rights, they are increasingly asked to take back their emigrants, with security assured. A growing responsibility weighs on countries bordering the European Union, now transformed without preparation into buffer zones or host zones for asylum-seekers. Re-entry accords have been signed, particularly by Germany, with Poland, the Czech Republic, Hungary and Slovenia. The newest countries in the European Union are especially exposed to the problem of asylum, by virtue of the European Dublin II accord, in effect since June 2003, stipulating that it is the first country a migrant arrives in that must deal with him.

The North African region, as a transit zone, is equally concerned by the hardening of European migration policies. The Barcelona Process, which launched the Euro-Mediterranean partnership in 1995, seeks to establish the basis for multilateral dialogue and cooperation between the European Union and the twelve Mediterranean countries and territories (Algeria, Morocco, Tunisia, Egypt, Jordan, Lebanon, Syria, Israel, the Palestine territory, Cyprus, Malta and Turkey). The Commission has considered that 'migratory pressures could, based on a lack of planning for cooperation on methodical management by concerned countries, easily generate friction, to the detriment of both international relations and immigrant peoples'.

Three phases of the Euro-Mediterranean partnership are defined (policy and security, economic and financial, socio-cultural and human), a process that the newspaper *Le Monde* announced, not without scepticism, in April 1998 under the heading 'Les illusions d'un codéveloppement sans moyens'.

This collaboration–cooperation on the migratory aspect of the partnership, which was then followed up in another form by the constitution of the '5 + 5 Dialogue',[22] has an effect. The collaboration is characterised by a large range of agreements (shared information and investigations) intended to stop clandestine fluxes: the production of legal texts with the goal of sanctioning organisers and participants in clandestine departures, the training of personnel to survey coastlines, and the acquisition of new material for detection. Thus, Romano Prodi, then president of the European Commission, lauded the strengthening of the Euro-Tunisian partnership during a conference in Tunis in March 2003. However, since 2003, we have seen the hardening of policy in Tunisia regarding free circulation of human beings: police controls have multiplied, new legislation (February 2004) foresees new passports and travel documents, and it aims especially to reinforce the repression of crimes connected to clandestine traffic. This has been extended to apply to any person having a direct or indirect connection to the incriminating act.

To compensate, re-entry accords between European and Mediterranean countries envisage economic openings, financial and technical aid, plans for cooperation and development, and quotas for regular immigrants coming from countries showing a real will to combat clandestine immigration. On the basis of these repatriation accords involving the intervention of consulates, contracting countries are required to readmit into their own territory their own emigrants – and, to a somewhat lesser degree, clandestine foreigners who have transited their country.

Among the first re-entry accords between European countries and Mediterranean countries was one signed in 1992 between Spain and Morocco: it was, however, necessary to wait nearly four years before Rabat agreed to readmit 65 clandestine immigrants from sub-Saharan Africa who had transited their territory. This long interval was used to gain certain improvements in the situation of Moroccans in Spain as well as a reduction in foreign debt. The situation of migrants concentrated in Ceuta and Melilla led to exceptional measures being taken by Spain to manage these fluxes (annual evacuation of 1000 migrants with the benefit of social aid), which was like an invitation to the sub-Saharan migrants, and thus aggravated the situation.[23] In 2000, the government halted the host programmes because of their high cost and because of the in-coming government's new orientation, which sought to discourage irregular immigration. The reduction of migratory pressure in the zone today is the result of improved border controls, the signing of repatriation treaties with countries of sub-Saharan Africa, and the repression used against immigrants who cannot be deported. The reinforcement of controls in Ceuta and in Melilla have displaced the problem towards the Canary Islands. Since August 2000, the halt of transfers to the peninsula has provoked an increase in migrants in temporary entry centres. The solution applied up to the present is to print up deportation orders for migrants and to allow them to cross the border with Morocco in the hope that they will voluntarily return to their country of origin.

If the media and various reports inform us more and more about routes taken by migrants, from the point of origin to the projected destination, we know little about the details and the conditions of return routes, taken by migrants who were refused entry. After several experiments, the charter-plane solution to repatriation, rapid but expensive and judged to increase traffic, seems to have been abandoned in favour of trucks that transport migrants from holding centre to holding centre all the way to the border of neighbouring countries. We are seeing repeated trips to the border for the same migrant, via formal (or informal) re-entry accords (by stages, for example, between Spain and Morocco, then from Morocco to Algeria, from Algeria to Niger, and, finally, from Niger to Mali; or else from France or Italy to Tunisia, then, possibly, from Tunisia to Libya).

Co-development has been put forward by European Union countries as a solution to the migratory issue. Since 1998, countries such as Italy signed no less than thirty accords of this type (coupled with aid for training of police from countries of emigration, with plans for development and cooperation, and with the establishment of quotas, which gave preferential entry to certain categories of workers according to an annual plan),[24] in particular with Morocco, Tunisia, Algeria, Egypt and Turkey, along with an operational understanding with Libya regarding management of migratory fluxes in the Sahara zone.[25]

This process has not occurred without a reaction from the North African countries. On 9 October 2001 Morocco presented an official demand to the European Union for sharing of responsibilities in managing clandestine migratory fluxes. During the European Council in Seville (21–22 June 2002), Khaddafi declared for his part that he was giving back to Europe the responsibility for multiplying development projects meant to slow down the flux of illegal migrants to North Africa.

These countries certainly did not wait for re-entry accords with Europe to undertake migratory policy. It can be said, however, that a policy is being formalised openly in the Euro-Mediterranean partnership, thanks to these accords and to guarantees in the negotiation protocols by international institutions, such as the International Organisation for Migrations (IOM).

With what seems to be the abandonment of conventional asylum and with the establishment, for better or worse, of Community regulation, we are seeing, paradoxically, a strong expansion of an international system, a multiplication of binational accords between Europe and the countries of the South. This strategy can be considered as one more means of reinforcing the inequality of wealth by transferring the costs of migration via pressure on the most fragile countries, with no assurance for them of anything in return. Is there really a relation between migration and development? For Reginald Appleyard,[26] this relation has yet to be demonstrated. In short, the crisis in asylum policy is only one change resulting from the policy disconnect in favour of economics or, at worst, a new episode in neo-colonialism.

On the other hand, it can be said that the crisis in asylum policy is the sign of a mutation, an alteration in North–South relations, in which the countries of the South are considered to be in an unequal economic situation but also as political partners partly responsible (and on the basis of negotiated compensation) for their departing emigrants whom it is no longer possible, whatever dramatic situations they might find themselves in, to consider as refugees seeking charitable asylum but rather as foreigners engaged in migration.

These two interpretations are not mutually exclusive. For example, North Africa's eventual participation in the European free-trade zone can only profoundly modify Euro-Mediterranean relations; which only displaces the asylum problem, particularly towards sub-Saharan regions. Today it is Europe, along with North Africa, that must ask the ethical question: to whom do we wish to grant asylum?

Notes

1. Translated by Penny Allen.
2. Excerpt from 'Sadness of Olympio', a poem by Victor Hugo quoted by a Mauritanian migrant in Tunis.
3. 'La France, première destination des demandeurs d'asile en Europe', was the headline in *Le Monde* on 30 April 2004. At the national level, the number of requests for conventional asylum was 50 000 in 2003, to which must be added 25 000 territorial requests for asylum, according to the accounting of the OFPRA and the Ministry of the Interior. These figures are approximate. They do not take into account, among other things, the number of people making multiple requests. In France, Turks make the most requests for asylum.
4. Aristide R. Zolberg, 'Chemins de la faim, chemin de la peur', in *Actes de recherche en sciences sociales (ARESS)*, no. 99, 1993, pp. 36–42.
5. D. Perrin, 'Evolutions du droit d'asile en Occident: le refuge refoulé', in *Ecritures de l'exil* (collection under the direction of A. Giovannoni) (PUF, 2004).
6. Rémy Bazenguissa, 'Les réfugiés dans les enjeux locaux dans le Nord-Est du Congo', in *Exilés, réfugiés, déplacés en Afrique centrale et orientale* (collection under the direction of André Guichaoua) (Paris: Karthala, 2004), pp. 379–423.
7. The notion of internal asylum appears in the new French asylum law of 10 December 2003.
8. Rémy Leveau, Catherine Wihtol de Wenden and Khadija Mohsen-Finan (dir.), *Nouvelles citoyennetés: réfugiés et sans-papiers dans l'espace européen*, Institut français des relations internationales (Paris: IFRI, 2001).
9. Godfried Engbersen, 'Sans-Papiers: les stratégies de séjour des immigrés clandestins', in *Actes de recherche en sciences sociales (ARESS)*, no. 129, 1999, pp. 26–38.
10. Didier Fassin, Alain Morice and Catherine Quiminal (dir.), *Les Lois de l'inhospitalité: Les politiques de l'immigration à l'épreuve des sans-papiers* (Paris: La Découverte/Essais, 1997).
11. See Andrea Rea, 'Le travail des sans-papiers et la citoyenneté domestique', in *La Fin des norias? Réseaux migrants dans les économies marchandes en Méditerranée* (collection under the direction of Michel Peraldi) (Paris: Maisonneuve & Larose, 2002).
12. Giacomo Luciani (dir.), *Migration Policies in Europe and the United States* (Boston: Kluwer Academic Publishers, 1993), and Salvatore Pallida, 'La Criminalisation des migrants', in *Actes de recherche en sciences sociales (ARESS)*, no. 129, 1999, pp. 39–49.
13. Loïc Wacquant, 'Des ennemis commodes', in *Actes de recherche en sciences sociales*, no. 129, 1999, pp. 63–7.
14. Zygmunt Bauman, *Globalization: the Human Consequences* (Oxford: Oxford University Press, 1998).
15. See Sylvie Mazzella, 'Vie et mort du droit d'asile territorial', in *Sociétés contemporaines*, no. 57, May 2005, pp. 105–18.
16. Albert Ogien, *L'Esprit gestionnaire: Une analyse de l'air du temps* (Paris: Editions de l'Ecole des hautes études en sciences sociales (EHESS), 1995).
17. Gérard Noiriel, *Réfugiés et sans-papiers: La République face au droit d'asile. XIXe–XXe siècle*, collection 'Pluriel' (Paris: Hachette, 1999) (new edition).

18. François Julien-Laferrière, 'La situation des demandeurs d'asile dans les zones d'attente et les centres de rétention administrative en France', in *Cultures et conflits*, special number 'Circuler, enfermer, éloigner', 1997, pp. 7–43.
19. Catherine Wihtol de Wenden, *op. cit.*, note 8.
20. Daphné Bouteillet-Paquet, *L'Europe et le droit d'asile* (Paris: L'Harmattan, 2001).
21. Alain Morice, *op. cit.*, note 10.
22. A group composed, on the North African side, of Tunisia, Algeria, Libya, Morocco and Mauritania and, on the European side, by Italy, France, Portugal, Spain and Malta.
23. According to a report by the BIT 2002, 'L'immigration irrégulière subsaharienne à travers et vers le Maroc'.
24. Ferruccio Pastore, 'Aeneas's Route: Euro-Mediterranean Relations and International Migration', in *Migration and the Externalities of European Integration* (Oxford: Lexington Books, 2002).
25. See Giuseppe Sciortino, 'Le politiche migratorie europee tra convergenza e vincoli strutturali', *Europa*, 10 (3), 2001, pp. 207–18.
26. Reginald Appleyard, 'International Migration and Development: an Unresolved Relationship', *International Migration Review*, 30 (3/4), special issue, 2002, pp. 251–67.

4

The Mediterranean Divide and its Echo in the Sahara: New Migratory Routes and New Barriers on the Path to the Mediterranean[1]

Ali Bensaad

As the Sahara connects directly with the southern shore of the Mediterranean via revitalised and ever multiplying routes, it is taking on significance and altering the relational system of the Mediterranean space. The Sahara is growing in importance as a result of intense traffic crossing it on the way to Europe (even if it often falls short), confronting both shores of the Mediterranean with the realities of new links, sometimes with worldwide roots, while confirming and consolidating the space as a preferred route. Trans-Saharan corridors now directly link black Africa and the Mediterranean. Migratory fluxes are the corollary of this renewed link. They are also its engine and fuel.

These migratory fluxes illustrate how the 'inclusive-exclusive' European pattern extends into always larger and more far-flung territories. They also illustrate, via the Sahara, how new territory adds more space for manoeuvre, space which is itself the scene of interactions between various players. It is because of the Sahara, that the Maghreb and the larger Mediterranean area are experiencing dynamic globalisation that alters both migratory patterns and the idea of borders.

This globalisation is not just limited to the draw of the North and the attraction of Europe. It is at base a product of a regional dynamic, a drawing together across the Sahara of North African and sub-Saharan regions. The changes the two sides are undergoing, and which unite them, have provoked and increased the volume of traffic within the region towards the Mediterranean portal to Europe, where it joins and adds to the Euro-Maghreb traffic.

If the Mediterranean is a line of demarcation between Europe and the South, the Sahara functions very much in the same way, an echo of the northern line, bringing Europe even further south. The worsening of tensions on the Mediterranean rift generates an echo underscoring the Sahara rift. The Sahara already carries within it a series of divides: it marks a difference in wealth and development within the southern continent; it is also the line of demarcation between two geocultural systems, the Arab-Berber and the black African, which, before the break introduced by the colonial period, already had a past of intense exchanges or struggles based on proximity. All this transpires on the physical fault line that the Sahara actually is: one of the most impenetrable places in the world, a vast expanse 4000 kilometres across.

Now Schengen Europe exports its tensions into this situation. By absorbing shock waves from the Mediterranean, which wash over and deepen the gulf, the Sahara is more than ever a Mediterranean outpost. As such it is also a periphery, a 'suburb' increasingly close to Europe and to which it is henceforth connected more directly.

It is this demarcation line, affirmed and deepened by the duality of attraction/repulsion it represents for its neighbours to the South, that Europe seeks to transform into a vanguard barrier.

Globalisation at the edge: the Sahara at the crossroads of new intercontinental links

Despite the danger – or, paradoxically, because of it – trans-Saharan routes have become major passages to Europe, clandestine migration routes for which the Sahara, because of its very impenetrability, functions both as a crossing/taking-off point towards Europe and as a holding zone. African emigration towards and via the Maghreb has become a significant factor since the beginning of the 1990s, reaching its peak in 2000. Armed repression and resistance on the Maghreb side, along with occasional violence, do nothing to turn back the ever-growing flux.

Difficult as it is to quantify the disorderly fluxes, their numbers can only be estimated. In 2001, we were able to establish the figure of approximately 65 000 migrants as the *minimum* transiting via Algadez, the migratory crossroads through which most of the flux passes (although 2.5 million are estimated to pass through Libya and about 300 000 through Algeria).[2]

If these fluxes are aiming for Europe, they do not always get that far. The numbers of sub-Saharan migrants remain slim as compared to migrants from other regions, notably the Maghreb. But the extreme danger of the routes, with crossings in nightmarish conditions, gives the impression of an endless push and creates in Europe the feeling of a fortress under siege.

At the same time that this immigration has taken on importance, the geographical origin of migrants has widened. Initially Saharan, it now involves all of Africa down to its most southern point. The function of the Sahara as a transit zone is such that it is now used even by international traffickers of Asian clandestines and, recently, of Latin Americans.

The borders of Europe are now situated and must be crossed much further south than the traditional demarcation line represented by the Mediterranean. They have moved all the way to the Sahara, where they are now the point of contact and a divide of intercontinental proportions. The Sahara, a marginal periphery, has now become a connecting factor on a planetary scale.

A new taking-off point for Europe, the Sahara is also a threshold whose extremely difficult crossing makes it a world apart, whose vast holding capacity is as broad as it is impenetrable. The Sahara has become a protective frontier zone for the Schengen region in which waves of migrants perish and whose barrier aspects Europe would like to reinforce; thus making countries of the Maghreb into holding zones for migrants who, unable to reach Europe, invade North Africa and are left in a precarious condition. Instead of a transit zone, the Maghreb is becoming a buffer zone for a Europe unwilling to open its gates, even though the shifting of the Euro-Maghreb border into the depths of the Sahara and the multiplication of obstacles have done nothing to quell the flow. However, these flows are feeding a paranoid vision: they are used to justify the holding zones Europe is creating on its southern borders, as well as the militarisation of North Africans or even Saharans as sentinels asked to operate camps or carry out cruel repression. This comes at the cost of further democratic and human failings, already extensive in these countries; of further unsettling of already fragile societies by structural demands imposed by Europe; of ethnic or community tensions; and of geopolitical tensions. All of this is a heavy and possibly explosive price to pay in a region already sufficiently torn apart.

What is the true reality of this 'invasion'? Its 'certainty' is based on two arguments stemming from a Eurocentric and paranoid vision: the draw of Europe and poverty as the engine of mobility. Supposedly there is an essential draw: Europe is attractive in itself, for its economic and democratic virtues. But both arguments are largely undercut in the case of trans-Saharan migrations.

In the first place, it is not the poor of these poor countries who come to Europe, but rather, instead, candidates for travel come most often from those who are best off. The cost is not necessarily an issue. The adventure, as the migrants themselves call it, is undertaken by the most enterprising.

Among them, the most educated, the most cultivated, those most open to the world are the most numerous and increasing in numbers: four years ago,[3] after an exhaustive study, we established that more than 20 per cent of clandestine migrants have a high level of education even though they come from countries where the largest portion of the population is illiterate. Polls done since then along various routes tend to confirm the percentage of educated migrants. It is not decrepitude or the lack of development in African countries that expands the exodus to new layers of society. It is the emergence of mobility as a supplemental strategy for developing resources, mobility acting as the soul and tool of the strategy.

Thus, it is not an accident that Nigeria furnishes the majority of migrants. The size of its population does not explain the disproportion. What explains the preponderance of migrants coming from Nigeria is, paradoxically, the relative wealth of this oil country (itself a country of immigration), its high level of development, the extraversion of its economy, and, especially, its urbanisation – well illustrated by the octopus-like Lagos, with its population larger than that of Ile-de-France! Many elements produce urban areas open to modernity, open to the outside world, and thus more open to the migratory vision.

But it wasn't always thus. The present evolution is like globalisation itself, in which it is those most open to the outside world who are the most likely to travel. They are like entrepreneurs, in our era where the entrepreneur is the ideal social type.

Unfortunately, criminalising the crossing, as well as the entry into Europe, means that it is those who are the best connected to Mafia networks who have the best chances of succeeding. This skimming off the cream of the crop is one of the paradoxes of Europe's closure with its consequential repressive measures. Interestingly, it is not that Europe has become increasingly attractive, but rather that the world is shrinking. If today a large part of migratory fluxes ends up in Europe or finds itself drawn in that direction, that is not the only place migrants go.

In reality, most migrants arriving in the Maghreb – whether as destination or as portal to Europe – are often already mobile, often having moved to an African country other than their own. Migrations within Africa are substantial and with a long history. The fact that a country such as the Ivory Coast has been able to attract as many as 1.7 million foreign workers, and that its capital is 46 per cent foreign, illustrates the amplitude of this phenomenon. If Europe has an effect, it is, first, the disruptions it produces in African economies. Already on the move, migrants continue to develop their mobility capital, by going as far as they can.

In the beginning of the 1990s, before becoming a massive movement of people, drawn from all over Africa and heading for Europe, this emigration originally sought to go only as far as the North African Sahara and consisted only of local populations (mainly the Tuaregs of Niger and Mali). The development of the North African Sahara (Algerian and Libyan especially), enriched by oil revenues, called out to everyone throughout the Sahara region. This attraction to the Sahara was enhanced by other events: after the discovery of mining resources in other regions (such as uranium in Niger) and faced with territorial conflicts (international or interethnic), certain nations were moved to develop other attractions in the Sahara in order to control it.

It was around such gravitational centres that the traffic grew, expanded in scope and linked together the sub-Saharan and North African sides of the Sahara, eventually reaching all the way to the southern shores of the Mediterranean. It was there, at its Mediterranean gate, that Europe became the obvious destination for migrations and drew them in. Here the southern migrations joined the Euro-Maghreb traffic, enlarging it and attracting other fluxes. By reconnecting black Africa to the Maghreb, the Sahara connected black Africa directly to Europe.[4]

The return to repressed spatial modes: an old and thwarted globalisation

The Sahara, land of transit and exchange, has once again found its secular function, but within contemporary parameters it is enhanced and is operated on a planetary scale. The spatial disruption that present trans-Saharan connections introduce is like an echo of the situation in the seventh century, when the Sahara had already promised to enlarge the 'limits' of the world with the opening up of Africa, then unknown, to trans-Saharan commerce, which would lead, for more than ten centuries, to important exchanges between black Africa and the Mediterranean, the centre of the world up to that point. This opening and this new connection were proportionally as much, if not more, of a spatial shock as the one engendered by new oceanic routes and the discovery of America seven centuries later.

The Sahara is therefore re-emerging from a latent period brought on by competition with oceanic routes and fixed in place by colonisation. The renewal of its transit function is like a new beginning for an earlier globalisation process: held back for a time, it is now revitalised by contemporary dynamics.

It is interesting to note how this traffic is in the process of modifying spatial orientations by bringing life back to old routes, to old trans-Saharan centres that had been marginalised by colonisation (which itself had countered the meridian-based spatial organisation that had existed up until then, instituting a region-based organisation and turning the Sahara into a discontinuity). The renewal of meridian-based circulation, trans-Saharan, is a return to repressed spatial orientations. Like any resurgence of something repressed, it is today the source of concern, because these meridian-based modes do not correspond to, and break out of, the categories instituted to contain them.

The growth of urban frameworks around old trans-Saharan centres (such as Agadez expanding at the expense of Niamey, the capital), or around new cities created in the Sahara on the potential meridian trade axes (Sebha, Tamanrasset), shows the new meridian-based organisation of various national spaces and the inevitable drawing together of the Maghreb and black Africa. Competing trans-Saharan routes starting in Morocco, Algeria and Libya, including those under construction, will only consolidate this organisation; the pioneer route starting in Algeria played a considerable role in the development and channelling of traffic towards a central axis even though one scarcely existed then.[5]

These routes, which North African countries and countries such as Nigeria invest in (by financing sections of highway even outside their national territory, as Algeria and Nigeria do for the Niger highway), become the echo of those that crossed the Sahara for centuries, linking the Maghreb to black Africa.

The Sahara: a double line of demarcation

Modern traffic, drawn towards Europe, comes from more and more distant sources; it illustrates, among other things, the extension of the 'inclusive–exclusive' European process. As a spatial vector of this extension, linking the two peripheries, the North African and the black African, the Sahara is also the spatial incarnation of the rift that occurs in the region and the relations between its various elements. It is a rift from the point of view of Europe, as it accentuates and exacerbates the ultimate line of demarcation with the South, the most obvious one, which is the vast border zone lying between the two shores of the Mediterranean.

The Saharan rift functions as a geographical echo, an extension and amplifier of the Mediterranean rift that is a consequence of Europe's closing of its borders. In the South, also, within the periphery, the Sahara is its own rift, of differentiation and of confrontation.

The simultaneous growth in Europe's attraction and in its fame, on the one hand, and in its closure, on the other, generates within the various elements of its periphery a tendency to move closer, to discover, while also exacerbating differences: the space of transit and of connections. The Sahara is also a major terrain of confrontations and of violence.

The Sahara: a divide echoing the Mediterranean divide

While North African immigration has been a major societal and political issue for decades, feeding political actions and security phobias, and while the question continues to be a sensitive issue in Euro-Maghreb relations, the appearance of an increasingly strong sub-Saharan contingency among clandestine migrants coming from the Maghreb adds a new dimension to the crisis and its tension points. However, these sub-Saharans are not very numerous proportional to other migrants, notably North Africans. What becomes a source of concern is the fact that their numbers are increasing and that a significant number of them, unable to reach Europe, become clandestine migrants in the Maghreb. Estimated to number between two and three million, they are seen as a sort of reserve army ready to deploy towards Europe.

Border control has become an essential preoccupation and a priority sensitive dossier in relations between European and North African countries. The latter are not only asked to survey their borders with Europe, they are also considered accountable for their southern borders in as much as they open onto migratory routes that then cross their own territories.

The question of migrations figures nowadays in ministerial conferences about foreign and domestic affairs occurring in the context of the Euro-Mediterranean partnership. Since the beginning of 2000, the question explicitly includes the subject of trans-Saharan migrations for which North African countries are both held responsible and solicited as sub-contractors. Libya's return to the international scene and its indirect participation in the Barcelona accords, through the 5 + 5,[6] allow the European Union to claim to deal globally with the issue with all North African countries.

The handling of the question of clandestine migrations – and more particularly sub-Saharan migrations – is, in fact, a required negotiating clause for North African countries, even if it is not officially so. Certain spoken blunders confirm this: Nicolas Sarkozy, as Minister of the Interior, going beyond internal French political rivalries, has, along with his European homologues, shown his muscle in relations and cooperation with North African countries on the question of migrations. Commenting on and justifying to the Algerian press the cooperative police agreements just signed, he stated this conditionality: 'If we are able to work in complete confidence on questions of security, it will be possible to work in a friendly manner on all other subjects.' At the same time, he launched into an argument in favour of the 'security zone on the western Mediterranean that would involve Spain, France and Italy in the North with the three North African countries in the South'.[7]

Since 2002 this conditionality has become explicit, collectively and institutionally. While the heads of state in the European Union already affirmed at the Seville summit (June 2002) 'their determination to struggle against illegal immigration while working with exit countries', this became explicit in 2004–5. The European summit in Brussels on 4–5 November 2004 declared its desire to 'completely integrate the immigration question into existing and future relations of the European Union and with other countries'; seeking 'the reinforcement of southern borders of the EU' it promised aid to 'countries that demonstrate their willingness to carry out their obligations'. The Ministers of Domestic Affairs and of Justice, meeting two months later on 27–29 January 2005, made this concrete with clear conditions: 'The intensification of cooperation with transit countries in questions of asylum must be part of the new neighbours' policy.' Earlier, the meeting of the G5 in Florence had called upon the three North African countries to collaborate on a security zone.

Capitalising on their role as 'sentinel outposts', North African countries have made trans-Saharan migrations a means for negotiation with and to put pressure on European countries. Libya used this widely to negotiate its return to the international scene and, with Algeria, to demand the extension of the lifting of the embargo on certain military surveillance equipment. More generally, the question becomes a tool for North African countries to use in soliciting and selling development aid, a recurrent theme in periodic Euro-Maghreb meetings of the 5 + 5 group. If this group has become active again in the last three years, in contrast to the blocked Barcelona accords process, it is because it is focused almost exclusively on the question of security and clandestine immigration.

This movement towards the western Mediterranean axis is not a simple geographic movement. It is instead a thematic movement, recentred on migration at the expense of development; it indicates that in place of the democratic conditionality, established at the beginning of the Barcelona accords process, there is now a migratory conditionality, which translates into an increased repressive role for North African countries.

Those imprisoned outside of the Schengen space: the Sahara as a holding zone

Border controls have become an essential preoccupation and a high-priority, sensitive, dossier on relations between European and North African countries has been compiled. The latter are asked to do more than survey their borders with Europe. They are considered accountable, also, for their southern borders in as much as they open onto migratory routes that cross their territories.

Going back to an earlier point, European demands extend now as much to control of foreign territory (pressure on Algeria and Morocco to get rid of migrant camps which were spectacularly raided and razed in early 2005) as to control of borders between North African countries (notably the Algerian–Moroccan border) and especially to control of southern borders. Obligated by agreements to readmit migrants who crossed their territory, they also have to organise these migrants' return to their country of origin, and European police assist them directly in the surveillance of migratory fluxes.

Thus the Sahara is now transformed into a kind of border outpost with the forced recruitment of North African countries as outpost sentinels, who are asked to maintain a retaining zone and to be sub-contractors of an outsourced repression far from European borders and public awareness.

Spectacular repressions that have taken place in the Maghreb in the last couple of years (and which North African governments have trumpeted in a flow of communiqués) revealed that said governments have already donned the uniform of 'repression recruits'. Although no legal measures dealt with the migration reality, practically all North African countries, between 2003 and 2004, took restrictive measures regarding circulation in their territories, measures which served legally to cover repressive acts that infringe guarantees of individual protection, as well as public liberties in the countries doing the legislating.

Paradoxically, it is the North African countries that, having resisted the large migratory presence in their territories, now point to it, as well as their proximity to Europe, in hopes of vaunting themselves as a geographical value that can protect Europe. Each of the countries presents itself both as the true corridor and crossroads of African migrations. Redefining the notion of who is the victim, the official North African discourse now presents local populations as victims of invasive migratory fluxes and repeats the European security argument that sees foreigners as a threat. The words of Mr Chalgham, Libyan Minister of Foreign Affairs, illustrate this reversal: 'Certain quarters of Tripoli are under the control of immigrants. They impose their laws; drugs and prostitution flourish. When I said that for us it's an invasion, that is exactly what I think.'[8]

The media headline 'clandestine immigration' has become an almost daily occurrence, notably in Algeria and Morocco, and it turns up under different themes, from communiqués enumerating repressive actions all the way to the demonising of migrants who bring with them delinquency or the spreading of sexually transmitted diseases.

For two years now, crack-downs are not only continuous, they are also publicised for all to see, even if the conditions in which they occur are kept hidden, as they could reveal serious violations of human rights. Different security branches (police and gendarmerie) do not hesitate regularly to leak their communiqués, enumerating the arrests, repressive actions and sacrifices made by security services as guarantees asked for and given by North African countries as evidence of their cooperation with Europe.

However, as they carry out their role as barriers, they amplify the repressive nature characteristic of their own governance mode. In regard to African migrants, North African countries multiply the excesses and violations they already practise on their own citizens. The repression of migrants becomes a new activity for corrupt bureaucrats, encouraged by government weakness, thereby aggravating the already dangerous conditions of crossing. In Algeria, there was so much police abuse in the commerce of deportation that it was necessary to have the gendarmerie monitor the process – which, according to migrants, has the effect of multiplying their baksheesh payments. In Algeria as well as in Morocco, rackets and violent round-ups of migrants (beatings, destruction and theft of property, illegal entry into homes, etc.) are widespread, and despite limits imposed on public expression, and associations and the press drawing attention to them, they continue to this day.

The most worrisome result of this repression is that massive expulsions push migrants into a desert no-man's land. This makes for a new kind of space in the Sahara as a holding zone. Migrants sent there build their own enclosures to survive in the desert. This leads in turn to a new kind of background space: self-imposed holding camps. So migrants find themselves locked up in the Sahara, far from the Schengen space, where their confinement occurs outside of any officially repressive space. These kinds of spaces appear in a discontinuous line from Niger–Libya to the Algeria–Mali outback. This is where migrants from round-ups and deportations are released.

In Tin Zouatin, on the Algerian–Malian border, one of three deportation points for African migrants sent from Algeria (the two others being

Bordj Moktar, 400 kilometres further west on the same border, and In Guezzam, on the Algeria–Niger border), we were able to verify that, in the course of December 2004 and January 2005, deportations of 300–600 persons occurred twice a week, an average of 3000 people a month (according to Niger consular authorities, there were as many in In Guezzam). Rounded-up migrants are released a few hundred metres from a dried-up river bed marking the border near the ruins of a destroyed Malian Tuareg village where they manage their survival, making an open detention zone of this ruined village.

Even though Libya publicises the return of migrants to their own countries by plane, most deportations are by truck towards Dirkou, in the interior of Niger, and often to Tumu or Madama, near the border, where migrants are supposed to be picked up by African counterparts. What happens in reality is that the deportees are stacked up at the border in deplorable conditions. Dirkou, which we described five years ago as the transit city where this sort of activity had spread, was becoming a holding pen where deported migrants were held. Libya announced that it alone had deported 54 000 people in 2004. This is almost as many as passed through the major point of passage, Agadez, at the moment of its heaviest traffic.

It seems as if we have been seeing a reversal of immigration waves since 2003. Practically speaking, this is not the case. Aside from those deported by plane (fewer than a tenth of those deported from Libya), very few migrants return to their country of origin. In Tin Zouatin, clandestine transporters, warned by their police accomplices, speed ahead of the deportation convoys in order to propose to the deportees to take them back (payable on credit) to Tamanrasset from where they were just deported.

If the European debate about setting up transit camps in North Africa has an antecedent in the European management of migrations beginning in 1986, with propositions for outsourcing already being made by the Danish government,[9] the practice of sending people to holding camps shows that reality is already ahead of the debate, and in the worst sense. These are not new practices either, because, five years ago at the very moment Libya was still presenting itself as a country of immigration, we pointed out the existence of retention camps there, with medieval conditions of incarceration, some of them active since 1996.[10]

In deporting and outsourcing the dysfunctions of the Mediterranean human space, there is the risk that instabilities on the southern flank of Europe will become worse and more numerous. The first risk is that in trying to reinforce the repressive function of North African countries in the struggle against immigration, we end up fatally reinforcing their generalised repressive practices, even though passivity is already deliberated in these countries.

Furthermore, in tightening the vice, we place North African countries themselves in difficulty. In pressuring them and recruiting them to carry out our repression, we end up voiding the notion of the sovereign state and reducing their capacities for social and spatial regulation – control of their own territory. It is a weakening of the state that does not stop the people creating the fluxes – from agents who organise or are complicit with the traffic, to leaders who, in order to perpetuate their own jobs, negotiate, based on new risks, the role of outpost sentinels and accomplices in the repression. Libya's acceptance of Italian soldiers on its soil to survey migrants already serves to legitimise those in charge.

Migrations contribute to the context of fragility surrounding Europe's southern gates, and the temptation of European countries to deport their dysfunctions can only aggravate the situation, or make it explosive.

The Sahara: a line of demarcation and confrontation between southern countries

Candidates for emigration, faced with a closed Europe – failing to reach it or still harbouring hopes of doing so – become clandestine immigrants in the Maghreb. Once a transit space, the region has become more and more one of immigration, and it is in this region that the effects of migratory fluxes, seeking Europe but falling short, are felt.

These fluxes are the source of an informal economy rooted in reality, and any idea of undermining it is an illusion. This economy generates resources tied to the transit function in countries south of the Sahara. It takes on importance for transit spaces, among the poorest areas in the world, such as Niger, now a crossroads of migrant traffic that has become a vital resource. An economy of transport has arisen, legally prospering out in the open, around this illegal and clandestine emigration.

The relative importance of this resource is such that the state is its first organiser and direct beneficiary through a system of transit taxes. Beyond that, it is a political resource, as employment tied to transit (notably transport of migrants) is meted out based on politics and patronage. The ancestral nomadic tribes (mainly the Tuaregs), affected by the fluxes, operate as guides and conveyors known as 'mules'. Functioning as guides, these tribes take on characteristics typical of nomadic tribes, such as playing the double role of conveyor/robber: they earn money by guiding and by robbing, robbery reinforcing their necessary function as guides. Among the migrants guided, many are relieved of their personal property and abandoned.

It is in the Maghreb that the economic stakes of this migration appear. African migrants constitute a floating reserve of labourers, whose paltry remuneration and availability for hard labour, especially in the Saharan environment, make them an appreciable source of profit for local economies. Entire sectors of the Saharan economy – notably in construction of buildings and public works and agricultural processing – owe their success to this labour. However, these labourers are also increasingly present in the northern part of the Maghreb, where they supply a growing portion of domestic labour.

The strategic importance of the Sahara for North African states, the importance of development projects initiated there, and the encouraged presence of entrepreneurs all create a tolerance for such entrepreneurs using labour that increases profits. The entrepreneurs are often local notables and the powerful who, in practice, have ample opportunity to locally manage the issues of migration to their own profit.

In many ways this clandestine immigration reproduces almost systematically the characteristics and the place it occupies in Europe. It is the same sectors that make use of it and that create prosperity based on it: construction of buildings and public works, agriculture, restaurant and hotel work, the clothing industry, and domestic labour.

Concerning the clothing industry, the position of African migrants is made stronger by the obvious Africanness of clothing worn in the southern part of the Maghreb as well as by their skills in this area. As for domestic labour, a kind of social tradition – heritage of a fictive egalitarianism going back to the war of independence, which made Algerians resist this type of labour despite their poverty – turns black Africans into workers in a sector that inequality encourages. On this subject, we cite Andréa Réa on clandestine status and its perpetuation in Europe: 'It is known on all social, economic, and political levels . . . and it meets the economic needs of certain work sectors.'[11]

The presence of migrants is so much a part of local economic realities of Saharan towns that even large waves of expulsion are, in fact, selective. They always spare a good number, those who are employed and who benefit, temporarily, from the protection of their employer and his connections. A slavery economy is being built, with a mix of local notables and entrepreneurs, local and south-Saharan mafias, and agents of the state: a slave market of labourers for construction and for domestic work, white slavery (although in this case, it is 'blacks') for prostitution, networks of racketeers, and 'mules' for transit. North African newspapers even call it a slavery economy.

It is a very profitable economy, in which representatives of the state are implicated; it is in the most dictatorial countries, such as Libya, that such traffic has assumed the largest proportions. Boats that recently sank on their way to Europe had set sail from Libya; such an event would have been unimaginable a few years ago, when the Libyan government, seeking power, militarised its territory. The current weakening of countries in this region makes control an illusion, as traffic is a source of corruption.

North African societies find themselves confronted with a new and delicate reality: the boom in African immigration creates a, hitherto unknown, problem for societies already in the throes of social crisis and the dysfunctions of underdevelopment; societies are made unstable by drastic structural changes. Forced into a clandestine world – or at least an ambiguous status – migrants are dealt with randomly and are always precarious. On top of police harassment and manipulations by employers is the daily racism, which sometimes becomes violent. This became extreme during the Libyan massacres of several hundred African migrants. The realities of daily life reveal a xenophobia and intolerance for African migrants. North African societies are proving that no society has a monopoly on intolerance.

Beyond its precariousness and its exploitation, immigration leads to an essential questioning of values within North African societies: there are mixed marriages between Algerians and clandestine migrants (about 200 in the town of Tamanrasset alone), and their children are born in Algeria deprived of legal status and with the possibility of education problematical. All of this brings into question the status of a foreigner there (no legal process takes into account or opens on to the possibility of regularisation), the code of nationality (practically inaccessible to a foreigner and not transmissible by a woman), and the status of women (mixed marriage is socially unacceptable for a woman and in any case is religiously forbidden with a non-Muslim, even if the majority of such marriages are with African Muslims or at least declared as such).

Between two identity front-lines: the Maghreb as meeting point with the other

As a result of the flux of African migrants towards the North, contacts multiply and expand between North African and black African socio-cultural groups. Migrations are redrawing the front-lines of identity and reformulating the question of 'the other' as multicultural contacts multiply. From the view from another horizon, the other 'other', the new immigrant in these countries of emigration adds his perspective to that of the Occidental – the traditional mirror in which North Africans have habitually seen their own image.

The new societal problem presented by African immigration is thus exacerbated by the doubly destabilising confrontation with a new 'other' – even though the Maghreb had already known serious identity crises related to colonial shock waves, prolonged by the attraction to Europe (and enhanced by its near proximity), and made more real, finally, by a growing socio-economic distortion that accentuates frustrations and leads to violent alternative affirmations of identity. It is in this context of fragility and crisis that North African societies face the challenge of a new 'other'.

All this occurs, in relation to Europe, in a reverse perspective: the new contact with black Africa, as it presently unfolds, perpetuates a long history of unequal relations between the two regions. The black African migrant is not a simple 'other' but an 'other' within historical memory, with an assigned place in the imagination. The inequality today is anchored, at least in the imagination, in the past, which justifies it.

Inequality has for a long time and until the very recent past marked relations between the two regions because of the slavery practised in the Maghreb until the end of the nineteenth century and even into the twentieth, (although this slavery was largely in Morocco). The presence of slaves – almost exclusively of black African origin – until the beginning of the twentieth century was a strong part of the social structure: they were estimated to be between 1 and 7.5 per cent of the total Moroccan population, and transactions concerning them amounted to several thousand a year.[12] More than ten centuries of trans-Saharan trade – of which the slave trade was the principal vector along with gold – contributed to a structure in the Maghreb that represented Africans as of unequal worth.

It was this inequality that was the basis of the construction and historical memory of relations with black Africa. The edifying shorthand and multiple meanings contained in the term *abd* (servant or slave), used formerly in the Arab-Muslim world to designate a function (servant-domestic), a status (slave), and a skin colour (black, of the black race), confirmed the tendency to equate servile status with race.[13] This historical memory is reactivated today where, in Libya for example, the term *abd* is the public and almost unique usage to designate migrant black Africans.

It is the same mental constructions, historically sifted down, that come into play today in the ambiguous attitude of the Moroccan elite city dweller regarding domestic help, which explains why certain forms of domestic labour persist even though they are denounced as modern forms of slavery.

It is again these mental constructions that contributed to the ostracism of black populations in Algeria – even of the elite – during the war of liberation, in a national movement that was nevertheless highly exclusivist.[14] The stigmatisation by skin colour (black) is a practice that illustrates the injurious meaning of the word *kahlouche* (swarthy).

It must be noted here how this historical memory has found life more recently in the European imagination to better situate its own representations: thus *eigro* (the word *nègre* in Creole) is reappropriated as a doubly charged insult. So this new 'other', the African migrant, is arriving in a universe where historical memory confines him to an already defined and assigned place. But his presence, casting light on the ambiguities of relations with foreigners, also casts light on relations within the immigrant society itself.

The presence of foreigners illustrates the malaise surrounding the status of Hartanis (descendants of servile people). Whereas in Algeria and in Libya, such people have benefited as much from the good will of political powers to improve their status, as from the willing rejection of modern structures by the Tuaregs, they have been able to acquire a socio-economic status that places them above their former masters (bureaucracy is in the hands of Hartanis in Saharan regions, where they are dominant). However, with the presence of black Africans in the Maghreb, the rejection and racism they suffer differ from the symbolic marginalisation that the Hartanis continue to experience. The Hartanis' desire to differentiate themselves from black African migrants is expressed by violent rejection of them and an exaggeration of nationalist sentiment.

In Tamanrasset, black African migrants find places to live with the Tuaregs, while they are completely absent in Hartani quarters, which are closed to them. And if in old cities such as Ouargla (the Soukra quarter) or Tripoli, black African migrants are found in the same quarters as the Hartanis, this physical proximity is with only the most marginal Hartanis and leads to no exchanges between them. Their cohabitation is a source of tension. In a learned denial, descendants of servile people treat the black migrants as slaves! Nevertheless, it is in the Hartani milieu that migrants find their bearings. Mixed marriages that are now occurring are only with people with Hartani roots.

As for the Tuaregs, although they practise and make use of archaic hierarchical concepts that can be shocking in the present North African context, paradoxically they are the ones who reject xenophobia the most. If their desire to maintain a hierarchical distance is strong (with explicit slavery or slavery disguised as servitude), they also demand rights for black Africans and resist clichés. So, hiding perhaps another form of racism, and even though AIDS is blamed on the migrants in both the press and on the street, the Tuaregs (and we verifed it in interviews) believe that black Africans are not the ones introducing this evil, since they have always been present in the Sahara, but that it is the fault of foreigners who come from the North!

This thinking cannot be explained simply by the benefits the Tuaregs receive from organising the transit of migrants. The explanation is found, perhaps, in experience gained during the centuries of trans-Saharan trade convoys that made the black African more familiar than the newcomer from the North.

The new migration paths, revitalising old routes and shrinking geographical distances, are reconnecting the threads of history, an obligatory passage for integration from the bottom up, already begun.

Chase them from the North, they come back via the South: the reintroduction of cosmopolitanism via the margins

Even though North Africa has recovered from the shock waves of colonisation, developing since independence a monolithic cultural and religious quality that has eliminated every cosmopolitan dimension – notably in Algeria and in Libya (and in Morocco and in Tunisia, the foreign presence from tourism does not have any real social effect) – trans-Saharan migrations reintroduce a cosmopolitanism through the back door, on the ground or in the street, because it is brought by modest peoples seeking to attach themselves to the local social fabric for their survival. This cosmopolitanism – an evident reality in the large Saharan border cities – sends out waves, although modest ones, all the way to the large cities of the North.

This cosmopolitanism is first of all black African, presenting a new and radical otherness for North African societies cut off from all contact with this dimension, but also a kind of renewed otherness, because there is a history of contact and a common heritage between the two regions. Black Africa has in any case sifted into North African culture, with certain fossilised elements suddenly thrown in contact with their source, for example the old and the new *griots* (soothsayers), or the renewal of the practice of voodoo, which exists in forms adapted to the Maghreb.

The most unexpected and spectacular effect of this cosmopolitanism, beyond its Africanness, is the return, or introduction, via migrant African populations, of the French and English languages and the Catholic and Protestant religions. This effect can be seen already in the reopening of churches, reduced before to remnants of the past but now reinvigorated by the presence of migrants, a portion of whom are Christian. These churches play a charitable role for the migrants, filling in for the lack of NGOs. This presence produces a sort of commonality – what with the different practices of migrants who come from every direction plus the practices of local cults – amongst people whose experience of difficult crossings can increase religiousness. It is a presence that can be seen also as an intrusion in the North African cultural and religious traditions, an intrusion which, despite some rejection, is not yet producing tensions, even though a country like Algeria, for example, has been shaken for at least a year by passionate debate on the subject of conversions, presumably numerous, owing to proselytism practised by evangelical churches, which profit from the decline of Islamism or the disaffections generated by extremism.

In a counter-movement, there is a diffusion of the Arabic language in countries of the South thanks to the migrations and processes of their crossings. Bringing with it an experience and knowledge regarding mobility, Arabic is gaining favour, both with black African peoples and with the Tuareg Berbers. In a crossroads city like Agadez, Arabic has become one of the main languages.

Cosmopolitism is infiltrating lifestyles as well. The exuberance of the South is encountering the relative austerity of North Africans. Hasty assimilation of non-conforming behaviours into the local North African rigour regarding prostitution reveals the discomfort produced by confrontation with other lifestyles. Prostitution, an undeniable reality accompanying and living with the fluxes – and financing them sometimes – is the most visible aspect of this confrontation, probably because it is the most easily stigmatised, especially in Libya or in Algeria, where, under pressure from Islamist lobbies, public prostitution has been wiped out. Such repression can save on soul-searching but weighs heavily on the malaise of young people, for whom rigour is not the least of the administrative disciplines they experience.

Blurring the lines on the identity front, altering the question of otherness, mixing of peoples, the trans-Saharan migrations introduce into the Maghreb, once a land only of emigration, another 'other', the immigrant, which offers to North African societies the opportunity to look long and hard at themselves. The migrations demand attention, which sharpens the way North Africans look at themselves and jolts them out of habits developed as a result of interacting only with Europeans, who held the only mirror for so long.

Notes

1. Translated by Penny Allen.
2. Ali Bensaad, 'Agadez carrefour migratoire sahélo-maghrébin', in *REMI (Revue Européenne des Migrations Internationales)*, no. 19 (1), 2003, pp. 7–28, and *La Grande Migration africaine à travers le Sahara*, Méditerranée, Aix-en-Provence, no. 3–4, 2002, pp. 41–52.
3. Ibid.
4. Thus globalisation advances also on the margins, such as the Sahara, even though it is originally a product of peripheral spaces. Opening to the world is essentially the product of internal logic and an internal process, in peripheral spaces as well as in the Sahara, which see people gravitating to the urban centres in the North, yet reduced to ever more peripheral and marginal functions, leading to the eventual deconstruction of borders and the connection to the world's gravitational centres of the peripheral spaces themselves. This happens via the linking together, on the ground, of neighbouring socio-economic and cultural gathering places, leading eventually to an opening onto the world.
5. Ali Bensaad, 'Agadez carrefour migratoire sahélo-maghrébin'; Louis Blin, *L'Algérie du Sahara au Sahel* (Paris: L'Harmattan, 1990); Emmanuel Grégoire, *Touaregs du Niger: le destin d'un mythe* (Paris: Khartala, 1999).
6. A group composed of, on the North African side, Tunisia, Algeria, Libya, Morocco and Mauritania and, on the European side, Italy, France, Portugal, Spain and Malta.
7. The daily *El Watan*, Alger, 26 October 2003.
8. Statement to *La Stampa*, reprinted by *Le Monde*, 25 August 2004.
9. C. Rodier, 'Les camps d'étrangers, dispositif clé de la politique d'immigration et d'asile de l'Union européenne', in *La mise à l'écart de l'étranger, centre fermés et expulsions* (collection under the direction of P. A. Perrouty) (Labor, 2004).
10. Ali Bensaad, 'Avec les clandestins du Sahel', in *Le Monde diplomatique*, Paris, September, 2001, pp. 16–17.
11. Andréa Réa, 'Politiques d'immigration: criminalisation ou tolérance?', *La Pensée de midi*, no. 10, Summer, 2003, pp. 106–12.
12. Rita Aoued Badouel, '"Esclavage" et situation des "noirs" au Maroc dans la première moitié du 20ième siècle', in *Les Relations transsahariennes à l'époque contemporaine* (collection under the direction of L. Marfaaing and S. Wippel) (Paris: Khartala, 2004).
13. Ibid.
14. Mohamed Harbi, *Une vie debout: Mémoires politiques*, vol. 1 (Paris: La Découverte, 2001).

Part II
The Challenges of Identities and Cultures

5
Identity, Nationalism and Anthropologists

Maria Couroucli

East meets West?

This chapter is about the ambiguous relationships between Europe and the Mediterranean as they are revealed in the anthropological studies on modern Greece. The European enlargement of 2004 incorporated into the Union countries that once belonged to the Soviet bloc, and more anciently to the Russian or Austro-Hungarian Empire. Europe goes East, but not towards the Orient: Turkey is knocking on the door and Balkan countries are next in line. It is a changing landscape where member states and aspiring states negotiate their relative positions and the divide between West and Rest, i.e. West = Us, Orient = Them, organises the newest inclusions and exclusions. In South-Eastern Europe and the Balkans, the divide separates Europe from the Ottoman lands, along the frontier where the two worlds fought each other from the fifteenth until the nineteenth centuries.

Since the publication of Said's *Orientalism* (1978) the question of Western identity and the definition of the 'other' – the Oriental – has been very much debated in anthropology. Said's criticism of the image of the Orient insists on the radical opposition between West and Rest and also on the timeless essentialism of the Orient. James Carrier (1992) has shown how anthropology cannot get away from this essentialism, so that even when studying the Western world, 'the Other expands to include most people in Western societies, people who, after all, are not middle-class academics' (1992: 188). He reminds his reader that anthropologists working in Western societies are trained in the same way as classic anthropologists: they are out to study the exotic and that, consequently, anthropologists essentialise the two categories, the West and the 'others', so as to arrive at an exaggerated sense of difference (ibid.: 203). It has also been pointed out that 'native anthropology' is a contradiction in terms but also that anthropological understanding may be inadequate, because it is impossible to speak both from a native and from an anthropologist's position (Hastrup, 1995: 148–59). The problem of anthropological understanding had also to do with the uneasy relations between anthropology and history, both as regards relations to time and as regards relations to historical research producing new knowledge about societies studied by ethnographers.

One of the many examples is the Greek case, where anthropology has stayed away both from social time and from historical and political science research within the country and has found itself more or less isolated from local intelligentsia. It could be the case that this is due to a difference between the native and the non-native points of view and that this difference is itself a result of the post-World War Two world order, where the 'Western' model dominated unhindered in the 'free world', creating inequalities between the centre and the periphery.

The anthropology of Greece is a relatively important field in the Anglo-American anthropological literature, with more than 50 books published since the 1960s. Indeed, post-war Greece can be described as an anthropologist's Eden: the only South-Eastern European country outside the communist bloc, the only Balkan state to have joined the EEC (since 1981), Greek society is both familiar and exotic, part of Europe but also marginal to it (Herzfeld, 1987). In the last twenty years Greek anthropology has established itself in Greece, where two university departments are thriving. These recent developments have induced changes in fieldwork methods, choice of research subjects and use of analytical categories.

Nationalism: ambiguities and questionings

Nationalism and national identity are among those analytical categories which have been redefined in later years through ethnographic analysis. It is also an area where fieldwork is most obviously dependent upon the conditions of study and the interaction between foreign observer and native observed, who find themselves in structurally opposed positions, in Greece as elsewhere. And, one may add, all the more so when political conditions in the country under study are not optimum conditions of democratic rule, as was the case in Greece during the military regime of 1967–74 when civil rights and freedom of expression were not fully enjoyed by citizens.[1] This crucial dimension of modern Greek society has been largely ignored in anthropological writings, not only because historical research on the question until the late 1990s was very limited, but also because of the mutual ignorance which characterises the relations between anthropologists and historians.[2]

Today, categories such as nationalism, national ideology or ethnic identity have been largely questioned after having been present in most debates in the fields of both political science and anthropology in the 1980s and 1990s. The historical context of the debates concerning South-Eastern Europe is of course the Cold War period, the collapse of the Communist world and its subsequent division into smaller 'nations' aspiring to be independent states. In Greece, the military regime and its 'Christian-Hellenic' ideology (the colonels' slogan was: 'The Greece of Christian Greeks') had triggered a long process of rethinking notions like fatherland (*patridha*), nation or Hellenism among historians and more widely among social scientists.[3] More recently, the Yugoslav war, often presented as a sudden burst of violence following the fall of the Berlin Wall, shook apart many firm beliefs about ethnic identities and the reality of nation-states among Balkan specialists, provoking a reconsideration of the categories involved in anthropological and sociological analyses.[4]

Fieldwork conditions have always been considered of crucial importance for the anthropologist, especially when the themes of the study include national or collective identity, ethnicity, minorities and the like. Yet, although the 'reflexive' tendency is certainly there in Greek anthropology, few deal with the subject directly. Margaret Kenna, who addressed the issue thirty years after her first fieldwork in Anafi – a small island which served more than once as an exile camp – is an interesting exception illustrating the importance of fieldwork conditions for subsequent anthropological analysis which I will return to later in this chapter.

The Greek case

Anthropologists arrived in Greece after World War Two, pretty much at the same time as the first foreign tourists. Both groups were visibly educated, belonging to one of the great Western nations and often linked to the foreign institutes in Athens that usually host archaeologists working in the country: the British, the American and the French schools. One should add that until the late 1980s anthropology was very much a rural practice, so that the anthropologist was in most cases more 'learned' than the village people he or she studied.

Village ethnographies published during this period follow the general trends of the time, focusing on the local and the synchronic and taking little notice of the conditions of the exchange between observers and observed and even less of the difficulties of comprehending categories and their use according to context. Questions related to interpretative anthropology, to the anthropologist's work in terms of history and memory (Geertz, 1983; Marcus and Clifford, 1986), or to native versus non-native anthropology (Hastrup, 1993), need to be addressed in relation to the more recent post-colonial analyses which have questioned the 'objectivity' of anthropological representations, stressing the fact that they are themselves part of a given and dominant culture (Argyrou, 2002; Herzfeld, 2002).

In Greece, observers and observed seem to be both culturally and socially distant, yet the separation between the two worlds is not as clear as elsewhere. Skopetea (*The Sunset of Dawn*, 1992) has pointed out how Greece, by the very fact of being marginal to Europe, was also part of it during the emergence of collective identities (European, Ottoman, Balkan, Greek) in the nineteenth and twentieth centuries. The 'European' category included part of the urban populations of the Ottoman Empire just as, later, it included the national elites of the Balkan countries precisely because the 'West' was in fact present within Ottoman society. Skopetea asserts that the West *is* in the East, i.e. the West defines itself and becomes West by opposition to the East and in relation to it; 'the West is here', she writes, meaning inside the Empire. In her study of women's education in the nineteenth century, Bakalaki (1994) also points out that Greece was in several ways part of Europe well before joining the EC in 1981. She analyses the influence of urban elites, who had adopted Western lifestyles, upon rural populations and she also criticises the ethnographers' naive assumption that rural lifestyles of the nineteenth century have survived until the ethnographer's fieldwork in the second part of the twentieth century. In her view, the populations studied by ethnographers do believe that in many ways they live in the same world as Europeans. One can therefore assume that members of rural communities studied by *xenoi* (foreigners) thought they all belonged to the same hierarchical system, which included both local society and the global world, inside a familiar – and dominant – model where Western society occupies the top of the pyramid, while 'other' societies dwell in the inferior apartments, according to their closeness to the dominant pattern.

Fieldwork

Anthropologists have always maintained that long periods of fieldwork are more profitable, because they allow the ethnographer to establish a relationship of mutual trust between himself and the people observed, this making the observation more accurate. Experience has shown that informants' narratives vary according to circumstances and that the patient ethnographer will finally get a more interesting version of events than the hastier surveyor. But however long the fieldwork, one cannot pretend that the structural oppositions at work in the relation between the two parties can be annihilated. The anthropologist who may become 'one of us' during his fieldwork does not in fact become part of the society under study. As an ethnographer he needs to maintain some distance in order to observe, thus occupying an ambiguous position, more outside than inside. Native anthropology, for its part, although criticising foreign anthropologists' misunderstandings, has not proposed new fieldwork rules and practices.

Although the native's point of view is impossible to apprehend, one may try to understand the social interaction involved during fieldwork (Goffman, 1967). One may assume that when a 'foreigner' enters a conversation in a Greek village coffee-shop the exchange will be determined by the mutual understanding of the categories in use, each other's identity and social status among these.[5] The first exchange between a local and a foreigner in Crete was described by Jacques Lacarrière as the 'hospitality ritual', the interaction between the landlord and the guest consisting of conventional questions and answers which inform about the segmentary oppositions at stake and end up in the negotiation of each other's status: 'Where do you come from? France, Germany, England, America? Then: How old are you? Are you married? Do you have children? Are your parents still alive? What is your profession? . . . Then comes "the ultimate question": "do you like Greece?" After which, one starts relating his travels, talks about Paris or, even better, about politics' (Lacarrière 1975: 126).

The segmentary principle is here at work in much the same way as among the Nuer of the Sudan: people identify with larger and larger groups the further up they go into the generations and common ancestry: brother is closer to cousin, who is closer to co-villager, who is closer to fellow-countryman.[6] In the case of the Cretan villager welcoming Lacarrière or Herzfeld, for example, later, it is the *Greek* welcoming the *foreigner* that are the categories concerned in the first place: the separation of identities takes place at the national level. One may here assume that during interaction the parties take this 'maximal' distance into account.

It is plausible that the first encounters between the anthropologist and the people observed take place along similar lines, i.e. that the exchanged information about each other's identity is part of the first meetings. We may also assume that the answers to the questions a foreign anthropologist asks would take into account his 'foreignness', i.e. his assumed ignorance of the national society. In fact, we are also within the hospitality sphere and its rules, one of which being that the guest, when in the master's house, must abide by the rules of the house. The ethnographer does the same: if he is to continue his fieldwork, he must become the guest of the local community under study and act according to its rules of hospitality.[7]

In 1960s Greece, the military coup and its social consequences certainly played an important role in the way a foreigner was perceived. I think that contextualising contemporary ethnographies within this Greek space-time can shed some more light on the question of the relations between observer and observed. It is useful to remember that during this regime (1967–74) the country was ruled by military law allowing no freedom of expression and the suspension of elections.[8] One may add that the presence of foreigners – free citizens in their own countries – among the local people living under martial law and experiencing repressive politics was perhaps not always easy to live with. The lack of equality of status vis-à-vis the authorities – a disparity of social rights reminiscent of colonial situations between natives and Westerners – and the humiliation of having to admit the obvious fact that the country was drifting away from Western society under this regime complicated the relationships between Greeks and non-Greeks. Finally, one should remember that those resisting the regime presented themselves as patriots defending national dignity, while the junta's rhetoric was nationalistic, anti-Communist, and full of stereotypes on Greek history and identity; hence nationalist representations of cultural, social or political Greek identity in the period 1960–90 can be a complex phenomenon to study.

A characteristic case briefly mentioned above is Anafi, an island which hosted political exiles in the 1930s and the junta period, studied by Margaret Kenna, who published a book on her fieldwork many years after her first stay. In this later study, which is a reflection on the relation between the anthropologist and his/her field, Kenna gives a very detailed account of her experience of the military coup in 1967 while she was on the island and proposes a retrospective analysis of the event. She also writes about the reasons she was unable to properly research the island's recent history during these early times:

> I became conscious that, for the islanders, trying to turn my attention away from the present and the recent past to the more distant past was a strategy to keep me away from the sensitive contemporary issues ... the history of Anafi to which I was encouraged to turn, however, was an uncontentious past; mythical Anafi revealed to Jason and the Argonauts by Apollo; classical Anafi ... Venetian Anafi ... patriotic Anafi (1821) ... post-Independence Anafi, sending its

young men to help build King Otto's palace … I was too naïve to understand why Anafiots would not freely answer questions about those (more recent) times. If I had thought about my own experience, as a six-year-old Australian 'alien' in Berkeley, California, in the McCarthy Era, hearing my parents talking of the Loyalty Oath, I might have understood a little better. (2001: 148)

The ethnographer was in this case not only ill-prepared to take history into consideration, but also not welcomed to do so by the local community.

The case of Karakasidou's work on the town of Assiros/Guvezna in Greek Macedonia in the 1990s revealed very clearly the inherent tensions between ethnography and politics: the ethnographer was harassed in Greece and abandoned by her English publisher.[9] The book is a historical anthropological study based on a variety or sources: local legends recorded in the field, local archival material, recent historical research and national ideology in its different forms (school books, political rhetoric). Karakasidou distinguishes three types of historical narratives at the local level. The 'generic' national history taught at school as a series of events (Turkish oppressive rule, Bulgarian aggression, anti-Communist struggle) constitutes the first kind. The second narrative links local events and landmarks to the grand national heritage. The third kind, not considered 'history' by locals, refers to the past through personal and family experiences. These family histories, though they might refer to non-Greek-speaking ancestors migrating to the area in the 1860s – and thus clash with the standardised national narrative – are oddly not considered by the locals to be anomalous vis-à-vis national history learned at school and celebrated on national holidays (1997: 223).

From *diglossia* to split thinking

Anthropologists studying representations of Greek national identity have often pointed to a structural opposition, a dual model of identification: on the one hand, vernacular, familiar, popular (*Romeic*) Greece, close to traditional society with links to the Ottoman past; on the other hand Hellenic Greece, official, cultured, urban, close to the West. The analysis corresponds to the classical opposition elite/lower classes found in historical literature. For political scientists, this duality represents two distinct social groups: those of rural origin constitute the first group, the second being the urbanites, originating from the Greek urban elite of the Balkan and Anatolian cities. The cultural expressions of these two groups have been labelled *underdog culture* and *reformist culture* respectively

(Diamantouros, 1994). The same kind of duality has been identified as an opposition between the language of the people and that of the state (Herzfeld, 1982; Couroucli, 1991, 1995). Herzfeld's work deals extensively with the representations of Greek national identity and the coexistence of two models, the one referring to intimate Greece, synonymous with tradition and the Ottoman legacy, the other being the official Hellenic model, which claims direct descent from classical antiquity and at the same time justifies the existence of a Greek nation-state among other European nation-states. Herzfeld criticises top-down analyses of nationalism and the nation-state and their inability to take into consideration the 'rueful self-recognition' the anthropologist is able to observe during his long-term fieldwork; he also calls this duality *disemia*, that is 'a formal tension between official self-presentation and what goes on in the privacy of collective introspection' and proposes the concept of *cultural intimacy*: national identity would then be a mixture of embarrassment and idealised virtues (1997b: 6–14).[10]

Bakalaki (1994) has observed that anthropologists' analyses imply a 'problematic isomorphism between 19th century rural attitudes and those encountered by ethnographers working in Greece after the 1960s'. In fact, she claims, the two models are not at all equivalent, since the Hellenic (modern) discourse dominates over the *Romeic* (traditional) in modern Greek society. The two parts of the duality being unequally represented in everyday exchanges, some of the elements observed may be present as verbal and behavioural stereotypes rather than as usable analytical categories for the social scientist. Duality then seems to be closer to sociological imagination, a pitfall that foreign analysts seem to have trouble in avoiding.[11]

The diverging interpretations of local or national 'representations' are indeed one aspect of the question of how ethnographic research may be related to historical and political science research. I have mentioned above that anthropological work has failed to take into account one major opposition characteristic of twentieth century Greek society, between 'those who think nationally', the *ethnikofrones*, and the others, considered as enemies of the authorities. This dualism corresponds to a greater or lesser extent to the division between left and right and has been at work for the best part of the century, from the early 1930s until today; among its latest manifestations, are those triggered by the publication of Karakasidou's monograph that Cambridge University Press decided not to publish in the early 1990s.[12]

I think that the dualistic model has persisted among students of Greek society because the basis on which it stands is still there: first, the synchronic character of the great majority of anthropological analyses which, ignoring history, reinforce the a-temporal aspect of the phenomena being investigated, as if these have always belonged to the society under study. This kind of reasoning reached its climax during the ex-Yugoslavia crisis: the Balkans, one could read in the Western press, is a traditionally violent region, ethnic conflicts are endemic, therefore it is not necessary to look for the causes or the forms of interethnic violence because these are quasi-natural.[13] It is possible that behind anthropologists' hesitation to tackle the political side of social phenomena lies an uneasiness about the junta years. The opposition between Greek and foreigner cannot be fully understood without reference to its special dimension during this period: it symbolised the separation of those who had a right to enjoy democracy (the foreign observers, journalists, anthropologists among them) and those natives living inside the country who were denied freedom and civil rights in the name of the balance of power and world peace during the Cold War.

The ethnography of Greece brings out problems of method related to cultural distance between observer and observed in a context where this distance is less explicit. While many have studied the paradox of Greece's incomplete inclusion in the West, the opposite question has not been dealt with: is the 'Western' ethnographer 'at home' in Greece? How is one to define what distinguishes the ethnographer's world from the world where the observed belong? Although one knows that each party's status influences the content of the discourse, i.e. while it is generally accepted that status differences (i.e. social, cultural or political distance between observer and observed) do in part determine the content of the exchange, this fact remains very much implicit in anthropologists' analyses of discourses on local identities. Some of the complexities of fieldwork may be revealed by contextualising within the social space-time of the study, analysing how far foreign ethnographers are not perceived in the same way as local ones, how their respective identities are being determined in relation to complex and changing factors, varying with time, even within a single stay.[14]

The West as looking-glass

The term *disemia* (Herzfeld, 1997b) is an extension of *diglossia*, a term coined by Ferguson to analyse similar phenomena in Greece, in the Arab world, and among the Creole-speaking societies, i.e. the double language structure, where one is linked to the high culture, the one closer to the West via history, and the other to popular culture, the most distant from Western culture. This paradigm sums up the way (Western) anthropologists have analysed the less exotic societies and the Mediterranean in particular: neither primitive nor civilised, with a glorious past and a miserable present. The paradigm is the expression of the traditionally Western point of view, the implicit model against which, as with Procrustes' bed, the 'others' are being measured; as Herodotus and Marco Polo did before modern travellers and anthropologists. Is it possible, then, that the concept of *disemia* is 'good for the West'? – that it is addressed to the foreigner, in his own terms, those of the opposition between the incomplete local and the universal ideal of humanity?

Today it seems that the Western model is no longer considered as 'good to copy' by the 'almost Western' societies; their elites – westernised or not – question its uniqueness and its superiority. Carrier argues, for example, that anthropological research which traditionally sought out the alien and the exotic, has become less possible and less necessary because of 'political changes in the third world, economic changes in western universities and intellectual changes in anthropology' (1992: 195). Moreover, as anthropology moves from the exotic towards the urban field, questions of fieldwork methods are being reconsidered and Goffman's warning that 'the observer's need to rely on representations of things itself creates the possibility of misrepresentation' (ibid.: 251) is useful to remember in this discussion.

I have tried, through the Greek example, to highlight the implicit but inevitable comparison of West and East, whatever this East may be, as long as it acts as a mirror of *us* in ethnographic work.[15] I should add that the usefulness of oppositions is relative. Apart from the opposition between local and global, which establishes an inequality of scale, the other couples are, in the last analysis, just conventions.

It is, of course, impossible to avoid all ethnocentric analyses, but one must also be able to avoid sweeping generalisations stemming from largely ancient and unconscious constructions, and question Occidentalism and its implications. It is vain to think that one may completely get rid of one's cultural point of view; but one way is to try to analyse the intricate relations between observer and observed, especially when these belong to two different worlds. For example, in nineteenth-century Ottoman society, the West intervened through its missions and observed through its journalists. The role of these early reporters is important, in so far as they depicted Ottoman society in their writings and influenced Western countries' public opinions. They made frequent references to the 'barbarian' character of the Balkan peoples, regularly allotting them a specific place along the scale of civilisation, changing their relative positions according to current events. In these cases, 'the westerner, whatever his nationality or his political party, represents himself by an abstraction, "the West", and believes that he belongs to an ideal society that, ungracefully, immoderately, hopelessly sometimes, Ottomans and Balkan people try to imitate' (Skopetea, 1992: 68).

Behind the ethnographic endeavour lies the same kind of abstraction; the point of view of the ethnographer relies on a particular representation of the West which produces absurd comparisons: the Chinese, African or Mediterranean peasant is measured against the liberal intellectual living in European capitals or American campuses. The comparison is not between communities of fishermen, say, of East and West, but between Mediterranean fishermen, for example, and 'the West'. Moreover, an English observer, for example, would convincingly argue that fishing communities are not 'typical' of English society, while anthropologists do not hesitate to generalise on other cultures from fieldwork experiences among just as marginal communities. It is clear that as long as the Western model remains dominant, the centre's point of view is also adopted by those at the periphery. It has been argued about those peripheral elites that while identification with Europe may generate both pride and humiliation (because unattainable), *'the pride generated by an emphasis on difference may also result from the internalization of a "European" fascination with the exotic'* (Bakalaki, 1994: 101).

Anthropological production on Greece can be a useful sample for the investigation of the relation between the ethnographer and his or her field, especially when the relationship involves separate identities. For example, it seems that a 'foreign' and a 'native' observer are perceived in different ways, especially when he or she asks questions dealing with identity.[16] The ambiguous position of the guest renders the analysis of these categories even more challenging: for if one is to get interesting answers one has of course to ask the right questions. The quality of these questions and answers depends on how knowledgeable one is not only about anthropology but also about the social and political history of the society studied; in other words, on the contextualisation of the ethnographic enquiry.

Notes

1. This seems to characterise post-war Greek society more generally, Cf. Mazower (2000).
2. This is not true within Greece, where anthropologists and historians work together on a regular basis.
3. Cf. Couroucli (2002, 2003).
4. Cf. Cowan and Brown (2002); Mazower (2000).
5. One may look at the encounter between anthropologist and people observed along Goffman's analysis: 'When an individual appears before others, he knowingly and unwittingly projects a definition of the situation of which a

conception of himself is an important part' (Goffman, 1959: 242). 'The individual tends to treat the others present on the basis of the impression they give about the past and the future. It is here that communicative acts are translated into moral ones., (ibid., 249).

6. Cf. Evans-Pritchard on the segmentary principle and the opposition between segments which regulates the political relations and conflicts among the Nuer: 'The members of any segment unite for war against adjacent segments of the same order and unite with these adjacent segments against larger sections' (1940: 142).

7. Cf. Julian Pitt-Rivers (1983) (*La Loi de l'hospitalité*, published in English as: *The Fate of Shechem of the Politics of Sex: Essays in the Anthropology of the Mediterranean*, Cambridge: Cambridge University Press, 1977).

8. The regime had imprisoned and sent into exile thousands of people without trial, accused of being political opponents, often on the basis of some local police report. Authorities were particularly repressive in villages and urban neighborhoods who had voted for the centre or left parties during the previous election; in the same spirit, villagers with no electricity were promised to be connected if they voted 100 per cent yes in the one referendum organised by the military junta in 1973. One needed to first obtain from the local police a 'certificate of social beliefs' (that is, of anti-Communist opinion), before one applied for a driving license or passport. The numerous civil servants who failed to obtain such a document were simply sacked from their jobs, and this is how universities were stripped of their professors during this time. Greeks abroad organised meetings and protests against the regime, including campaigns against tourism in Greece. This is why many intellectuals in the opposition considered foreign students who went to Greece at the time (with or without scholarships from the Greek government) as *de facto* collaborators of the regime. Cf. Clogg and Yannopoulos (1972), who estimate the number of political prisoners in 1967 as 4567.

9. Cf. supra note 8.

10. 'If the nation is credibly represented as a family, people are loyal to it because they know that families are flawed – that is part of love and so they rally to the defense of its compromising but warmly familiar intimacy (1997b: 172).

11. It is noteworthy that the 'dual' analysis is based more on the national narrative found in rather old (pre-1970s) historical and folklore works and relies much less on work published locally in the last twenty years. For more about the role of the military regime's ideology (1967–74) in transforming later nationalist representations and historian's production, cf. Couroucli (2002).

12. On the history of institutions and anti-communist legislation, cf. Alivizatos (1983); on modern Greek history, cf. Campbell and Sherrard (1968); on the Karakasidou affair, which is related to the early 1990s Macedonian question in Greece, cf. for example http://www.h-net.msu.edu/~sae/threads/CUP/protest.html and http://members.tripod.com/giorgi10/id52.htm.

13. For a critical analysis of these cf. Cowan, 2002.

14. Cf. for example, Kenna (2001), and also James Faubion (1993) on these questions, even if the argument is less explicit. Kenna insists on the ambiguity between the Western world and the local society in his study of Athenian intellectuals. His book received a scathing review in a Greek newspaper, pointing out the very many factual errors and suggesting that the author should have written a travel book instead of a book of anthropology.

15. Note the very interesting choice of the title of the first French monograph on Greece: *La violence et la Ruse (Violence and Slyness)* by Handman (1983), a phrase Hegel used to characterise the state of nature as opposed to human society, Cf. Russ (1999: 331).
16. Cf Karakasidou's discussion on this in the afterword of her monograph, and Herzfeld's discussion of the Rhodian police attitude during his short stay on the island. One last, personal, remark: while on the field in Corfu in 1977–8 (cf. *Les Oliviers du Lignage*), none of the people I worked with had the idea of informing me about Greek national history. My identity, as a native with university education, was one probable reason, the other being that during my stay no political crisis prompted any inquiry about these matters. One of my oldest and better educated informants had pointed out my status in his eyes by addressing me in official Greek (*kathareuoussa*), that being the appropriate language to address members of the learned elite and authorities in general.

References

Alivizatos, Nicolas (1983) ' "Nation" contre "Peuple" après 1940', in D. Tsaousis (ed.), *Hellinismos kai Hellinikotita* (Athènes: Hestia).

Argyrou, Vassos (2002) *Anthropology and the Will to Meaning: a Post-colonial Critique* (London: Pluto Press).

Bakalaki, Alexandra (1994) 'Gender-related Discourses and Representations of Cultural Specificity in Nineteenth and Twentieth Century Greece', *Journal of Modern Greek Studies*, 12.

Bourgois, Philippe (1991) 'Confronting the Ethics of Ethnography: Lessons from Fieldwork in Central America', in F. V. Harrison (ed.), *Decolonizing Anthropology* (Washington, DC: Association of Black Anthropologists).

Campbell, J. K. and Sherrard, P. (1968) *Modern Greece* (New York: Praeger).

Carrier, James (1992) 'Occidentalism: the World Turned Upside-down', *American Ethnologist*, 19.

Clogg, Richard and Yannopoulos, George (eds) (1972) *Greece under Military Rule* (London: Secker & Warburg).

Comaroff, John and Comaroff, Jean (1992) *Ethnography and the Historical Imagination* (Boulder: Westview Press).

Couroucli, Maria (1985) *Les Oliviers du Lignage: Une Grèce de Tradition Venitienne* (Paris: Maisonneuve et Larosse).

Couroucli, Maria (1991) 'Diglossie et double langage: Langues et langages d'honneur en Grèce', *Langage et Société*, 57, pp. 71–92.

Couroucli, Maria (1993) 'Heroes and their Shadows: the Hungry, the Humble and the Powerful', *Journal of Mediterranean Studies*, 3 (1).

Couroucli, Maria (1995) 'Le *Lalein* et le *grafein*, parler et écrire en grec', in *Oral et ecrit daus le monde turco-ottoman*, Revue du Monde Musúlman et de la Méditerranée (REMMM), no. 75–6 (1–2), pp. 257–71.

Couroucli, Maria (2002) 'Le nationalisme d'Etat en Grèce', in A. Dieckhoff and R. Kastoriano (eds), *Nationalismes en mutation en Méditerranée orientale* (Paris: CNRS editions).

Couroucli, Maria (2003) *Genos, ethnos*, Nation et Etat-nation, *Ateliers*, 30.

Cowan, J. (ed.) (2002) *Macedonia: the Politics of Identity and Difference* (London: Pluto Press).

Cowan, Jane and Brown, K. S. (2002) 'Macedonian Inflections', in Jane Cowan and Keith Brown (eds), *Macedonia: the Politics of Identity and Difference* (London: Pluto Press).

Diamantouros, Nikiforos (1994) *Cultural Dualism and Political Change in Postauthoritarian Greece*, Madrid: Centro de Estudios Avanzados en Ciencias Sociales, Instituto Juan March de Estudios e Investigationes (Greek edition: *Politismikos Diismos kai politiki allagi stin Ellada tis metapoliteusis*) (Athens: Alexandria, 2000).

Evans-Pritchard, Edward (1940) *The Nuer* (Oxford: Oxford University Press).

Faubion, James (1993) *Modern Greek Lessons: a Primer in Historical Constructivism* (Princeton: Princeton University Press).

Ferguson, C. A. (1959) 'Diglossia', *Word*, 15 (1).

Geertz, C. (1983) *Local Knowledge* (New York: Basic Books).

Goffman, E. (1959) *The Presentation of Self in Everyday Life* (Garden City: Doubleday).

Goffman, Erving (1967) *Interaction Ritual: Essays in Face-to-face Behavior* (New York: Pantheon Books).

Gossiaux, J.-F. (2002) *Pouvoirs ethniques dans les Balkans* (Paris: PUF).

Handman, Marie-Elisabeth (1983) *La violence et la ruse* (Paris: Edisud).

Hastrup, Kirsten (1993) 'The Native Voice – and the Anthropological Vision', *Social Anthropology*, 1 (2), pp. 173–86.

Hastrup, Kirsten (1995) *A Passage to Anthropology: Between Experience and Theory* (London: Routledge).

Herzfeld, Michael (1982) *Ours Once More: Folklore, Ideology and the Making of Modern Greece* (Texas: University of Texas Press).

Herzfeld, Michael (1987) *Anthropology Through the Looking-glass* (Cambridge: Cambridge University Press).

Herzfeld, Michael (1997a) *Portrait of a Greek Imagination* (Chicago: Chicago University Press).

Herzfeld, Michael (1997b) *Cultural Intimacy: Social Poetics in the Nation-State* (New York: Routledge).

Herzfeld, M. (2002) 'The European Self: Rethinking an Attitude', in Anthony Pagden (ed.), *The Idea of Europe: From Antiquity to the European Union* (Cambridge: Cambridge University Press).

Journal of Modern Greek Studies, 14 (2), October 1996, Special issue: Macedonia.

Kaplan, Martha (1990) 'Meaning, Agency and Colonial History: Navosavakadua and the Tuka Movement in Fiji', *American Ethnologist*, 17(1): 3–22.

Karakasidou, Anastasia (1997) *Fields of Wheat, Hills of Blood: Passages to Nationhood in Greek Macedonia, 1870–1990* (Chicago: University of Chicago Press).

Kenna, Margaret (2001) *Greek Island Life: Fieldwork on Anafi* (New York: Harwood Academic).

Kovats-Bernat Christopher J. (2002) 'Negotiating Dangerous Fields: Pragmatic Strategies for Fieldwork Amid Violence and Terror', *American Anthropologist*, 104 (1), pp. 208–22.

Lacarrière, Jacques (1975) *L'été grec* (Paris: Plon).

Laidlaw, James (2002) 'For an Anthropology of Ethics and Freedom', *JRAI*, 8, pp. 311–32.

Marcus, G. and Clifford, J. (eds) (1986) *Writing Culture: the Poetics and Politics of Ethnography* (London: University of California Press).

Mazower, Mark (2000a) *The Balkans: From the End of Byzantium to the Present Day* (London: Weidenfeld & Nicolson).

Mazower, Mark (2000b) *After the War was Over: Reconstructing the Family, Nation and State in Greece, 1943–1960* (Princeton: Princeton University Press).

Nugent, Stephen (2001) 'Anthropology and Public Culture: the Yanomami, Science and Ethics', *Anthropology Today*, 17 (3).

Ortner, Sherry (1991) 'Resistance and the Problem of Ethnographic Refusal', in R. G. Fox (ed.), *Recapturing Anthropology: Working in the Present* (Santa Fe: School of American Research Press).

Pitt-Rivers, Julian (1983) 'La loi de l'hospitalité', in *Anthropologie de l'Honneur: La mésaventure de Sichem* (Paris: Le Sycomore), pp. 149–76.

Price, David (2002) 'Lessons from Second World War Anthropology: Peripheral, Persuasive and Ignored Contributions', *Anthropology Today*, 18 (3).

Rowbotham, Don (1997) 'Postcolonialités: le défi des nouvelles modernités', *Revue Internationale des Sciences Sociales* (UNESCO), 153, pp. 393–408.

Russ, Jacqueline (1999) *Les chemins de la pensée* (Paris: Bordas).

Said, E. (1978) *Orientalism* (New York: Vintage Books).

Skopetea, Elli (1992) *Le couchant du Levant: Images de la fin de l'Empire Ottoman* (Athens: Gnosi (in Greek)).

Todorova, Maria (1995) 'The Course and Discourses of Bulgarian Nationalism', in P. Sugar (ed.), *Eastern European Nationalism* (New York: American University Press).

Todorova, Maria (1997) *Imagining the Balkans* (Oxford: Oxford University Press).

6
Altering the Perspective[1]

Dionigi Albera

The question of cultural and religious identities is certainly one of the most sensitive issues of 'living together' in the Mediterranean. Crossed by the divide between Occident and Islam, the interior sea appears today more than ever to be a space of differences and of conflict. I would like to look at the issue of cultural challenges from a point of view other than the usual one that examines the meaning of cultural identities and differences – with the usual array of problems, misunderstandings and conflicts – and envisages the possibility of diminishing separations and encouraging dialogue. Instead, I would like to focus attention on the perspective of collective identities that exaggerates separations.

Covering Islam

A new spectre is haunting Europe: Islam and Islamist terrorism. The threatening faces of 'Saracens' and 'Turks' are resurfacing in today's troubled waters. Incitements to hatred ooze from the programmes and propaganda of extreme-right populist parties and gain a certain intellectual and media respectability. Debates (such as the ones about wearing the Muslim headscarf or about Turkey joining the EU) have shown the importance of the cultural and religious (two adjectives that often end up being synonymous) core as a factor in identity separation and polarisation.

The identity problematic is fed by a media barrage offering obsessive visions of the other, but the language of mutual incomprehension exists as well in more subtle forms, often laden with good intentions. A narrow and frozen view of cultural and religious identities shows up in speech that pretends to be pure and objective; it is apparent behind certain semantic shifts when stereotypes rise to the surface almost inadvertently. Passive, often nonchalant recourse to expressions as popular as they are imprecise contributes to the confusion or gives a false impression of clarity. Such is the case, for example, in the expression 'Islam', which carries within it several ambiguities. While it would be considered excessive to conflate Christianity and Christendom, the concept of 'Islam' invariably assimilates dogma and history and becomes a source of confusion.[2] The entity takes on almost metaphysical connotations when evoked in geopolitical scenarios, either in their authorised or their disreputable versions. Islam is a monolithic and uniform totality.

The same essentialist understanding is inherent in the use of expressions such as 'Islamist terrorism', unfortunately the current usage, which suggests an amalgam between violent practices and belonging to a religion, seen in an undifferentiated manner. (To measure the subtle bias of this formula, we must ask a simple question: Would we have spoken with the same casualness of 'Catholic terrorism' or of 'Protestant terrorism' in relation to events in Northern Ireland?) Further, even the formula 'Islamist terrorism' lends itself to the suggestion that all Islamists are ready to use violent means, which is far from the case. The neutral principles that control the choice of adjectives sometimes carry with them a generalisation of religious affiliations. Such inaccuracy can lead to an assimilation of religious aspects. The most grotesque example of this was the Spanish politician who, the day after the Madrid bombings on 11 March 2004, evoked the presence of 'Muslim bodies' among the victims.

Another kind of rhetoric, silent and deadly: images. An examination of the covers of principal French weeklies shows that, for ten years now, a special kind of visibility is accorded to Muslims: crowds bent over in prayer; demonstrators shouting and threatening; veiled women; worrisome bearded, sometimes armed individuals.[3] Year after year, this repetitive rhetoric suggests haunting and surreptitious associations between a religion and situations of blind submission, oppression and danger. The implicit persuasiveness of images is revealed especially on television screens, where they take on the power of evidence. Here, the media understanding of Islam often relies on *wahhabi* or *salafi* characteristics. The Islam arrayed on television is usually about the *sharia* or the mosque. The *oulémas* (theologians) or ayatollahs in interviews become emblematic figures who take on stereotypical qualities. The camera lingers on hidden faces that distil scriptural doctrine. The other very present iconographic element is the wide shot of praying or more or less threatening crowds. By itself the visual rhetoric produces, via editing and independent of the accompanying audio, an amalgam between terrorism, Islamism and Islam. It is not unusual to see on the news or in other journalistic programmes, sequences or images of attacks or of terrorist training camps mixed up or edited in sequence with Muslims praying in a mosque. I do not remember having seen anything like this when the programmes were about other tragic events in which a religious confrontation – but involving a different religion – was presented. For example, only a few years ago, programmes about the massacres perpetrated by Serbian militias in Bosnia were never illustrated by images of the faithful praying in a church. That would have been inconceivable, because of connotations of passivity which any reference to the Christian religion carries in European received knowledge. Thus the canons of 'the optically correct'[4] attack the failings of clichés and negative prejudices that surround the Muslim religion.

It would be wrong to attribute absolute power to the media in the business of creating stereotypes. In regard to the way the Muslim world is presented, they simply refer to its composite nature, building on shorthand already adopted by contemporary society.[5] This is the situation that Edward Said designated, almost twenty-five years ago, by a play on words: 'Covering Islam'. 'Covering Islam' refers to the journalistic role (providing information), but also to the act of hiding or disguising. This analysis of Said's has not aged. On the contrary, mechanisms he identified at the beginning of the 1980s have taken on breadth and intensity in the period that followed.

Said's work came in a context in which elements of a practice destined to become worldwide were already well established in the United States. Beginning in the 1970s Islam began to emerge in the media as a problematical, worrisome and threatening world. The petrol crisis and the Iranian revolution were important factors contributing to this concept. There was a flowering of clichés and simplifications in media coverage: bearded men, threatening crowds in the streets, corporal punishment, autocracy, medieval thinking – these were the main themes.

The turbulence experienced by several countries in the Muslim world and its growing (and often tragic) 'relevance' on the geopolitical level confirmed a cultural reading already begun in the 1970s. Confidence in the developmental ideology of modernisation and the sympathy sometimes aroused by the process of decolonisation began to fade. The arrival of fundamentalist movements and the hardening of authoritarian regimes built 'a screen of incomprehension and fear'[6] around the Islamic world. There was a retreat to a fatalistic reading that isolated a small number of persistent cultural traits, taken mainly from the religious matrix and, supposedly, the source of regression or stagnation in these societies – and also the threat they represent to the Occident. This vision has obvious analogies with the one put forth by reactionary and fundamentalist forces in Muslim societies. The growing success of these forces has only reinforced a haunting image of Islam. The intensification of means of communication has had the seemingly paradoxical effect of radicalising communities with opposing interpretations – to borrow another category dear to Edward Said – who demonise each other with the same selection of shorthand and clichés. As has been often noted, proclamations about the clash of civilisations hide the clash of fundamentalisms – and a war of reciprocal ignorance.[7]

The intellectual genealogy of the clash of civilisations

In a famous text, Charles Wright-Mills showed that we all live in what he called a 'second-hand world'. In a complex society, understanding of the world by nearly all populations depends on a set of received interpretations. We see images seen by others, we speak with sentences that others have used.[8] Beginning with this concept, Edward Said deconstructed the 'apparatus' that produced the representation of Islam.[9] He isolated three connected levels: the first is academic product; the second corresponds to strategic reflection, closely connected to the political sphere; the third is the media. The latter select from the repertory created by the other two elements that can be shown in images or understood in the short time frame of media communication.

The theory of the clash of civilisations became a powerful tool in the 1990s, linking together the three levels. This explains, in my view, its rapid and flamboyant success. The theory has the advantage of seeming to take scholarly knowledge into consideration while positioning itself solidly in the realm of strategic usage and furnishing the media with easily communicated formulas and slogans. The father of this theory, Samuel Huntington, incarnates the transition between the scholarly world and the strategic and media world.[10] Despite the way many distance themselves from the theses, they strongly condition the understanding experienced in contemporary life. Guy de Maupassant once noted, in regard to the influence exercised by Schopenhauer, that even those who despised him seemed, despite themselves, to keep some threads of his thinking in their own thoughts. If an analogous phenomenon appears to happen in Huntington's case, it is not due to the strength and originality of his vision, but rather to the fact that it facilitates a reification of a diffuse trend towards the politicisation of culture by providing a transition between different levels of communication.

If the clash of civilisations theory is inseparable from Huntington, we must not forget that he himself was inspired by an article by the Orientalist

Bernard Lewis. The notion of the clash of civilisations, later popularised by Huntington, was first introduced into the media debate by Lewis in a discussion of relations between the 'Occident' and 'Islam'. In a 1990 article, which itself is a good example of the shift from an erudite register to a political and media one, Bernard Lewis signalled 'the roots of Muslim violence':

> It must henceforth be clear that we are confronted by a state of mind and by a movement that go beyond the problems, the politics, and the governments that incarnate them. This is no less than a clash of civilizations – it is the perhaps irrational but ancient reaction of an old rival against our Judeo-Christian heritage and what we have become today, and against the expansion of both of them.[11]

In appropriating this concept, Samuel Huntington enlarged the context, embracing the whole planet. However, in his work the Islamic menace remains the most palpable and the most pressing for the future of the Occident, while the danger from the other great adversary, Chinese civilisation, is for the moment less tangible.[12] So, to close the circle, it must be emphasised that the reception of the Huntington theses has almost invariably seized upon the number one 'clash', that is to say the Muslim world, which is thus seen as a sort of preferred enemy.

The geopolitical scenario proposed by Huntington is well known. In his opinion, 'civilizations form the largest human tribes, and the clash of civilisations is a tribal conflict on a global scale'.[13] In the emerging modern world, inter-civilisation relations are the fundamental variable. They oscillate between indifference and violence. To define the theoretical base on which he constructs this vision, Huntington calls upon a large number of precursors (historians, anthropologists, sociologists . . .).[14] Referring to the mountain of writing produced by the comparative analysis of civilisations, he defines a series of theoretical propositions: the history of humanity is the history of civilisations; each civilisation is first a cultural entity; civilisations are all-encompassing, meaning they constitute 'the highest grouping and the highest level of cultural identity that humans need'; civilisations extend over a very long period of time; since civilisations are cultural entities, their political composition is variable.[15]

References to a vast intellectual domain in Huntington's overview compose a rather superficial digest. As Emmanuel Todd noted, 'one often has the impression reading his book of skimming a strategic pastiche of the *Decline of the Western World* by Spengler'.[16] On the whole however, even if Huntington's work is full of shorthand and simplifications, its placement in scholarly heritage is not illegitimate. In Bernard Lewis's article, which was his direct inspiration, one already sees the link between Anglo-American Orientalism and geopolitical theory that accentuates the confrontation between civilisations. The same cultural postulate supports research into the history of Islam and current outbursts.

We are thus confronted with a more general problem. The paradoxes and dangers of clichés that condition common knowledge via media discourse and strategic reflection lead to a questioning of scholarly elaboration – seemingly detached from current events, refined and often garbed in noble intentions – that provides its matrix of meaning. In other words, we must deal with the intellectual genealogy presented by Huntington (the same intellectual genealogy that so many of his opponents continue to revere).

We are thus led to envisage a radical option. Is it not necessary to question not only the meaning of *clash*, but also of *civilisations* and *cultures*? If we do not take this path, do we not risk falling back into the quirks of a dialogue of cultures and civilisations, paved with good intentions and circumstantial discourse that only reproduce, with politically correct accents, the same postulates of closure and reification of all uniform and closed cultures?

The success of culturalism

Anthropology has long specialised in working with the notion of culture, which no doubt is the main element in its favour in the 'commercial balance' with other disciplines. The idea of culture was the alpha of the discipline – and often also its omega. According to the words of two great figures in American anthropology, the notion of culture, foundation of anthropology, was to it what gravity was to physics or evolution to biology.[17] Anthropologists set the 'scientific' idea of transmitted culture in opposition to the elitist idea of cultivated knowledge. In the latter there is an absolutist gradual progress leading to perfection; in the former, a relativist vision. Despite the theoretical differences and the abundance of definitions (in 1952, Kroeber and Kluckholn counted 164 definitions of culture or civilisation, terms they considered 'almost synonymous', and added their own), for a long time anthropologists largely shared the idea that the world is an assemblage of cultures. The integrative vision of culture as a cohesive whole is also linked to the technique of fieldwork and to the adoption of a synchronic approach.[18] It is thus possible to sketch a sort of model portrait of the anthropological idea of culture. It refers to small as well as large entities, which are discrete and endowed with a set of distinctive traits. Each culture tends to reproduce itself in an equilibrium organised by a set of symbols and shared meanings, which are the heart of the authentic culture. Each cultural entity is an integrated and structured 'whole' reflected in the behaviour of individuals, the latter also being endowed with a powerful homogeneity. Exchanges or outside movements are sometimes eliminated. More often, these phenomena are acknowledged, but they are considered to be secondary as compared to patterns that arrange disparate elements into a coherent whole and regulate mechanisms of borrowing and rejection.

Naturally, this kind of model portrait simplifies the context and neglects variations of behaviour. Within the discipline, two primary positions can be distinguished. One is what can be identified as constructivist, according to which the culture is an artificial unit isolated for heuristic reasons. This is what Robert Lowie supports for example, adding that the only natural unit for the ethnologist is the culture of all humanity in all periods and all places. Similarly, for one of the founding fathers of British anthropology, Alfred R. Radcliffe-Brown, the word 'culture' does not correspond to a concrete reality, but is an abstraction. What one can observe are not 'cultures', but actions of individuals and the products of past actions of these individuals. For his part, another great figure of American anthropology, Edward Sapir, remarked once that the notion of culture, such as it was described by anthropologists, was a sort of statistical fiction.[19]

The second position can be defined as realist. In this case, the existence of 'peoples' or of 'societies' is recognised, and each of these entities has a 'culture'. A coherent version of this vision runs through the work of Claude Lévi-Strauss, who, thanks to the influence of his writings, has been an eloquent and influential spokesman for cultural determinism. In a brochure published in 1952 by UNESCO, Lévi-Strauss used, to describe the cultural relativism that characterises his position, the metaphor of a train, often employed to explain the first rudiments of the theory of relativity in physics. It is a long elaboration, of which I will use here only the passage that describes how each individual is enclosed in his culture train:

> So each member of a culture is as narrowly within it as the ideal traveller is within his train. Because at birth, our entourage imposes upon us, in a thousand conscious and unconscious ways, a complex system of references consisting of value judgments, motivations, centres of interest, including the reflexive view that education imposes on us of

the historic evolution of our civilization, without which it would become unthinkable or would appear to be in contradiction with real behaviour. We literally carry this system of references around with us, and cultural realities from outside are observable only through the distortions this system imposes on them, when it does not make it impossible for us to perceive anything at all.[20]

In a talk given in 1971, again for UNESCO, Lévi-Strauss again used this metaphor.[21] Cultures are like trains, each one on its rails and each one rolling at its own speed, in a different direction. There are no stations or transfers in this differentialist universe. Each individual is imprisoned in his train, he is within his culture and of it alone. Every connection, every overlap, every mixing between cultures is dangerous. Each culture must keep its distance, limit its exchanges to what is strictly necessary and maintain its difference vis-à-vis others. Even a certain degree of reciprocal hostility is healthy. On the whole, one has the impression that this (hyper)realist concept only replaces the old notion of race by culture.[22]

These positions are like two polarities by which we measure oscillations. The realist vision has certainly known more prudent characterisations than the one we just examined, as it is in this sector that most of the disciplinary practice in the concept of culture takes place. The constructivist vision was especially good for statements of honourable methodological intentions, destined soon to be forgotten in concrete analysis. It is not rare that an author, from one article to another – or sometimes within the space of several pages – goes from a constructivist vision to realist transmutations of culture. Despite epistemological vigilance, the assimilation of categories easily slips into discourse. In any case, it is more or less in the realist version that the 'anthropological' concept of culture – and of its 'cultural' identities – has in the last decades become a matter of common usage. Cultural claims support the struggles of minorities and stir up the post-colonial world. This consciousness of possessing a 'culture' on the part of former victims of imperialism has been called one of the most remarkable phenomena of contemporary world history by one major figure of anthropology.[23] Even in rich countries, the elitist sense of the word 'culture' has often ceded to an anthropological definition. The worlds of business, of advertising, and of law use this notion more and more. The idea of culture intervenes especially in political dynamics. Cultural differences are invoked in the most disparate contexts. We are experiencing the popularity of culturalist fundamentalism[24] in xenophobic positions in the debate on immigration. Old ingredients and old recipes are contributing to the construction of stereotypes, but the process is more and more legitimised by a culturalist option. Racial criteria are too stigmatised and cannot be openly used to designate difference. Culture lends itself to this task. It is a referent that unifies modes ranging from primary hatred to scholarly reflection. The other aspect of culturalist fundamentalism, already mentioned, is the understanding of geopolitical dynamics. Multiple manifestations of culturally received knowledge are solidifying around certain core areas, the principal one being the Muslim world, on the European scale as well as the planetary scale.

Once again, Samuel Huntington is a connecting figure. He describes the two kinds of culturalist fundamentalism, recommending a cultural closure in the United States in the face of foreign 'invasion', Hispanic first of all,[25] after pointing out the importance of the cultural variable in the politics of the Occident vis-à-vis the rest of the world. In Europe, the two versions, internal and external, can converge even more easily on the same enemy, 'Islam'. Orchestrated by a majority of the media, culturalist fundamentalism is spreading in our society, is becoming accepted truth. The decline of revolutionary and reformist ideologies, the end of the Cold War, and the process of European unification are all factors contributing to setting aside polarisations which, until yesterday, held a predominant position (nationalist, class . . .). The term 'Occident' has seen an exponential growth in its use by the media, replacing the term 'free world'.[26] The 'umbrella' of an Occidental cultural community is becoming increasingly seductive, beyond intellectual and humanist circles.

If previously the anthropologist was (or at least was considered to be) the culture expert, now everyone seems to agree that 'culture is everywhere'.[27] The blossoming of the notion of culture and its growing politicisation invite examination. Is it still possible to withdraw to one's scholarly den, or into the laboratory of fieldwork, ignoring concrete implications of the manipulation of concepts? The putting together of the ideological apparatus described by Edward Said is becoming increasingly visible. How, then, can one denounce the media shorthand and condemn Huntington's simplifications, while continuing at the same time to celebrate the intellectual and moral mastery of Lévi-Strauss's considerations on culture and society? Culturalist thinking showed itself essentially to be thinking about difference, and this has obvious political implications, whether one wants it or not. Reflexive prudence is needed then, with a reconsideration of categories and their history, as well as their shifts from one register to another. In short, it is a question of imagining a critical recognition of what talking about culture means.

Venturing into this kind of exploration means taking account of the complex overlaps in scholarly genealogies. The role of anthropology has been preponderant in the twentieth century, especially as a result of taxonomic effort, but the discipline cannot pretend to exclusivity in this regard. In reality, the 'scientific' notion of culture came out of a vast number of reciprocal influences from several intellectual and disciplinary traditions, which mingled together on the immense chessboard on which ideas of 'civilisation' and 'culture' have changed meaning in Europe since the eighteenth century, have opposed or become superimposed on each other, depending on the country, ideologies and disciplinary orientations. The meaning that is central here corresponds in any case to the main semantic space, coinciding with a series of variations on a theme that crystallised during the romantic reaction to Enlightenment universalism, when, from culture and civilisation in the singular, we went to the plural to designate coherent, homogeneous, and relatively fixed groups, exemplified above all by the idea of *Volkgeist*. The contours of these groups are extremely elastic. They can isolate a primitive group of a few hundred people, an isolation within a more complex society, or a segment characterised by professional activities, or by political, artistic, or sexual orientations in industrial and post-industrial societies. The notion of civilisation permits the maximum multiplication of entities conceived by culturalist thinking. Here, the ideas of high culture (literary, artistic, etc.) and of ordinary culture become superimposed and, in a certain way, melt together. A large number of influential works (among them those of the many 'ancestors' claimed by Huntington) refer to 'civilisations' in this sense. The evocation of Islam by Bernard Lewis in the passage cited earlier is also within this semantic space. In effect, Islam seems to be the most probing testing ground of the culturalist vision's pertinence.

Malaise in relation to Islam

In an essay devoted to the role of Islam in the main philosophies of history conceived by European thinkers, Albert Hourani noted that its presence was generally limited. From Hegel to Toynbee, moving through Comte, Renan or Burckhardt, the interpretive filters always tend to minimise the contributions of this 'civilisation' and make excessive simplifications. Not even the great Max Weber's imposing syntheses escape this rule. This state of affairs seems to him to indicate a particular difficulty in finding categories that allow one to grasp Islam. Islam, he adds, falls neither entirely within the Orient nor the Occident. Without being

Christian, it is not totally non-Christian and, in any case, it is tied to Europe by a prolix and intimate connection, by an ambiguous and generally painful overlap.[28]

In the opening of the last chapter of *Tristes Tropiques*, Claude Lévi-Strauss expresses an analogous consideration: 'This malaise felt in relation to Islam, I know too many reasons for it: I find in it the universe I came from; Islam is the Occident of the Orient.'[29] One must add that this malaise is explained very clearly in the pages that precede and those that follow, in which Lévi-Strauss evaluates the historic destiny of some universal religions. Men have made three great religious attempts, he says, separated 'by approximate intervals of a half a thousand years'. They are Buddhism, Christianity and Islam. Lévi-Strauss deploys his usual concept of history as regression as opposed to a dawning phase of happiness. If, in general in the history of mankind, the golden age seems to him to be represented by the Neolithic; as far as religion is concerned this age coincides with Buddhism. Thus, from Buddhism to Christianity to Islam, 'each stage, far from marking progress on the preceding one, is witness instead to a retreat'.[30] The negative role of Islam, 'the most worrisome' of the three religions, materialises also in historical interactions with the two other religions. Mohammed is but a rustic intruder who disconnected the Christian Orient from the Buddhist Orient, which were predestined to be joined. Islam 'cut a more civilized world in two', introducing a rupture that the Occident must reconnect: 'In placing itself between Buddhism and Christianity, Islam Islamized us when the Occident got caught up in the Crusades opposing Islam, thus resembling it rather than lending itself to this slow osmosis with Buddhism that would have made us more Christian, if Islam hadn't existed.'[31] These observations, both extremely abstract and eminently subjective, are livened up by remarks that reveal anti-Muslim sentiments whose violence and superficiality have little to envy in the recent propaganda tract by Oriana Fallaci.[32] Taking up the subject of Islam, Lévi-Strauss abandons his habitual attitude, renouncing the ethnologist's Olympian detachment that contemplates the swarming of human cultures from on high with a melancholy relativism according to which all are the same, all offer advantages and disadvantages, and none can be proclaimed superior to the others.

Another great figure of twentieth-century anthropology, Alfred Kroeber, examines Islam in other planetary triangulations with an underlying philosophy of history, which once again produces a rather hostile and reductive vision of Islam. In a famous text on the dynamics of civilisations in the ancient world, Kroeber proposes a sort of diffusion *à la sauce hégélienne.* Starting from the cradle in the Middle East, the spreading of great civilisations progressed towards the East (in India, China and Japan) and towards the West (in Europe first, then in America). Islam did not, as Lévi-Strauss suggests, come in to sever the Orient from the Occident, but it instead occupied an abandoned space, where the creative energy was used up. Here, at the moment of Islam's birth, there was no hope of seeing the birth of a new, truly creative great civilisation. This explains the particularity of Islam which, according to Kroeber, is a reduced civilisation, in the background, without art, without real intellectual curiosity, without depth.[33]

The framework hardly changes as one turns to professional historians. As Jean-Louis Triaud indicates, the malaise about Islam can be seen in the whole of European historiography, which contains a 'historiographical fault line' that, like the stolen letter in the tale of Edgar Allan Poe, is so flagrant it remains invisible.[34] The Arab-Muslim world has been wiped out of European historicity. Its place in the genealogy of Europe is at best under-estimated – when it is not entirely absent from the roster of ancestors taught in history. Competence in the history of Islam does not figure in the academic preparation of the ordinary professional historian. Its study has been confined to a specialised branch, Orientalism, occupying a sort of space apart, not integrated into the profession of an academic historian. With the decline of traditional Orientalism, political science has taken over the expert's role: 'Here again,' observes Triaud, 'the Arab-Muslim world does not derive from a historical analysis in the full sense of the term, but from a geopolitical and media short-term approach, an Islamology that becomes seismology.'[35]

Even the field of knowledge that has taken the greatest interest in Islam has been marked by ambivalence. The critique of Orientalism reveals shorthand, stereotypes, and political implications within the specialisation. The corpus of doctrines and intellectual and artistic practices through which Islam has been perceived developed around an unacknowledged set of beliefs, clichés and myths. The central thesis of Said's book, which was the culminating moment in this critique, is that the Orient is a constituted idea: 'Like the Occident, the Orient is an idea that has a history and a tradition of thought, an imagery, and a vocabulary that have given it reality and presence in the Occident and for the Occident. The two geographical entities thus support one another and, in a certain way, reflect one another.'[36] One of the most piercing analyses of the consequences of culturalism in relation to the Orientalist fear of the Muslim world is the critique formulated by Abdallah Laroui[37] about the methodological foundations of Gustave von Grunebaum's work. Von Grunebaum's work is exemplary, due both to the author's erudition and to the variety of intellectual influences that form it. The fundamental notion used by von Grunebaum is in any case culture, which he takes from Kroeber. In this way, by means of a long detour, von Grunebaum absorbs culturalism via American anthropology, but he also returns to the German roots of this kind of thinking.

As a basis for the culturalist approach, Laroui isolates 'the postulation of an invariable' at the centre of a culture, which acts both as 'a unifying principle' and as 'an elimination principle'. This invariable allows an accounting of exchanges, influences and transformations. Once the matrix of the culture is established, it determines the direction of the historical process, presiding over the choice of elements that will be kept and those that will be rejected, gradually. As a consequence of this postulate, the culture forms a closed and coherent system. Ordered by a common pattern, the components of the system – whether they be social, moral, aesthetic or political, etc. – are isomorphic.[38]

Considering from the beginning that Islam is a culture, von Grunebaum takes on the task of finding the unifying principle that organises Islam's history by examining a double comparative: 'One comparative aims for concordance and homogeneity between different domains within Islam, the other for difference and opposition outside.' The direction of the research is influenced by postulating the matrix: 'A theory of God that follows from a kind of piety, itself followed by a political theory, which forms the fundamental sequence, the matrix of Islam.'[39] The adoption of the culturalist mode makes it such that developments that do not fit into the logic of the matrix are ignored, or at best are considered as deviations, passing crazes that are outside the culture's 'plan for a good existence'.[40] Von Grunebaum's culturalism thus ends up with restrictions and distortions.[41] Not only does such a construction of Islam's 'matrix' give the impression of extreme subjectivism,[42] the theory of history impoverishes real history, for example by devaluating the realm of science and research on the subject.[43]

Caught up by the determination of an invariable, culturalist analysis becomes the description of a tradition. The search for the matrix leads to the isolation of the classical period, characterised by an equilibrium between different expressions of the culture. For von Grunebaum, Islam finds its 'matrix' after the eleventh century, while the earlier period, 'cannot constitute the central period for the culturalist, precisely because the situation was too much in flux; nothing was definitively integrated then, and nothing definitively eliminated.'[44] Once tradition takes shape in the period considered to be classical, there is henceforth but one Islam, which can fall into decadence or experience a revival. In Islam, when seen as a culture, there is no place for novelty. Islam's current dilemma is thus between fidelity to its fundamental aspiration by rejecting the Occident, and modernisation, which signals the abandonment of the matrix and the end of a culture.[45]

In this manner the culturalist approach implies an impoverished idea of history. While referring to each moment in history, it replaces history with a theory of history.[46] This is the essential point of divergence in Laroui, who maintains the contrary: 'the non-reduction of real history (abundance of events of different orders, different meanings in a single real time) to culture; in as much as culture is not reduced to ideology, that is, the theory of it offered at each moment, ideology in turn going at each moment beyond theology, which is itself a restrictive theory of the relation between man and God'. And that, he adds, is a valid principle for all historic-geography.[47]

Even as he shuns the pitfalls of a culturalist fear of Islam, Laroui indicates reasons that explain the fascination with this approach:

Of course one can never emphasise enough that, in a culturalist approach, the history of Islam is seductive and dangerous. Seductive because it calls for system and structure; everything is given from the beginning in the framework of culture and ideology: we have a theory of religion yet little testimony about the experience of the religion, a theory of politics yet few precise political documents, a theory of history yet few dated events, a theory of social structure yet few individualised 'acts', an economic theory yet few statistics, etc. The danger is the constant risk of confusing theory and with practice, because the one is available, while the other requires research and elaboration. It is this situation that gives culturalist analyses the appearance of truth, because the temporality they postulate agrees with what Islamic tradition has itself imposed.[48]

Refusal to reduce history to a theory leads to a countermanded perspective. While the Orientalist and the Islamic cleric make the same methodological choice, which consists in considering the sacred as the heart of the system, as the engine determining the culture, peoples' behaviour, and history's unfolding, for Laroui it is a question rather of beginning with real history, without burying concrete situations in pre-existing typologies, and of avoiding the positions taken by tradition and by theoreticians.[49] This conclusion is not unlike the critique formulated by Marx in relation to Hegelian idealism.

Laroui's analysis seems to me exemplary, because it implacably peels away the distortions, the reductions, and the subjective flights of the culturalist option, while showing as well the semblance of reality that such an approach produces, and which is particularly perceptible in the case of Islam. Laroui's methodological critique is pertinent in relation to a panoply of culturalist characterisations of Islam, some of them less sweeping and erudite than those of von Grunebaum. However, it can also apply to much more moderate culturalist readings, more open ones, more on the left as it were, such as for example the one put forth by Jacques Berque in the preface to the French translation of *L'Identité culturelle de l'Islam* by von Grunebaum.

The title, Berque observes, constitutes a taking of position. It is a position to which Berque fully subscribes, opposing all those sceptical of the notion of collective identity, those who have doubts as to the very existence of cultures: 'This existence, Islam experiences it and proclaims it with an energy that throws any doubts right back in the face of the scholastic dispute.' If only they will look at it, this will put an end to their dithering. The Orientalist knows well that the 'personality of Islam makes itself felt with recognisable force in the most diverse forms in both time and space'.[50] Berque heralds the synoptic amplitude of von Grunebaum's theses and agrees with the reduction made therein, gathering a vast variety of situations into a simple matrix, with a single theme capable of explaining 'everything regarding the collective behaviour of Islam from the time of the Abbaside caliphate throughout the contemporary period'. He limits himself to suggesting an integration of the strictly culturalist analysis with the 'less directly expressed configurations – the relationship to territory, the world market, the evolution of technology for example'.[51] The only real difference is a less pessimistic vision of contemporary events. For von Grunebaum, Islam's maintenance of specific cultural traits is the source of its inadequacy faced with modernism. Islam must choose between staying itself and stagnating, or advancing and dissolving into the Occident. Berque retorts that this pessimism, although partly justified, does not take into account 'a number of facts, observable for a good quarter of a century, that reveal, on the part of Afro-Asiatic populations, and notably Islam ones, an energy and vitality that, through disappointments, errors and failures, seem to have delivered advantages over the Occidental system'.[52] The process of decolonisation and the development of certain third world countries seem to him to authorise a more optimistic vision. 'Why not attribute current changes in the world to a non-Occidental positivism?' he asks himself. The reformist or revolutionary action that is occurring in the Orient promises a 'reconstruction of the world' that will also involve Occidental populations. These are positive traits showing, according to Berque, that Islam can keep its collective identity while modifying its content. The current disturbances do not mean the end of a cultural system: 'This is, on the contrary, what will allow it to endure in a variation.' This allowed Berque to conclude by prophesying a pluralist world, based on the cooperation 'of all the cultural identities in the world'.[53]

Berque's open and generous vision does not go so far as to liberate inherent culturalism from the Orientalist approach. Once the third worldists' enthusiasms have cooled, how to contrast, with such arguments, the apparently much more coherent reasoning of classical Orientalism and the meta-historical theories of the culturalist orientation, which surface consistently within the contemporary political debate? How to oppose their reductive implications for societies and humans ranged within the nebula of Islam?

Altering the perspective

We have noted the complex overlapping between pure knowledge and political knowledge, their contiguousness in the apparatus producing media presentations, and the inertia of received knowledge. All of this leads to a certain epistemological pessimism, confirmed by current events. In the ideological mind-set that creates the understanding of Islam, the last decade saw the victory of the 'Bernardists' (Lewis) over the 'Edwardians' (Said), to use Jean-Claude Vatin's formula.[54] Faced with a culturalist consensus throughout the political-media universe, critical thinking appears increasingly necessary.

In the last pages of *L'Orientalisme*, Edward Said asks if 'the concept of distinct culture (or of race, religion, civilisation) is useful, or rather is it tied either to self-satisfaction (when one speaks about one's own culture), or to hostility and aggressiveness (when one speaks about the Other)?'[55] This reflection remains current in the face of incantations of culturalist and essentialist visions, which seem paradoxically to furnish fixed and sure points for increasingly hurried observers in a worldwide landscape marked by the blurring of borders and by the ubiquity and instantaneity of information flows. Whence the success of this culturalist geo-strategy which, as Olivier Roy notes, 'since the collapse of the Soviet Union, dominates salons and cafés, where everyone goes on at length about the nature of Islam, and where it happens that the expert mouths the same banalities as his neighbour'.[56] Whence the growing and massive good fortune of what Maxime Rodinson calls 'theologocentrism', consisting of thinking that 'practically all observable phenomena in societies adhering primarily to the Muslim religion are explainable by this adhesion'.[57] Whence the vogue for the expression 'Judeo-Christian' which, as Sophie Bessis[58] explains pertinently, has the triple advantage of obscuring at no cost nearly 2000 years of Christian anti-Judaism, of annexing onto 'the Occident' the first enunciator of monotheist universality, and of expelling Islam from the Abrahamic revelation, which now concerns only the 'Judeo-Christian' duo.[59] Elsewhere, the same formula is taken up in Islamist circles, with a sort of 'polemical mimicry'. Of course, it has an inverse meaning when used to define the 'Judeo-Christian' enemy.

This ambient culturalism is largely, and often explicitly, dependent on anthropology. Faced with this success, the reaction of anthropologists does not look like a lapse into triumphalism. On the contrary, popularisation of the idea of culture is concomitant with an epistemological malaise that, in the same time frame, saps the old certainties and self-confidence of the discipline. One of the most obvious symptoms has been precisely the calling into question of the very idea of culture by a certain number of authors.

Doubtless the 'wild' proliferation of the idea contributed to this questioning. The critique of the idea of culture has thus taken an important turn in contemporary discussions in international anthropology. Must we abandon the notion of culture? Certain authors envisage this possibility or at least affirm the need to give it up. Others propose to keep only the adjective 'cultural', which lends itself less to reification. On the other side, defenders of the idea emphasise that critics are doing a selective reconstruction of the meaning of culture in the history of anthropology. They point out dissonances among anthropologists of the past, citing many authors who, conscious of the risk of reification inherent in the abstraction, were inclined to attribute a central role to actors and to recognise the fallibility of cultural borders.[60]

It is difficult to say whether abolition will have the upper hand in this debate. In any case, even the defence of the notion of culture has been transformed into a kind of reformism (sometimes conscious, sometimes tacit), which, by emphasising the precedents of a flexible vision of culture, changes the facts in relation to the version I have called realist, dominant in the past, and moves towards a constructivist vision. This reflects a change in research orientations that are distancing themselves from concepts meant to understand the social through totalistic, holistic, juristic and ahistoric categories.

The work of self-critical reflection – almost a mourning – in a discipline that for a long time held the copyright on the scientific notion of culture has larger implications. If culturalism finds few explicit defenders, it nevertheless maintains a powerful subterranean influence in several fields of knowledge. Like a partially extinguished star in the firmament of anthropological theories, it continues to throw intense light on many contemporary intellectual and political debates. Often a troubling light, or better, a light endowed with equivocal clarity. How to pave the way then for a renewed analytical path? Two important directions can be observed in recent research orientations. They adopt a position that alters the perspective, by looking both beyond and within the borders between civilisations and cultures.

In the first case, it is a question of a macro-analytical perspective that forces itself free from the endemic Eurocentrism that has conditioned and still conditions the vision of world history. In a certain manner, this perspective prolongs the 'Copernican' revolution begun at approximately the same time by anthropology and by meta-histories, in the vein of Spengler and Toynbee. Opposing the 'Ptolemaic' concept according to which European history was the centre around which the planet evolved, these theories dethroned Europe, making it only one 'culture', one 'civilisation', one history among others.[61] These trends were dependent on idealist perspectives issuing, sometimes with long detours, from German romanticism and pivoting around notions of cultures and civilisations conceived as closed wholes, such as the avatars of the earlier *Volkgeist* or of the Hegelian 'objective thinking'. The change of perspective that is happening in many sectors of macro-history seems intent on getting rid of the idealist burden. This movement is going instead in the direction of real history, concentrating precisely on traffic and exchanges between those who before were thought to belong to homogeneous and airtight blocks of civilisation. A group of relational processes (connected history, shared history, crossed history, world history . . .) questions, in recent years, the links between different historical formations. In this framework, the study of comparative contact situations appears to innovate even the comparative project, while allowing the rethinking of principles of homogeneity and of difference.[62]

Certain recent works by Jack Goody seem to be an example of the heuristic contribution of a perspective outside the norm.[63] Taking on, in the wake of Gordon Childe, the common heritage of the Orient and the Occident since the urban revolution of the Bronze Age, they allow a distancing from the Eurocentrism that inhabits the main explicative theories proposed by the social sciences to interpret the supposed 'unity' of the Occident. Until the industrial revolution, progress on the part of the European economy was only local manifestations of a much larger process, implying, on the Euro-Asian scale, the development of commercial economies and manufacturing activities. A broad vision appears, obliging us to modify the global vision of the history of Occidental and Oriental societies.[64] The Mediterranean is a node in this vast decentralisation. One must avoid making the other into a phantasmagorical catchall onto which constructions of identity are projected. Moving from the 'historiographical fault line' concerning Islam, it is a question of reintegrating the Arab-Muslim world into the same historicity, 'not as a marginal barbarian, but as a close actor and a partner with whom there is a shared history – and not only in the confrontational mode'.[65] Without forgetting that in a thousand years of exchanges, transfers and borrowings that contributed to the ecumenism of the ancient world, a primary role was played by Islam.[66]

The other direction in research leaves behind the local communities and seeks to define the postulates of homogeneity, coherence and fixity that characterise the culturalist postulate, giving central importance to events, actors and processes. Observed close up, without culturalist prejudices, the borders reveal themselves porous, the identities fluid. The configurations of symbols and contents that the latter carry have a historicity and never represent a coherent and unanimous whole. Even social microcosms are fields of struggle for hegemony.[67] It is hegemonic forms that appear coherent, systematic and consensual – that resemble a 'culture' in the old meaning of the word.[68] Among the most interesting explorations in this direction of research are those of Fredrik Barth, one of the most significant figures on the anti-culturalist front in anthropology. Here, the focus of attention is on interactions between individuals, whose behaviour is not seen to be the simple materialisation of a culture. Studying village communities in Bali, for example, he shows that the local community is not endowed with congruity and so falls apart in a series of paradigms for action and their interpretation of events present in a world that extends beyond the community.[69] In an analogous fashion, authors such as Paul Veyne and Albert Piette react to the over-interpretation and saturation of the religious aspect, insisting on the multiplicity and agglutination of practices, on ambivalences, and contradictions in beliefs.[70] As the recent book by Jean-Noêl Ferrié shows,[71] a perspective of this sort provides the key to a correct reading of ordinary Islam: this discrete Islam, hardly visible, yet the greater part. Michael Gilsenan had pointed out this path more than twenty years ago in a book that was an overview of several countries and contexts, concentrating on daily life, deliberately choosing to speak of what is banal, local, 'normal'.[72] Following Walter Benjamin's lead, this work was like a walker attentive to nuances, practising the art of wandering, capable of getting lost in the maze of swarming, complex and contradictory lives. This apprenticeship of the concrete has long been practised by ethnography, in relation to the Muslim world and elsewhere. Taking its rhythm from a stroller wandering through half-foreign realities, this perspective allows for inspections at ground level that are by themselves, beyond the interpretations they support, an important repertory from which we can derive necessary correctives of clichés that currently accompany the spectacular reading of Islamic events.

The distinction between the two directions I have described is not rigid. They can inter-mingle. The monumental work of Shelomo Dov Goiten,[73] did it not reveal, in studying a microcosm in the Geniza in Cairo, ancient connections between the Mediterranean and the Orient? The Mediterranean indeed seems to be a stimulating context for the overlapping of macro and micro perspectives. Its long-term multicultural aspect allows for construction of subjects that go beyond the divisions between 'civilisations'. Certain works accord a major importance to what remains indistinct, to the connivances that last longer than the confrontations, to what is held in common.[74] What emerges therein is 'a more limited, relative, less perennial vision of borders'.[75]

Under attack so to speak from above and below, the civilisational groups that result are less monolithic than usual. They are contradictory, stratified groups, inhabited by diversity. Interrogated at ground level, identities often appear mixed, inventive, conjunctural. They even authorise the crossing of religious boundaries generally considered to be impassable.[76] The process of constructing and maintaining more rigid identities must be studied and not assumed to be a stable given: it is part of belonging to imagined communities, it depends on the acts of intellectual, religious and political elites, it is influenced by the economic and social context.

The preceding considerations have tried to give shape to an excursion along the enigmatic horizon extending between what 'talking about culture' *can be* and *means*. Some examples of an essentialist understanding of Islam are the provisional navigational chart of reflective recognition; this has led us to consider works that attempt to change perspective. Yet the weight of intellectual heritage and the current socio-political context, in which the notion of culture is used in an often aggressive manner, does not lead to optimism. The essentialist vision of the race–nation–people conglomerate is still with us, in disguised forms, hardly more flexible. There are thus good ethical and epistemological reasons to develop critical thinking, capable of sustaining us against the 'Herder tyranny' that continues in understanding the contemporary world.

A first remedy can come from a constructivist vision that sees the notions of culture and civilisation as tools among others: no more than abstractions to create analytical order in the perpetual flow of events and the complex overlapping of processes. Escape from the hold of culturalism would be facilitated if we could formally abandon the notions of culture or civilisation. This sacrifice, perhaps beneficial, is nevertheless unlikely.

Culturalist absolutism operates particularly in relation to the Muslim world. It is therefore more urgent, in this case, to alter the perspective. We must, in other words, *un-cover* Islam, free it from the strata of theologocentric and essentialist interpretations, which conceal it and make of it the monist entity so loved by fundamentalist Muslims, the media and Orientalists, old and new. Without having too many illusions about the impact of such an effort, especially in the short term, we can at least aspire to insert a wedge in the paradoxical unanimity shared by endogenous culturalism and by most 'Occidental' experts.

Notes

1. Translated by Penny Allen.
2. Abdou Filali-Ansary, *L'Islam est-il hostile à la laïcité?* (Casablanca: Le Fennec, 1997), p. 24.
3. Bruno Etienne, 'La fabrique des regards', in *La Pensée de midi,* no. 9, Actes-Sud/La pensée de midi, winter 2002–3, pp. 90–102.
4. Paul Virilio, *Ville panique. Ailleurs commence ici* (Paris: Éditions Galilée, 2004), pp. 45–8. See also the interview with Paul Virilio by Thierry Fabre, 'L'art de l'effroi', in *La Pensée de midi,* no. 9, Actes-Sud/La pensée de midi, winter 2002–3, pp. 9–19.
5. As Vincent Geisser noted, 'the media does not create Islamophobia but generalises common usage about Islam and Islamism: a generalising via the selection of articles and reports, themes treated, images offered to readers and to television viewers; a generalising via the cooptation of legitimate figures apt to speak about Islam and Islamism (writers, essayists, philosophers, political experts, or more rarely Islamic experts); finally, a generalising via the focus on nationally or internationally famous Muslims, presented sometimes as positive heroes, sometimes as negative or evil heroes' (Vincent Geisser, *La Nouvelle Islamophobie*, La Découverte: Paris, 2003, p. 26).
6. Jocelyne Dakhlia, 'La "culture nébuleuse" ou l'Islam à l'épreuve de la comparaison', *Annales HSS,* 6 (November–December 2001), p. 1177.
7. Tariq Ali, *The Clash of Fundamentalisms: Crusades, Jihads and Modernity* (London: Verso, 2002).
8. Charles Wright-Mills, 'The Cultural Apparatus', in I. L. Horowitz (ed.), *Power, Politics and People: the Collected Essays of C. Wright-Mills* (Oxford: Oxford University Press, 1967), pp. 405–6.
9. Edward W. Said, *Covering Islam: How the Media and the Experts Determine How We See the Rest of the World* (London: Routledge & Kegan Paul, 1981), p. 32.
10. Samuel P. Huntington, *Le Choc des civilisations* (1996; Paris: Odile Jacob, 2000).

11. Bernard Lewis, 'The Roots of Muslim Rage: Why So Many Muslims Deeply Resent the West and Why their Bitterness Will Not be Easily Mollified', *Atlantic Monthly*, 266 (September 1990), p. 60.
12. 'Le problème central pour l'Occident n'est pas le fondamentalisme islamique. C'est l'islam, civilisation différente dont les représentants sont convaincus de la supériorité de leur culture et obsédés par l'infériorité de leur puissance' (Huntington, *Le Choc des civilisations*, p. 320). ['The central problem for the Occident is not Islamic fundamentalism. It is Islam, a different civilisation whose members are convinced of the superiority of their culture and obsessed by the inferiority of their power'.]
13. Ibid., p. 303.
14. The list is long. It includes among others Max Weber, Emile Durkheim, Oswald Spengler, Arnold Toynbee, Alfred Weber, Alfred Kroeber, Fernand Braudel. Huntington, *Le Choc des civilisations*, p. 43.
15. Ibid., pp. 43–50.
16. Emmanuel Todd, *Après l'empire. Essai sur la décomposition du système américain* (Paris: Gallimard, 2004 (2002)), p. 21. Other sources of inspiration often used are Braudel and Toynbee. This déjà-vu characteristic of Huntington's theses opens the way to confusion. In Italy, there was recently a publicity barrage around the re-edition of a book of Luciano Pellicani that would have anticipated Huntington by some years. In reality, he only re-assessed Toynbee. See Luciano Pellicani, *Jihad: le radici* (Rome: Luiss University Press, 2004).
17. A. L. Kroeber and C. Kluckhohn, *Culture: a Critical Review of Concepts and Definitions*, vol. 47, no. 1, MA. Papers of the Peabody Museum, Cambridge, 1952, p. 3.
18. It is elaborated in a series of approaches: culture and personality, structural-functionalism, structuralism, interpretive anthropology, up to certain currents of postmodernism. Different visions correspond to different trends as regards the placement of culture: in the social structure, in people's heads, in a network of symbols that organise public behaviour, etc.
19. Robert H. Lowie, *The History of Ethnological Theory* (New York: Farrar and Rinehart, 1937), pp. 235–6; Alfred R. Radcliffe Brown, 'On Social Structure', *Journal of the Royal Anthropological Institute of Great Britain and Ireland*, 70, 1940, pp. 1–12; Edward Sapir, *Selected Writings in Language, Culture, and Personality* (ed. D. G. Mandelbaum) (Berkeley: University of California Press, 1949), pp. 515–16.
20. This text has gone through several editions. Here I am quoting from Claude Lévi-Strauss, *Anthropologie structurale deux* (Paris: Plon, 1996 (1973)), p. 397.
21. This talk is published in the first chapter of Claude Lévi-Strauss, *Le Regard éloigné* (Paris: Plon, 1983).
22. This is what Lévi-Strauss does explicitly by affirming a continuity as compared with Gobineau. See Claude Lévi-Strauss and Didier Eribon, *De près et de loin (suivi de 'Deux ans après')* (Paris: Odile Jacob, 1990 (1988)), pp. 222–3.
23. Marshall Sahlins, 'Two or Three Things that I Know about Culture', *Journal of the Royal Anthropological Institute* (NS), 5, 1999, pp. 399–421. See p. 401.
24. See Verena Stolcke, 'Talking Culture: New Boundaries, New Rhetorics of Exclusion in Europe', *Current Anthropology*, 36, 1995, pp. 1–24.
25. Samuel P. Huntington, *Who Are We? The Challenges to America's National Identity* (New York: Simon & Schuster, 2004).

26. See Huntington, *Le Choc des civilisations*, pp. 65–6.
27. 'Suddenly people seem to agree with us anthropologists; culture is everywhere. Immigrants have it, business corporations have it, young people have it, women have it, even ordinary middle-age men have it, all in their own version' (Ulf Hannerz, *Transnational Connections: Cultures, People, Places* (London: Routledge, 1996, p. 30)). Jack D. Eller notes that almost all sectors of American society have learned the language of culture, to the point where it is possible to speak of a sort of 'culture cult' in civil society ('Anti-multi-culturalism', *American Anthropologist*, 99, 1997, pp. 249–60: see p. 253).
28. Albert Hourani, *Europe and the Middle East* (London: Macmillan, 1980), pp. 19–73. See in addition, on German thinking, Hichem Djaït, *L'Europe et l'Islam* (Paris: Le Seuil, 1978), pp. 81–103.
29. Claude Lévi-Strauss, *Tristes tropiques* (Paris: Plon, 1955), p. 485.
30. 'The merit of Buddhism is to have eliminated the beyond (everything is reduced thus to a radical critique, "at the end of which the wise man emerges into the refusal of the meaning of things and of beings"). Christianity re-establishes on the contrary the beyond; Islam completes this decadence, narrowly linking the supernatural and temporal' (ibid., p. 489).
31. Ibid., pp. 489–90.
32. Antipathy towards Islam is well rooted in Lévi-Strauss's work. See for example Claude Lévi-Strauss and Didier Eribon, *De près et de loin*, pp. 210–11.
33. Alfred L. Kroeber, 'The Ancient Oikoumene as an Historic Culture Aggregate', *Journal of the Royal Anthropological Institute of Great Britain and Ireland*, 75, 1945, pp. 9–20.
34. Jean-Louis Triaud, 'L'Islam vu par les historiens français', *Esprit*, no. 246, October 1998, pp. 110–32. See p. 110.
35. Ibid., p. 118.
36. Edward Said, *L'Orientalisme. L'Orient créé par l'Occident* (Paris: Le Seuil, 1980), p. 17.
37. Abdallah Laroui, 'Les arabes et l'anthropologie culturelle. Remarques sur la méthode de Gustave von Grunebaum', in *La Crise des intellectuels arabes. Traditionalisme ou historicisme?* (Paris: Maspero, 1974), pp. 59–102.
38. Ibid., pp. 66–7.
39. Ibid., pp. 70–1.
40. Ibid., p. 67.
41. Ibid., p. 83.
42. Ibid., p. 86.
43. Ibid., p. 84.
44. Ibid., p. 77.
45. Ibid., p. 79.
46. Ibid., p. 83.
47. Ibid., pp. 89–90.
48. Ibid., pp. 91–2.
49. Ibid., pp. 94–8.
50. Jacques Berque, preface to *L'Identité culturelle de l'Islam*, by Gustave E. von Grunebaum (Paris: Gallimard, 1969, pp. vii–xv). See p. vii.
51. Ibid., p. x.
52. Ibid., p. xiii.

53. Ibid., pp. xiv–xv.

54. Jean-Claude Vatin, 'Orient-ations', in *D'un Orient l'autre*, vol. 1, *Les Figurations* (Paris: Editions du CNRS, 1991) pp. 11–32. See p. 23.

55. Edward Said, *L'Orientalisme*, p. 351.

56. Olivier Roy, *L'Islam mondialisé* (Paris: Le Seuil, 2004), p. 234.

57. Maxime Rodinson, *La Fascination de l'Islam. Les étapes du regard occidental sur le monde musulman* (Paris: Maspero, 1980), p. 129.

58. Sophie Bessis, *L'Occident et les autres. Histoire d'une suprématie* (Paris: La Découverte, 2002), pp. 281–6.

59. Certain authors, such as Jacques Ellul and Alain Besançon, go explicitly in this direction, reducing Islam to a form of paganism.

60. For an idea of the debate, see Robert Brightman, 'Forget Culture: Replacement, Transcendence, Reflexification', *Cultural Anthropology*, 10(4), 1995, pp. 509–46; Susan Wright, 'The Politicization of "Culture"', *Anthropology Today*, 14(1), 1998, pp. 7–15; Christoph Brumann, 'Writing for Culture. Why a Successful Concept Should Not be Discarded', *Current Anthropology*, 40, Supplement, 1999, pp. S1–S27; Robert Borofsky et al., 'A Conversation About Culture', *American Anthropologist*, 103(2), 2001, pp. 432–46; Fran Markowitz, 'Talking about Culture: Globalization, Human Rights and Anthropology', *Anthropological Theory*, 4(3), 2004, pp. 329–52.

61. It would be possible to follow a certain number of overlaps between the two orientations by showing for example the influence of Spengler on the anthropological culturalism of Ruth Benedict, Alfred Kroeber and Claude Lévi-Strauss.

62. For stimulating discussions on these perspectives, see Serge Gruzinski, 'Les mondes mêlés de la Monarchie catholoque et autres "connected histories"', *Annales HSS*, 56(1), 2001, pp. 85–117; Lucette Valensi, 'L'exercise de la comparaison au plus proche, à distance: le cas des sociétés plurielles', *Annales HSS*, 57(1), 2002, pp. 27–30; Michael Werner and Bénédicte Zimmermann, 'Penser l'histoire croisée: entre empirie et réflexivité', *Annales HSS*, 58(1), 2003, pp. 7–36; Gale Stokes, 'The Fates of Human Societies: a Review of Recent Macrohistories', *American Historical Review*, 106(2), 2001, pp. 508–25.

63. Jack Goody, *L'Orient en Occident* (Paris: Le Seuil, 1999); *Famille et mariage en Eurasie* (Paris: Presses Universitaires de France, 2000); *Capitalism and Modernity: the Great Debate* (Cambridge: Polity, 2004).

64. See also André G. Frank, *ReOrient: Global Economy in the Asian Age* (Berkeley: University of California Press, 1998).

65. Jean-Louis Triaud, 'L'Islam vu par les historiens français', p. 110.

66. Jack Goody recently wrote a book about this showing that Islam is part of the history and the present of Europe: *L'Islam en Europe. Histoire, échanges, conflits* (Paris: La Découverte, 2004).

67. Tatal Asad, 'Anthropology and the Analysis of Ideology', *Man* (NS), 14, 1979, pp. 607–27.

68. Susan Wright, 'The Politicization of "Culture"', p. 10.

69. Fredrik Barth, *Balinese Worlds* (Chicago/London: University of Chicago Press, 1993).

70. See Paul Veyne, 'L'interprétation et l'interprète. A propos des choses de la religion', *Enquête*, 3, 1996, pp. 241–72; Albert Piette, *Le Fait religieux. Une théorie de la religion ordinaire* (Paris: Economica, 2003).

71. Jean-Noël Ferrié, *La Religion de la vie quotidienne chez les marocains musulmans. Rites, règles, et routine* (Paris: Karthala, 2004).
72. Michael Gilsenan, *Connaissance de l'Islam* (Paris: Karthala/Iremam, 2001 (1982)).
73. Shelomo Dov Goiten, *A Mediterranean Society: the Jewish Communities of the Arab World as Portrayed in the Documents of the Cairo Geniza*, 5 vols, Berkeley, Los Angeles and London, 1967–88.
74. See for example, Ammiel Alcalay, *After Jews and Arabs: Remaking Levantine Culture* (Minneapolis: University of Minnesota Press, 1993); Henk Driessen, *On the Spanish-Moroccan Frontier: a Study in Ritual, Power and Ethnicity* (New York & Oxford: Berg, 1992); Haim Gerber, 'Muslims and Zimmis in Ottoman Economy and Society: Encounters, Culture and Knowledge', in *Studies in Ottoman Social and Economic Life* (collection under the direction of Raoul Motika, Christoph Herzog, Michael Ursinus) (Heidelberg: Heidelberg Orientsverlag, 1999), pp. 9–124.
75. Jocelyn Dakhlia, 'La "culture nébleuse"', p. 1198.
76. See for example Dionigi Albera, 'Sanctuaires ambigus et pèlerinages mixtes en Méditerranée', in *Les Pèlerinages au Moyen-Orient: espaces public, espaces du public* (collection under the direction of Sylvia Chiffoleau and Anna Madoeuf) (Damas: Institut Français du Proche-Orient, 2005).

7
Identity Crises and Value Conflicts[1]

Abdou Filali-Ansary

The dialectic of identity and value

In principle, identity and value refer to incommensurable realities. Platonism offers perhaps the most convenient means for illustrating this incommensurability: the two belong to different 'worlds'. Identity defines the *reality* of each individual or group of individuals. Value comes from the *ideal* projected beyond all reality. Identity and value refer then to two different realms in the universe marked by language. However, their contents and their paths have been intimately linked. Identity, when it is conscious, carries also the givens imposed and inherited, such as physical characteristics, as well as projected self-images, in which the ideal and the imaginary work with the given to compose something. Value is always expressed in a language that remains in one way or another local, rooted in a particular path.

In the history of human groups, the relation between collective identities and value systems has been one of the most complex, and it has led to developments that are the most difficult to reduce to simple logic. It can be said that the dialectic of the universal and the particular has found its best illustration in this relation. Human groups express their particularities by invoking universal categories. Their specific personality is described in terms of physical or moral qualities. The particular is as such only because of the implementation of universal dimensions. However, by a supplementary complication, the universal is spoken in and by particular languages. There is no existence separate from the particular forms that incarnate it. The categories used to signify it are constructed in and by different symbolic systems. The question asked from the beginning, as soon as different human groups entered into contact with one another, was that of communication, of translation – but at a superior level. How to come to terms with communication between value systems? Can one say in one language the values expressed in another? Can one practise what Reinhard Schulze calls 'code switching',[2] the transcription of the same values into different symbolic systems, the passage from one system of symbols to another? This question sends us back to other much more complex ones. Are so-called universal values universal in the sense that they transcend the symbolic systems that 'express' them, or rather because they are constructions produced by (or by means of) these systems and projected into a transcendent space? Spontaneous Platonism, which could be an innate disposition, a naive attitude of our consciousness, or a characteristic of our linguistic usages, makes us lean towards the realism of values. This spontaneous Platonism has been subject to systematic suspicion on the part of various philosophers (Sophists, Ash'arites, Nietzsche, Foucault), but seems to resist the mistrust, or the lucidity, that everyone feels about it.

Between identity and value, we find ourselves caught up in one of the most powerful whirlwinds of history. It can even be said that the tension between the two, the dynamic created by their fusion and repulsion, has been the most powerful engine of history, at least in the political, spiritual and intellectual realms. Even if one must admit that they are only reflections of the relations of production, a language in which other conflicts and other interests are expressed, they have defined the universe as meaning where human societies have evolved, have produced and formulated their plans, and have projected their frustrations and aspirations.

The relations between the two have given rise to what certain authors[3] have described in terms of flux and reflux, with strong variations between moments of intense mobilisation – in which a particular identity melts and becomes part of the defence of a value system (moments of religious and/or national fervour) – and moments of demobilisation, in which individuals withdraw into their immediate interests, when individual identity takes over from collective identity and the value systems that support it. Ibn Khaldoun has offered perhaps the strongest illustration of this dialectic and of the paradox in which the *açabiya* (collective and intensely felt identity) is indispensable to the mounting of religious goals. It is this that allows the construction of empires in the service of faith, that imposes the moral and political order necessary for a life conforming to religious precepts.

David Hume and Ernest Gellner have taken up the idea of the cycle whose different stages represent modalities of interaction between identity and value. The events of such a relationship produce the different states of individual and collective consciousness. Value seems to dominate when open religion triumphs, the negation of egotism[4] in the collective conscience of humans. Here, humans feel themselves to be situated in a cosmos whose existence has meaning and whose functioning obeys certain laws, and they begin to consider that their actions and their lives have purposes that lie beyond the satisfaction of immediate needs. The value systems that emerge refer thus to perceptions in which man has a place in the universe, in which the universe is in a sense connected to man's existence. A vision of the world and moral meaning become one in order to open up humanity to new horizons, either in the intellectual and spiritual sphere or the political and social. The two spheres are realised, formulated in the language of a people – which, through their intermediary, feels as *one* in relation to other peoples, with its own vision and destiny. Particular forms of collective identities are born, reinforced by confronting others of the same nature. The first value 'conflicts' take place, even if (and perhaps 'because') each value system aspires to universality. These first systems succeed, nevertheless, in breaking the limits of local identities, because they succeed in encompassing populations settled in large spaces yet divided by obvious cultural characteristics (languages, customs, heritage).

Religions break the constraints of identities that existed and marked the path up until then, in order to build others. Becoming Buddhist or Pythagorean, one denies one's local connection, but one reaches or forges a new connection. Visions and value systems proposed by the great religions contribute thus to the reconfiguration of consistency and distribution of collective identities. They facilitate the emergence of great empires, which unify diverse populations, which create new spaces of cultural and economic exchange, and which help in integrating – and sometimes in homogenising – disparate human groups dispersed in large spaces.

Islam, which came after what Karl Jaspers called 'the axial age', illustrates in the best way the functioning of this process. Born in a tribal milieu fragmented in the extreme, it succeeded in unifying Arab tribes and in mobilising them against the powers of the time, the Byzantine and Sassanide Empires. In the second stage, it pushed out or eliminated these two long-term rivals and created, in the territory conquered at their expense – and, further, at the expense of other political entities – a vast territory in which diverse peoples interacted intensely and produced cultural expressions, social forms and new politics, in which the local style was more or less immersed in acquisitions or borrowings from the new platform of religion.

The system of values and religious beliefs soaks into local identities and causes them to evolve towards new forms. The resulting integration is made real also by differentiation in regard to other groups, which develop around other value systems and other world visions. It is such a moment one can describe in terms of value conflicts and identity crises, even if the word 'crisis' is happening to vast identities constructed on universal principles, rather than as a result of belonging to tribal or national segments, as if adhesion to these principles created new tribes. The opening that occurs at a certain level (between peoples who had believed in the same religious concepts) is at the same time closure on other levels, in regard to other peoples who choose to believe in other religions. Certainly, clerics who were in charge of maintaining and teaching dogma felt that their rival value systems converged to a certain degree, that their ultimate purposes were the same. They envisaged the possibilities of 'dialogue' between believers in different systems. Intellectual and spiritual motivation for such dialogue was not lacking and could be powerful, decisive at certain moments. One must not forget, though, that sectarian spirit and dogmatic purity could exercise an equally powerful attraction, sometimes even more powerful, than opening to the other in the name of universal religious and moral principles. Spiritual, intellectual and moral preoccupations were not the only ones present in minds. They led often to situations in which moments of confrontation, coexistence, even cooperation came one after the other without interruption. Even inside large groups, the same dynamic produced comparable effects between sects, regimes, peoples, etc. The great religions offered new means of 'coming together/differentiation', but did not put an end as such to the practice of tribal and local forces, etc. They certainly attenuated, sometimes reduced to nothing, the intensity of these dynamics, often by channelling them into other forms and sending them in new directions.

With the arrival of modernity, another principle of 'coming together/differentiation' became operational and produced new entities, new attitudes and new configurations. Politics separated from religion when the nation emerged as the most appropriate entity to organise, mobilise and symbolise human groups. The modern state is conceived as the means of giving form to the potential of the nation. Nationalism, without eliminating predominant religious attitudes in societies in which it emerges, offers to people new visions of the world and of themselves, new concepts of history and new collective aspirations. It produces in turn overarching narratives but encourages different hopes and offers new principles of organisation.

The religious moment allowed the mobilisation of large human groups around moral visions that transcend the real givens of existence. Certain religions offered perspectives on life after death. All of them kept alive the hope of deliverance from suffering experienced in life, and they created order, by means of this hope, in the relations between members of human groups, amongst themselves and with others.

The political moment, to borrow Burhan Ghalioun's expression, not only mobilised the masses in the name of a cultural and linguistic identity and a common history, but 'enflamed them with the hope of acquiring terrestrial gifts', such as economic prosperity, cultural flowering and political participation. On these three planes, the new movement helped human societies accomplish substantial progress (or served as a framework for the accomplishment of progress). It allowed for better participation in economic competition by integrating vast populations into national markets, by establishing infrastructures, and by encouraging modern economic enterprise. It created homogeneous cultural spaces, by establishing a political education that generalised access to writing in unified idioms regulated centrally. Finally, it produced structures that allowed for better participation by people in political processes, by building institutions, principles and procedures that shaped those in power into new moulds and forced them to act according to agreed-upon rules.

Throughout this process, the dynamic of values is reinforced by the question of identity, although according to different mechanisms. Once again, it is the invocation of particular identities, national identities, their reinforcing and sometimes their exacerbation, that allows for proclaiming and establishing universal values. Economic prosperity, cultural accomplishment and democracy are not conceivable except within and by means of nation-states. The principle that allows certain populations to identify themselves as nations permitted them at the same time to build the framework in which they could pursue – and realise – the most prestigious objectives within modern value systems. An identity 'crisis' – or rather a rising identity fever – allows for certain values to be reclaimed, defended and affirmed.

Does history have meaning?

Reviewing so rapidly and so summarily certain major transformations in the history of humanity, one is soon tempted to see an unfolding, a kind of progress in which humanity passes from primitive forms marked by irrationality, savagery, etc. to intellectually and morally superior forms. Even more, one recognises in the flux and reflux visible in certain episodes the mark of a temporary stagnation or an inherent process at particular moments in the long path of humanity. One may even be tempted to integrate them as illustrations of the 'work' of history (the Hegelian terminology cannot be avoided too long), as spasms that prepare for the arrival of great change to follow. Perhaps the identity tension is the negative moment that allows the positive moment – the realisation of values – to happen?

Even if, on the whole, history seems to have permitted humanity to go from the simplest to the most complex, from the free play of instincts and impulses that define the animal state to processes and mechanisms that organise human beings into denser systems, the reality is much more complicated and calls for more nuanced judgements. The amalgam that assimilates the greatest complexity into qualitative superiority comes from an arguable value judgement and from a highly contested fact we have learned to regard with suspicion. Variations, if one can say so, have been so extreme that one would be blissfully happy to grab onto the idea of real progress. It is not our role here to re-examine the immense questions raised by naive belief (naive, but not innocent) in the continual progress of history.

Questions that can stop us here have to do with the wide gap one can observe today between perceptions and aspirations in different contemporary societies. Gaps that make one think – and which have indeed pushed many to think – that we are in a situation in which different cultures must coexist without being able to really communicate, that insurmountable barriers exist between distinct value systems, and that we have entered into an era of total confrontation between irreducible modes.

One of the concepts that seems to have acquired the status of orthodoxy insists that humanity has arrived at the formula that guarantees the best possible realisation of values accepted by the great majority: market economy, pluralist democracy and the state based on law. The latter, a system of obligations and rights, is supposed to create the optimal context for free play of private initiatives, for a total deployment of individual and collective creativity, and for the greatest good for the global community.

Given this, one does not understand how large segments of humanity – especially in societies in which Muslims are a significant component – can reject such a 'covenant' despite the successes which the state based on law has brought, how they can invoke religious ideals of obedience to norms of supposedly transcendental origin but belonging visibly to another age and to societies 'situated' in very particular contexts. It is here that one perceives today the most violent conflict of values – and, whether it is said explicitly or not – the deepest fault line in humanity today.

This encourages a certain number of thinkers to proclaim that as long as Muslims are not converted to a certain form (or to a minimum 'dose') of secularism, the road to democracy will remain closed to them, and their real insertion into modernity will be postponed indefinitely, and their interactions with the rest of humanity will be profoundly and durably troubled.

In fact, the historic path of Muslim societies seems both to have placed them ahead and outside of the general evolution in the configuration of the religious and the political. As we have seen, the moment of religious revolution saw the emergence of equality ideals and the establishing of a socio-political order allowing the historical creation of the equality and justice promised by religious teachings. Muslims have known the supreme frustration of seeing their dreams smashed by political reality. The *fitna kubra* (great discordance, or great anarchy) that instilled, in the deepest consciousness, a particular kind of tragic sense, was the first confrontation between the ideal of a community – in which the political is subject to the religious (meant as an ethical ideal of equality and justice) – and the reality of politics, in which primitive forces (*açabiya*) believed to be quelled, arose again.

The custodian of full legitimacy, Ali Ibn Abi Talib, the fourth of the 'well-guided' Caliphs for the Sunnis and first Imam for the Shiites, was replaced by Mu'awiya, a usurper who mobilised a bureaucratic apparatus and a professional army. A dynastic secular power using religion to achieve worldly objectives replaced the power established to bring to life the religious ideal.

The trauma in the face of this first and unique secularisation was immense and its effects long-lasting. Instead of power considered to be truly *legitimate* – the power of the Caliphs was said to be 'virtuous' – the worldly power of dynasties supported by force was imposed. The secular power was experienced as a usurper. Its attempt to subjugate religion, to coopt it, was experienced as extreme violence done to the profound aspirations which Muslims had internalised. The ultimate developments, which showed the impossibility of restoring legitimate power, led to the emergence of a kind of compromise, in which those in power, a power acquired through armed force, were accepted as legal (but not as legitimate), in so far as they accepted an important limitation on their prerogatives, in so far as they respected the religious symbols and abandoned all attempt to interfere in the formulation of social norms and their realisation.

Thus political power was secularised and conserved a certain room for manoeuvre in the maintenance of order; but it was refused any role in domains in which full legitimacy was required: the formulation and execution of laws. Temporal and religious power were well separated. They coexisted, managed different domains in collective life, lived their shared life with difficulty. If there were moments of complicity between the two, or hegemony of one over the other, tensions were dissimulated. They coexisted in reality, not in conviction. Still, such a configuration produced what one could consider to be a first approximation of what was going to become a system of law. Political power (or what remained of it[5]) was reduced to managing public order with extremely reduced responsibilities. Religious power, held by the clerics, the *oulémas*, took on the maintenance of the educational system (religious teaching, formulation of law) and what constituted the minimum necessary for the functioning of social order. For the rest, Muslim societies following various procedures took charge themselves of the systems of rules and distribution of functions connected to local contexts, urban or tribal.

The dream of legitimacy, of returning to a legitimate order, was 'sublimated', so to speak. It took on utopian form, which was expressed for Shiites by the myth of the return of the Imam who had gone into hiding and, for Sunnis, by that of the restoration (or return) of the 'well-guided' Caliph. In all communities, Sufism arrived to seal the historic 'compromise': for the masses, by maintaining that Sufi exultation liberates one from the real world and restores, via incantation, direct access to virtue and happiness.

Is it necessary to go back to the distant past, to these medieval forms, to find the origin of Muslims' apparent resistance to secularism and intellectual and political modernity? The painful divorce between the legitimate and the legal certainly left a profound mark on the collective consciousness of Muslims, notably the intense attachment to one form or another of utopia, in which a religious government (Caliphate, Imamate) returns or is put in power to restore justice and establish a true *system of law*.

Thus before the emergence of the modern ideal of a state based on law, Muslims had the hope of an ideal regime and tried to establish what one could call a *society of law* – a society in which political power is reduced to nothing (since it deals simply with the administration of public order and the defence of territory) and in which making law sacred keeps it free from manipulation by the powerful and places its maintenance in the hands of a class of experts (*fuqaha*) authorised to read the texts and explain their contents.

Utopia would appear to prefigure what has become a powerful ideal today: law as ultimate reference for the regulation of politics and social matters. In the form in which Muslim consciousness became immersed, it is unattainable, but still capable of mobilising the masses, of enflaming imaginations. It stands as a marvellous and inaccessible alternative to today's reality and as the possibility of embracing ideals that are themselves realisable, even if they remain stripped of seductive effects.

But if utopia is there, available for use, its real effect cannot be explained uniquely by itself nor by its seductive powers. The question is then: how can such a utopia return to power, how can it take hold of imaginations and produce the general elation one observes in such a vast space as the one occupied by Muslim societies today?

Nations of the 'fifth type'?

Ernest Gellner, evoking the history of nationalism as a force that has produced major effects in modern history, suggests the image of time zones to explain the different paths via which the first modern nations were born in Europe. According to this point of view, Europe should be divided into four zones going from the west to the east like time zones.

The first of these zones includes countries in which nationalism manifested itself the earliest. It happened that political units around Lisbon, Madrid, Paris and London corresponded to linguistic and cultural groups in which knowledgeable traditions ('high culture', according to Ernest Gellner) had prospered for a certain time. When the age of nationalism arrived, linguistic and cultural homogenisation of peoples, as well as the creation of new boundaries required for forming modern nation-states, were relatively minimal. The problem for young nations in this zone was to transform peasants speaking different 'patois' into citizens speaking a national language and sharing the same cultural references. The challenge was to transform peasants into citizens by inculcating the language and high culture of elites in the capital, rather than to invent a new national culture based on the particularities of peasant populations.

The second time zone corresponded to territories united into the Holy Roman Empire. The two cultural spaces of these territories, which were to become Germany and Italy, had long maintained prosperous knowledgeable cultures and particular languages sustained by active and productive intellectual classes. Emerging nationalism aimed therefore to endow existing and strongly developed cultures with moulds – or, as Ernest Gellner says, with politically appropriate 'roofs'.

The third zone, further to the east, includes territories in which neither politically consistent, long-lasting units nor particular knowledgeable cultures had emerged (central Europe). In the marriage between culture and politics that nationalism was meant to accomplish, the two partners had to be literally 'invented'. It was necessary to create knowledgeable cultures in local dialects and to define geographical contours of states that had never existed. The task of nationalists was more arduous, and thus more brutal: to create knowledgeable cultures out of local peasant traditions and to endow them with state-like forms (or 'roofs').

The fourth zone, still further to the east, saw its nationalist development 'frozen' (but not extinguished) by the rise of absolutist socialism, which did not tolerate economic, political or ideological pluralism, and which destroyed civil society. This zone absorbed, for a certain time, the third zone. It deferred – and thus made more virulent – the effect of rising nationalism. It did not modify its major effect – the identification of a human group with a high culture in the framework of a unified political entity.

What is the nature of the birth of modern nations in territories in which Muslims constitute a significant majority? Should other 'time zones' be added to those mentioned by Ernest Gellner? The first impression is that, here again, the situations are diverse. In the multiplicity of paths that have led to the emergence of modern nations, one can recognise the extremes. There was, for example, the creation of states based on artificially drawn borders on geographical maps by colonial powers of the period. Jordan and Kuwait are such examples. Alternatively, other states have been created in the framework of territories marked by a long political centralisation (Egypt, Morocco). In yet another example, certain states have been created by replacing religious allegiance with ethnic allegiance (modern Turkey created from the ruins of the Ottoman Empire), while others have resulted from the replacing of ethnic identities with religious identities (Pakistan detached from the Indian whole to create a Muslim state).

Each time, a different element has played a role in the life of the new nations. Language, which helped to bind together modern Turkey and Iran, contributed to the destabilisation of Arab states, owing to the lack of synchronisation between language and nation-state. Religion, which was the foundation of the existence and form of other states (Pakistan, Saudi Arabia), functioned both as a means of linguistic and cultural homogenisation of disparate peoples as well as an obstacle in the creation of modern institutions.

Whatever the consequences for the feelings of peoples (Jordanians feeling themselves to be Arabs cut off artificially from their great mother nation, or Pakistanis defending ferociously their Muslim identity), conflicts have been exacerbated, and the construction of states endowed with modern institutions has been troubled. Aside from Turkey and Iran (even if, in Iran, the revolution seemed to give priority to religious belonging as compared to national belonging, and the predominant religion at the local level is Shiite, which allows one to imagine a correspondence between the religious and the linguistic and ethnic identity), in which long concomitant histories contribute to strong and continuous national sentiments, the modern nation does not appear to have found a feeling and a basis that legitimise it in the name of the people. Modern politics are slow to take hold.

One can deduce from these remarks that, despite the diversity of situations, the passage from the premodern ideal of the *society of law* to the modern ideal of the *state based on law* has experienced many difficulties. The modern ideal, having had a humanist and secular tradition, economic success, and real politics in its favour, has been able to take root in European societies. It is the background of political life as well as a permanent source of ideals and concepts that organise collective life in the European context.

In contrast, the youth and fragility of the modern humanist tradition in the Muslim world and serious demographic, economic, political and cultural problems have led certain movements to imagine the return to premodern ideals, to conceive of a form of religious nationalism (Islam as organising principle), and to oppose modern ideals, not realising their continuity and affiliation with premodern ideals. The humanist tradition, born in the 1920s, was, one must remember, rapidly submerged by nationalist and extremist currents not unlike the absolutist socialism that submerged the 'fourth zone' of Europe.

The Islam/Occident, Islam/modernity polarisation – in which terms are frozen and impoverished in meaning – is the result of this process. It is reinforced today by the work the media began several decades ago, giving new life to and amplifying certain prejudices that prevailed in ancient societies. Our societies today oscillate between the prolonging of nationalism – with its positive and negative consequences – and universalist elation. The question today is the following: When will sporadic elation become a constant trend, strong, and with cumulative effects?

Notes

1. Translated by Penny Allen.
2. Reinhard Schulze, *A Modern History of the Islamic World* (London: I. B. Tauris, 2000).
3. See, notably, Ernest Gellner 'Flux and Reflux in the Faith of Men', in *Muslim Society* (Cambridge: Cambridge University Press, 1981).
4. Henri Bergson, *Les deux sources de la morale et de la religion* (Paris: Librairie Felix Alcan, 1932).
5. Marshall G. S. Hodgson, *The Venture of Islam: Conscience and History in a World Civilization* (Chicago: University of Chicago Press, 1974), vol. 1.

8
The Face of the Foreigner: Reflections on the Case of Lebanon's Palestinians[1]

Daniel Meier

For some years now, one way of thinking about the issue of North–South relations is to examine local initiatives and internal processes in countries of the South. This perspective opens the way for observations of social interactions in the South and East of the Mediterranean and shows these interactions to be the modalities for management of problems shared by many countries around the Mediterranean. Among these problems, the question of migrants and foreigners is central, especially in regard to questions of identity.

To discover the identity of the foreigner, we upend the classic perspective: instead of questioning the status, practices or representations of foreigners in European countries, our reflection deals with countries of the South and their relations with their own foreigners. The country that interests us here is Lebanon; the foreign group studied, the Palestinians,[2] is emblematic of a certain foreigner, the individual dispossessed of what makes up his identity: his country of origin.[3]

Turning first to the definition of what is a Lebanese, we see there is already an ancient link to the Palestinians. Next, a brief examination of variations in perceptions of this population since its exile in 1948 leads us to the post-war period, where we look at the Palestinian question via laws that concern them or debates about their settling in Lebanon. Finally, we will attempt to show the face of the foreign population in the current situation and, consequently, what this face shows in terms of a more general reflection on the identity of foreigners beyond Lebanon and, notably, in the understanding of refugees and others wanting to enter European countries.

Lebanese nationality: the shadow of the Palestinians

The limits to what is foreign obviously find their source in what is defined as 'national'. At the level of individuals, Lebanon has had a law on nationality since the fall of the Ottoman Empire and the creation of 'Greater-Lebanon',[4] following the San Remo conference in 1920.

Directive no. 15 of 19 January 1925, modified by the law of 11 January 1960, set the limits of Lebanese nationality (Art. 1): 'Those who were born of a Lebanese father or born in the territory of Greater-Lebanon and have no nationality or were of unknown parents'. As the articles that follow also show, the father remains the administrative figure in terms of identity: it is by him alone that nationality passes. The foreign woman becomes Lebanese via her marriage with a Lebanese (Art. 5). The foreign man, on the other hand, cannot acquire nationality by marriage. He can, however, become naturalised Lebanese (Art. 4), in which case he can transmit his new nationality to his wife and to his children. One way for a man to obtain Lebanese nationality before 1975 was judicial naturalisation, if the individual had spent five years in Lebanese territory. This measure was frozen at the beginning of the civil war. Palestinians, from their arrival in 1948, have been subject to a special status and placed under the authority of UNRWA,[5] making this judicial measure inoperable. Another difference between other foreign men and the Palestinian man occurs if there is a marriage with a Lebanese woman: while the former can obtain a visitor's card giving him the right to work, the latter has no rights nor access to the labour market.

There is in the law an optional right defined at the time of modern Lebanon's foundation. This right, which was valid until the end of the 1950s – and which was renewed for several periods of ten years each – gave to each person in the territory of the Ottoman Empire the possibility of requesting nationality from the new state in which he found himself after the disappearance of the Empire.[6] Two censuses were taken, one in 1923 and the other in 1932. However, at those times, Palestinians were either not yet there, or had chosen to opt for Palestinian nationality, Palestine having been much more prosperous than Lebanon in 1920. This also led to the emergence of two categories of Lebanese 'abroad'. The first category grouped those who, as refugees in 1948, were Lebanese of long duration but were living in Palestine and had taken Palestine nationality. The other category included those who had emigrated elsewhere, to Europe and especially to America (North and South), and who, even though born in Lebanon, had taken the nationality of the country in which they resided (they are still called 'emigrants'). This second category recurrently provoked demands for their naturalisation by Christian milieux, as these emigrants were, for the most part, Christian.

There is here a second aspect linked to Lebanese nationality, which again involves Palestinians: that of identity overlaps brought about by migrations between Palestine and Lebanon before 1948. This history, recently clarified by new Israeli historians,[7] emphasises an often established fact: Palestine was a prosperous land for all who lived there, notably for the large Lebanese community.

In 1948, several thousand Palestinian refugees in Lebanon were in fact of Lebanese origin. Some tried to get their Lebanese nationality back, while others preferred to wait for better days to return in Palestine. If they were Christian, they had the luck of benefiting from naturalisations facilitated during the term of President Camille Camoun (1952–8),[8] but if they were Muslim and had no personal wealth, they were caught up in the stigmatising of Palestinian identity that began in the 1950s.

Vagaries of history, wandering collective identity

Some time after their arrival, Palestinians were oriented towards zones that rapidly became camps situated near the principal cities of the country. Currently, the people living in the twelve camps represent about half of the Palestinians counted by UNRWA in Lebanon. As some Lebanese say, when speaking about these refugees during the first years after their arrival, 'They were invisible'. Those who had the means or relations, or family with Lebanese nationality, could live outside the camps, among the Lebanese. They still felt the same anxieties as those in the camps, but with a stronger feeling of isolation, which often produced feelings of guilt. Certain individuals ended up denying their origins, and many dissociated 'their identity' from the one the PLO began to proclaim at the end of the 1960s.

During those years, Palestinians were victims of disparagement and were the object of legislation that developed progressively, following the establishment of the Direction of Palestinian Affairs, in 1959. This organisation limited Palestinians' access to the labour market by reserving certain professions for Lebanese or for those with work permits, which required connections to obtain. In parallel, the camps were closely watched, travel was limited, and Palestinians paid the cost of heavy security apparatuses installed during the term of Fouad Chéhad (1958–64).

In 1964, a group of Palestinians founded the Palestine Liberation Organisation and decided to carry the fight onto Israeli territory. Rapidly, Lebanon looked like an ideal base for launching commando operations, thus favouring regional changes that advanced the role of Palestinian resistance.

The perception of Palestinians changed in Lebanon for a large part of the population, from the moment the Six Day War (June 1967) revealed the weakness of Arab armies and the inanity of fiery discourse from politicians in charge. One must add to that the emergence of the Palestinian question as a political problem in terms of security beginning in 1965, as *fedayin* commandos had begun their anti-Israeli operations from Lebanon by then.

In a few years, Palestinian identity had thus become the object of radically opposed perceptions within the Lebanese population, and two contradictory arguments about the Lebanese nation came of this: one, Arabist, sought to unite Lebanon to the Palestinian cause and to become its main support; the other, Lebanist, wanted to preserve neutrality regarding the Israeli–Arab conflict, severely reprimanding the Palestinian resistance if need be.

In 1969, accords were signed in Cairo to attempt to find a *modus vivendi*: they gave to the Resistance the possibility of leading operations against Israel from Lebanon, in coordination with the Lebanese army.[9] However, in reality, these accords only deepened the gulf between the two camps, and the golden age of Palestinians in Lebanon ended in confrontations beginning in 1975 between Lebanese groups, then by the Palestinian Resistance joining the combat on the side of the National Movement in 1976. Palestinian military alliances soon found themselves in an awkward position with regards to Syria and the Christian camp.[10] On top of this, tensions with the Shiites of South Lebanon angered the latter against those they had expected so much of; those on whose behalf they had tolerated excesses and bombings on the part of the Israelis.

It was in this already strained context that the Israeli invasion took place in June 1982. Losses were considerable, and the PLO was forced to withdraw from the capital, then from Tripoli a year later, this time under Syrian military pressure.

This multiplication of enemies,[11] and especially the military weakening that resulted, opened a new era: marginalisation. Far from putting an end to the struggle, the end of the war in 1990 led to a prolonging, mainly in the judicial realm, of the Palestinian social-exclusion dynamic.

Post-war illusions

The end of combat and the return of civil peace with the disarming of militias gave the general impression of a return to normalcy that seemed to have its future in reconstruction. In reality, it was first and above all the social link, reconciliation, that was the object of reflection and of various collective actions within the Ministry of the Displaced.[12]

Centred on the Lebanese mountains, these actions largely under-valued other regions and ignored Palestinians as part of a new post-war consensus. In other words, the Palestinians of Lebanon did not receive recognition of their suffering nor the right of return to where they had been living. The reason is obvious if one recalls that many camps (Quarantaine, Tall e-Zaatar, Naba) had been destroyed. Yet this does not explain the 'oblivion' of these foreigners in the midst of the Lebanese. To understand that, one must look at the redeployment of regional forces and also the attitude of the Lebanese elite, as seen in laws and discourse.

The origin of the Palestinian situation in Lebanon after the war can be blamed on a blind spot in the discussion: the civil war. Post-war political discourse mostly blamed the Palestinians for having launched the country into war, for having been the fifth column in a 'war for others', to use President Hraoui's expression. The reason for such an accusation began with a structural problem in the Lebanese post-war political system: the former heads of the militia were co-opted within the government of the Second Republic. That is, everyone had an interest in shifting the responsibility for what happened onto someone else, preferably someone foreign. Furthermore, one cannot eliminate from the Lebanese political equation the Syrians who were the *deus ex machina* of the Taëf accords (1989) and of the political entente between ex-militia and notables in the new post-war contract. At the same time, Syria did everything to turn the Lebanese struggle in its favour[13] and, by marginalising the Palestinians, Syria arranged that the Palestinian question in Lebanon was a problem of internal security and for Lebanese politicians, while at the same time it was an asset in the regional political game, especially in negotiations with Israel.[14]

From the judicial point of view, the marginalising was first accomplished through a new constitutional text of 1990, which stipulates in its preamble the refusal by Lebanon of all settlement (*tawtin*) of Palestinians on its territory. This strategic 'red line' was mostly a Syrian position in negotiations that took place the following year in Madrid. The failure of the multilateral negotiations in 1992 and the Oslo accords in 1993 pointed out the absence of the right of return, even though its incorporation is primary for Lebanon in the sense that its omission means a *de facto* 'settlement' of hundreds of thousands of Palestinians living in the country. Beyond the injustice of the process, it was its danger that was noted by commentators of the era, especially in light of the persistent image of the Palestinian as a combatant (*fedayin*).

Thus a debate developed around the Palestinians of Lebanon: what was to be done with them? Some people proposed rehousing them in better living conditions,[15] or even rapidly giving them civil rights. Others, complaining about the betrayal regarding the right of return, favoured inflexibility, with the secret hope that Palestinians would decide themselves to leave a country with no future for them. In all cases, the debate about settlement allowed the authorities to legitimise with good conscience measures of control and restrictive laws. In short, 'settlement' functioned and functions today as 'a weapon of mass destruction',[16] to use the expression of a Lebanese journalist, in the sense that it pops up at regular intervals to remind everyone of the internal menace victimising Lebanon.

Measures taken regarding Palestinians in the post-war period led to a progressive increase in the number of forbidden occupations, leading up to the creation of a law in 2001 forbidding the ownership of property and, for owners, the non-transmissibility of property rights. All realms of social life are concerned and tend to exclude from Lebanese society individuals identified as Palestinian, stigmatising them and making them pariahs who live in zones with no rights.[17]

The most spectacular of the anti-Palestinian measures was created in 1995 to support a Libyan protest against the Oslo accords. The Libyan government expelled all Palestinian workers from Libya, a certain number of whom were registered in Lebanon and had their families there. By Decree 478, of 22 September 1995, the Lebanese government reacted by introducing a travel visa for Palestinians, for leaving but also for re-entering Lebanon. Lebanese consulates around the world have issued very few return visas to Palestinians from Lebanon who were abroad.[18] This too obvious measure to 'get rid of' Palestinians was finally dropped in 1999.

The present situation of Palestinians in Lebanon

More than half of Palestinians in Lebanon (57 per cent) currently live in camps. These are permanent but relatively old structures in which families are crowded together, and more than half of individuals of working age are unemployed.[19] This professional precariousness indicates a dependence on the aid of UNRWA, whose statistics speak volumes: 45 146 cases of extreme poverty among the 223 956 individuals UNRWA has counted in the camps.[20] Access to health care and basic needs are widely publicised by UNRWA and target mainly Palestinians in camps.

The camps were at first relatively closed and controlled zones. After the Cairo accords (1969), they became more open to the outside, to the point where it was sometimes difficult to determine their geographical borders.[21] But since the 1980s and the spatial separations that the war introduced, they have once again become well-defined zones.

There is a difference between the camps of the north and the south (Saïda and Tyr): their openness to the outside depends on the influence of pro-Syrian political parties that are active there. The camps in which the Arafatist movement is the strongest (in the south) are those that require multiple permissions to visit, and they generally have two checkpoints, one for the Lebanese army and one for Syrian intelligence. This different treatment is related to the development of housing there: 'A secret administrative decision from general security forbids any increase in the surface area of camps as well as building additional stories.'[22] This rule was hardened for the camps of the south in the 1990s – including forbidding any construction material – while it was softened for camps of the north that are traditionally pro-Syrian.

In psychological terms, the segment of society rendered most fragile by this situation is not the one living in the camps, with networks of mutual aid, but the one made up of individuals, essentially men between the ages of eighteen and thirty, who live near the camps, having daily contact with employers and the Lebanese population. In a series of interviews,[23] we were able to learn that the perception they have of themselves is very negative, because of the responsibility they must assume for family tasks and, later, for supporting a family. A certain number of them have thus become interested in emigration and, with the consent of their entourage, work several years and borrow from those close to them in order to assemble the large sums necessary to enter into secret emigration networks.

The idea that exile is necessary is part of the positive understanding of the situation: the departure abroad of one or of several sons is seen as a strategy for circumventing problems. As a current solution for families interviewed, departure abroad is seen as a necessary phase in the betterment of their collective situation, especially for the accumulation of sums allowing other members of their family to continue living in Lebanon.[24] It is this same justification that lets 'mules' justify their role and claim that the lot of young Palestinians in Lebanon is the same as that of young Lebanese. In fact, the latter also choose more and more often to emigrate in order to escape a destiny heavily marked by political and community corruption in Lebanon.

Another face of the Palestinian presence in Lebanon is the Lebanese–Palestinian mixed couple. In such cases, one must differentiate the kind of integration possible and identify in particular whether it is the man or the woman who is of Palestinian nationality. In Lebanon, as we have seen, the male can transmit nationality to his children. A Palestinian father will have Palestinian children even if he marries a Lebanese woman. There is nothing surprising about that in the region. What is surprising is the fact that the Lebanese man can give his nationality to his Palestinian wife, but the Lebanese woman cannot in any case give her nationality to her husband, even if the marriage takes place in Lebanon. More radical still, she cannot give her nationality to her children either, which, according to several Lebanese women interviewed, can be an obstacle to a union with a Palestinian.

The Palestinian man in Lebanon is thus a 'bad catch' in the social sense. In the anthropological sense, he is in the category of those with whom it is preferable not to become allied (in the sense of matrimony). The comparison with a man of another nationality marrying a Lebanese woman in Lebanon is illuminating: the man, unlike the Palestinian, would receive his work papers.

Still, despite the obstacles, Lebanese–Palestinian matrimonial unions happen frequently and say the opposite of what the statutory limitations assigned to Palestinians and the dominant negative image imply. For the most part, these mixed marriages take place in poorer social groups and lead in general to the exclusion that prevails. It is only in rare cases in which the man is a Lebanese with cultural and material resources that the marriage represents an improvement in status for the woman. In any case, the idea that these unions are a form of social integration is irrefutable: the increase in links between national groups has a symbolic value with social implications – solidarity in particular – that have been creating new forms of interdependence between the two national groups for several decades.

In conclusion, there is first the idea of a 'joined destiny', to use the Arab expression, between Lebanese and Palestinians. In fact, both national identity and the history of an independent Lebanon are tied to Palestinian refugees. Which makes us think that there can be no migratory phenomenon as large as this one without the countries involved being profoundly affected. Which ought to lead to a re-examination of how the security of migrations is handled, as little reflection is given to the reasons for the emigration occurring in Mediterranean countries, notably between the South and the North.

Secondly, the Lebanese judicial position in relation to Palestinians testifies without a doubt to a fear of this particular foreigner, going back to historical facts often of a phantasmagorical nature. Still, the post-war period could have unfolded differently, and political will is desperately needed regarding the manner in which a national refugee group is considered a problem. The media play a role too, giving voice to arguments of the political debate.

Finally – and this is probably not a small reward for looking at North–South relations – the historic wealth of relations between a group of migrants and the citizens of the host nation is itself a kind of lateral integration, in as much as it is organised through sentimental links, notably matrimonial. This said, these relations are open to plural identities. Whereas the isolation lived by individuals in camps is a form of withdrawal and a negation of the very existence of these individuals, since they take no active role in their situation. This is also a characteristic trait of the welfare logic currently found in the treatment of foreigners in northern countries. Finally, we have seen that the margins of manoeuvre available to migrants are limited by local vectors of social exclusion (community behaviour, divided society, impoverishment, creation of ghettos, etc.). Beyond certain initiatives, such as young Palestinians choosing emigration, these vectors are obstacles that remain unmoved by porous identity or opening of certain social sectors to migrants and refugees.

Notes

1. Translated by Penny Allen.
2. For an overview of the general situation of Palestinians, see Sari Hanafi and Mohamed Kamel Doraï, 'Des réfugiés qui ne relèvent pas du Haut Commissariat aux Réfugiés: les Palestiniens', in *L'Asile politique entre deux chaises. Droits de l'homme et gestion des flux migratoires* (collection under the direction of Michelle Guillon, Luc Legoux and Emmanuel Ma Mung) (Paris: L'Harmattan, 2003), pp. 287–310.
3. With this example, we wish to pursue the reflection begun by others regarding the social construction of collective identity in as much as it is prone to variations and usages likely to contribute to a larger reflection, notably at the level of the Mediterranean space. For this work, see Ahmad Beydoun, *Identité confessionnelle et temps social chez les historiens libanais contemporains* (publications de l'Université Libanaise, Beyrouth, 1984); Bernard Voutat, 'Objectivation sociale et mobilisations politiques. La question nationale dans le Jura suisse', *Revue française de science politique*, 46 (1), 1996, pp. 30–51; Jean-Claude Kaufmann, *L'Invention de soi. Une théorie de l'Identité* (Paris: Armand Colin, 2004).
4. As opposed to 'Smaller-Lebanon', claimed by the Maronite representatives to Paris in 1919 and confined to the mountains and the Mediterranean coastline.
5. United Nations Relief for Palestine Refugees.
6. For the judicial documents, refer to Article 5 of Directive no. 2825 of 30 August 1924 and then to the Lebanese–Turkish accord, ratified by the law of 3 December 1951, concerning the continuing option for Lebanese nationality.

7. Mainly Benny Morris and Ilan Pappé. On the subject, see Dominique Vidal, *Le Péché original d'Israël. L'expulsion des Palestiniens revisitée par les 'nouveaux historiens' israéliens* (Paris: Les Editions de l'Atelier & les Editions Ouvrières, 1998).

8. A lawyer of the court explained this policy as follows: 'He first naturalised the notable Palestinians who had money, then Palestinian Christians, for reasons of community harmony'. Conversation in Beirut on 12 September 2001.

9. Nadine Picaudou, *La Déchirure libanaise* (Complexe, Brus, 1989), p. 118.

10. Samir Kassir, *La Guerre du Liban* (Paris-Beyrouth: Kharthala-Cermoc, 1994).

11. Rosemary Sayigh, *Too Many Enemies: the Palestinian Experience in Lebanon* (London: Zed Books, 1993).

12. See Ministry of the Displaced, *The Achievements 1993–1997* (Beyrouth, 1998).

13. Joseph Bahout, 'Liban: les élections législatives de l'été 1992', *Maghreb-Machrek*, 139, 1993, pp. 53–84.

14. Bernard Rougier, 'Le "destin mêlé" des Palestiniens et des Libanais au Liban', *Maghreb-Machrek*, 169, 2000, pp. 43–54.

15. The deputy Walid Joumblatt proposed settling a large number of them in Kray'a, in 1994, but had to retract it when his proposition was seen by a significant part of the political class as a *de facto* settlement.

16. Gaby Nasr, *L'Orient le Jour*, 21 November 2003.

17. This refers to the journalistic definition of refugee camps, which effectively take on extra-territorial qualities. See Rosemary Sayigh, 'Palestinians in Lebanon: Implantation, Transfer or Return?', *Middle East Policy*, 8 (1), 2001, pp. 94–105.

18. Wadie Said, 'The Obligations of Host Countries to Refugees under International Law: the Case of Lebanon', in *Palestinian Refugees: the Right of Return* (collection under the direction of Naseer Aruri) (London: Pluto Press, 2001), p. 137.

19. Michael C. Hudson, 'Palestinians and Lebanon: the Common Story', *Journal of Refugee Studies*, 10 (3), 1997, pp. 243–60.

20. See the summary chart from 31 December 2003, available on http://www.unrwa.org.

21. Julie Peteet, 'The Dilemma of the Palestinians in Lebanon', in *Lebanon's Second Republic: Prospects for the Twenty First Century* (collection under the direction of Kail C. Ellis) (Gainesville: University Press of Florida, 2002), pp. 78–90.

22. Souheil Al-Natour, *Les Palestiniens du Liban* (Beyrouth: Dar al-Taqqadom sal-Arabi, 1993), p. 160.

23. Done at Tyr, Saïda, and Tripoli between September 2003 and August 2004.

24. See regarding Palestinians in Europe, Mohamed Kamel Doraï, 'Les réfugiés palestiniens en Europe et en Suède. Complexité des parcours et des espaces migratoires', in *L'Asile politique entre deux chaises*, pp. 311–31.

Part III
Political Challenges

9
Turkish Conservatism and the Idea of Europe

Hakan Yilmaz

Introduction

In this chapter we are going to explore conservative beliefs and attitudes in Turkey and how they deal with the idea of Europe and Turkey's integration with the European Union. First, we will offer a brief characterisation of conservative thought in general and of the major variants of Turkish conservatism today, namely Islamic and nationalist. Secondly, we will present, in two separate sections and in more detail, the nationalist and Islamic versions of contemporary Turkish conservatism, focusing particularly on their mind-sets on Europe. For both nationalist and Islamic conservatism, in addition to offering conceptual explanations of these modes of thinking and codes of operation, we will also make use of survey data to explain the degree to which these ideas have found an audience within the general public. In my account of nationalist conservatism, we will define and focus on two discursive patterns, the Tanzimat and Sèvres syndromes, which we believe constitute the core of the Turkish nationalist discourse on Europe. We will argue that while the 'deep policy' imperative of the Tanzimat syndrome is a delegitimation of collective and individual rights, that of the Sèvres syndrome is isolationism in the area of foreign policy and 'westernisation without the West' in the domestic arena. These two syndromes, we will argue, may help us understand the strategic shift of the nationalist conservatism away from Europe and the generally disapproving attitude of the nationalist conservative political parties and intellectuals to Turkey's integration with the European Union. The next section will be devoted to an explanation of the strategic turn of the Islamic conservatism towards Europe. In that regard, we will concentrate on the 'conservative democratic' governing party of today's Turkey, the Justice and Development Party (JDP) of Tayyip Erdogan and

Abdullah Gul, and examine how this party has distinguished itself from political Islam and why it has so wholeheartedly embraced the cause of Turkey's unification with the European Union. We will argue that Islamic conservatives' strategic choice for Europe involves, first, distancing themselves from the political Islamist project of anti-Kemalist revanchism and top-down Islamicisation of society, and, secondly, Europeanising the public sphere in Turkey in such a way as to make it amenable for the manifestations and performances of Islamic identity in that arena.

Conservatism and its major variants in Turkey

In the eyes of the secular elites of Turkey, conservatism has traditionally been associated with 'religious reaction' or 'religious regression' (*irtica*), implying a latent or open opposition to the secular policies of the state, to the westernising reforms of Kemalism, to the western ways of life in the urban areas, and to the West in general. At the core of this conservatism, it has been argued, lies a reactionary attitude towards the status of women in private and public domains. In contrast to this classic-republican characterisation of conservatism, today's governing party, the JDP, has also defined itself as 'conservative'. Though the intellectuals close to the JDP have never defined this new conservatism in precise terms, it is clear from their thinking that it has little to do with the 'religious reaction' as characterised by the secularist elites. The Islamic conservative world-view in Turkey, as represented by the JDP, is certainly 'not modernist', but 'contemporary'. In other words, Islamic conservatism is not modernist in the sense that it is not committed to the Enlightenment ideas and values, particularly as they relate to the secularisation of knowledge, separation of religion and politics, and equality of men and women. However, the Islamic conservative stance is contemporary, in the sense of being committed to following and putting into use the most up-to-date technologies, instruments, ways of life and modes of thinking. In what follows, we will offer a working definition of conservatism and identify its main variants in Turkey, both nationalist and Islamic.

Conservatism, in all its types and varieties, is an ideology that is devoted to the maintenance, defence, revival or restoration of a certain 'tradition'. Conservatism is, therefore, a type of traditionalism. The point is that this 'tradition', which the conservative ideology so ardently tries to defend and sustain, is itself defined or even invented by that very ideology, although conservatives of all brands would almost always argue that the tradition they are defending is not a product of their own imagination and that it is real, authentic and genuine. In fact, all conservative ideologies first define (invent, construct, imagine, dream of) a tradition and then develop arguments in its defence. Tradition, for conservatism, represents the accumulated wisdom of the past, codes and modes of life that passed the hard test of time, and by doing so it must be preferred to an unknown change in view of all the uncertainties and risks associated with the latter. According to conservatism, tradition embodies the 'we' (*biz*) as opposed to the 'other' (*öteki*). In almost all conservative thinking, there is an imagined 'golden age' located at a place and time in the past. The golden age is perceived as a moment of genesis, in which the elements of an essential 'we-ness' (*bizlik*) are created, and it is those elements that distinguish 'us' from the 'others'. Conservatives believe that the tradition they want to revive or maintain was born and given its 'pure' form in this golden age, in the hands of the 'founding fathers'. As a result, the political struggles, thoughts and speeches of these founding fathers, as well as the way they lived their daily lives, the manner in which they responded to some critical situations, the many hardships (imprisonment, torture, poverty) they 'bravely' faced, the kind of music they listened to, the sort of books they read, the works of art they liked and disliked, the houses they lived in, their pastime hobbies, and even the fashions they followed are later on codified by the ideologists and made sources of inspiration to follow.

For the more radical and marginal variants of conservatism, fundamentalist Islamism and Turkist/Turanist nationalism, the golden age is to be looked for in the distant past and outside the current boundaries of Turkey. Hence, for instance, for some Islamic conservatives, of a fundamentalist variety, the golden age can be traced as far back in time as to the period of the Prophet Mohammed and the four Caliphs. For the Turkist/Turanist version of nationalist conservatives, on the other hand, the golden age can be found at the age of the great Turkic empires of Central Asia. The more mainstream conservative movements, on the other hand – Ottomanist Islamic conservatism, centre-right Islamic conservatism and Kemalist nationalism – bring the golden age nearer in time and space. Hence, for what can be termed the Ottomanist Islamic conservatives, followers of the so-called 'Turkish-Islamic Synthesis' (*Turk-Islam Sentezi*), the golden age must be sought in the classical age of the Ottoman Empire, during the 'glorious' century that begins with the reign of Mehmed the Conqueror and ends with that of Suleiman the Magnificent. For the moderate or centre-right Islamic conservatives, the golden age is between 1946 and 1960, covering the years of the rise and rule of the Democratic Party, under the guidance of the heroic figure of Adnan Menderes. Still a newer branch of the centre-right Islamic conservatism, the one that we can perhaps label as neo-conservatism, looks to the 1980s as its golden era and the late Turgut Ozal as its source of inspiration. For the Kemalist variety of nationalist conservatism, the golden age resides in the 1920s and 1930s, when Ataturk himself was alive and at the helm of the reform movement.

'Change', understood as a movement away from tradition, is always regarded with a high degree of suspicion by conservatism. In this regard, change is usually perceived as a negativity, a process of degeneration, corruption, decadence, disbelief and immorality. In the Turkish context, and for both Islamic and nationalist variants of conservatism, change is mostly believed to come essentially from the outside, namely from the 'West'. Hence, change is usually identified with 'Westernisation', and the general contrast between tradition and change, and the associated opposition between 'we' and 'others', takes the particular form of a conflict between the 'East' (tradition, we, positivity) and the 'West' (change, other, negativity). We may here note that this way of conceptualising the change–tradition contrast in the form of an East–West conflict is not peculiar to Turkey, and we can find a similar debate among the Russian intellectuals of the nineteenth century, most particularly between the Slavists and the Westernists.

Both major versions of conservatism in Turkey (Islamic and nationalist) have developed a certain criticism of a way of life, that they have labelled 'Imitation Westernism' (*Bati Taklitciligi*). Both conservatisms trace the beginning of this 'Imitation Westernism' to the Tanzimat period of the mid-nineteenth century, at a time when the Ottoman leadership had initiated a series of reforms, particularly in the area of the reorganisation of the state apparatus on the model of the West European states, and they all are very critical of the so-called 'Tanzimat Mentality' (*Tanzimat Kafasi*) or 'Wardrobe Westernism' (*Gardrop Baticiligi*). But, the two branches of conservatism disagree on where to locate the source of the Turkish authenticity or the golden age of the Turkish glory. Although this golden age may be located by each type of conservatism at a different epoch of history, the common point of each is that in that particular epoch the Turks were either equal or superior to the Europeans. Hence, for the Islamic conservatism, labelled above as Ottomanist, the age of Ottoman imperial construction, that had lasted from conquest of Istanbul by Mehmed the Conqueror in the mid-fifteenth century to the death of Suleiman the Magnificent in the mid-sixteenth century, is often alluded to as the cradle of Turkish authenticity. For nationalist conservatism, of the Kemalist variant, the golden age comes nearer in time and it is coterminous with the era of Ataturk (1919–38). It was in that era, according to the Kemalists, that the Turks won a twin victory: both against foreign powers (the 'Enemy', the

'West', *Dusman, Garp, Yedi Duvel*) but also over their own 'Gloomy Destiny' (*Makus Talih*).

However, it is interesting to note that in none of the two mainstream branches of conservatism has there been a total denial of the West and a defence of an unconditional restoration of the ways of life of the golden age, be it middle Ottoman or early Republican. On the contrary, both versions of conservatism have defended some type of synthesis or hybridisation between tradition and modernity, the East and the West, the past and the present, 'we' and the 'other', 'us' and 'them', the 'authentic' Turkish and the 'alien' western identities. Just what the right mixing or the correct formula is for the optimum synthesis between tradition and modernity has long been a matter of intense debate by the intellectuals of the two conservative currents. A famous formula was proposed by Ziya Gokalp, the ideological luminary of nationalist conservatism, to the effect that the right synthesis between the East and the West would be to blend together the western 'civilisation' (*medeniyet*) with the Turkish 'culture' (*hars*). Western civilisation was not limited to the material-technical culture of the West only, but also included ideologies and political institutions, such as nationalism and the modern state. The Turkish culture, on the other hand, had be searched for not in the corrupt culture of the Ottoman palace, not in Istanbul, which was labelled as 'Byzantium, that old whore' (*Kahpe Bizans* or *Kohne Bizans*), but in Anatolia, in the folklore of the peasants, who were seen as the 'repository' of the untamed, uncontaminated, authentic Turkish culture.

The strategic move of nationalist conservatism away from Europe: the Tanzimat and Sèvres syndromes

The Tanzimat syndrome and the Sèvres syndrome represent two premises of the genealogical narrative of modern Turkish nationalism. It was on these two premises that modern Turkish nationalism has constructed its historical narrative of the decline and collapse of the Ottoman Empire and the foundation of the Turkish Republic, covering roughly the 100-year period between the early nineteenth century and the first quarter of the twentieth century. The syndromes have essentially been consolidated by Kemalism, the founding ideology of the Turkish Republic founded in 1923, and they have been popularised in the larger society by the Kemalist-controlled school system, press and literature. However, the roots of the syndromes go back much earlier than Kemalism, to the reign of Sultan Abdulhamid (r. 1876–1909) and the Young Turks (r. 1909–18), embodying an ideological continuity between the late Ottoman and early Republican state elites.

As western powers played a determining role in both the collapse of the Empire and the founding of the Republic, both syndromes offer a specific interpretation of the nature of relations between the Ottoman Empire and Turkey, on the one hand, and European great powers, on the other, highlighting the turning points, major actors and their intentions. Although both syndromes give an account of the actions and intentions of the West towards Turkey, each encapsulates a different moment of Turkish–western history and emphasises a different facet of the West. Among the two, the Sèvres syndrome is more central, focuses upon Turkey's foreign relations, and offers a general account of the western strategy towards Turkey and of what Turkey should do in order to put off direct foreign intervention and subversion. The Tanzimat syndrome, on the other hand, focuses upon domestic politics and identifies the West's likely collaborators within Turkey itself. These potential collaborators of the West have typically been identified as the Christian minorities (Armenians and Greeks); Muslim but non-Turkish communities (Arabs and Kurds); Muslim and Turkish but over-westernised segments of the society.

The syndromes are rooted in the fact that the Turks, beginning with the Seljuks in the eleventh century, but particularly the Ottomans since the fourteenth century onwards, conquered and settled in the lands, Anatolia and then Rumelia, which had originally belonged to the Christian peoples. Anatolia had been a territory of the eastern Roman (Byzantine) Empire, and long after the Seljuk Turks had captured it piece by piece and made it their new home, they continued to call it the 'Land of the Romans' (*Diyar-i Rum*). Once the Ottoman Turks replaced their Seljuk predecessors as the new masters of Asia Minor, they changed the direction of their conquest and settlement towards Constantinople and the Balkan possessions of the Byzantine Empire. The Balkans became the Ottomans' 'Land of the Romans', who called the area *Rumeli*, a name that is still in common parlance today. The Turkish-Islamic conquest of the Christian territories, the Turkish nationalists believe, prepared the ground for a European-Christian revanchism and restorationism, which started with and is epitomised by the Crusades of the middle ages. The Europeans, in the Turkish nationalist narrative, never gave up their historical mission of driving the Turks away from the historic lands of the Christians and back to the steppes of Central Asia. Hence, in the Turkish nationalist narrative, the Crusades of the middle ages, the capitulations (trading privileges) that the Ottoman Empire granted to certain European states beginning with the sixteenth century, colonisation of some Ottoman territories in the nineteenth century, the occupation and the final division of the core Ottoman lands by the Allied powers after World War Two, and the American and European political, economic, military and cultural hegemony over Turkey in the period following World War Two, are all incarnations of the eternal European 'crusade' against the Turks.

The Tanzimat and Sèvres syndromes are syndromes, in the sense that they refer to a certain mode of perception, and a resulting code of operation, which are rooted in a traumatic past experience with the West, and which are not revised afterwards, no matter how the real relationship with the West has changed over the years. On the one hand, it is not rational to stick to a past memory of a relationship, and the corresponding reflexive reaction to it, even though the nature of that relationship has significantly changed over time. On the other hand, however, it is not uncommon for states and similar organised collectivities, like big corporations for instance, to develop syndrome-like perceptual and operational patterns and transmit them from one generation to another as the time-honoured wisdom of the past. This seemingly irrational behaviour may have to do with the overwhelmingly high transaction costs of adapting one's mentality and behaviour to the changing conditions, particularly for the big organisations like states. Because of the sheer size of a state-like organisation, it takes so much time and work for the acquisition, processing and possessing of information that there occurs an almost natural resistance within the organisation to revising that information and adapting organisational behaviour in line with the changing conditions. Particularly when the information in question has to do with the survival of the organisation in a world populated by rival organisations, the organisation in question may overvalue that information and develop an even stronger resistance to its revision. As such, the syndromes refer to the 'deep memory' and the associated 'deep policy' of the Turkish nationalist elites regarding the West and its domestic allies. In what follows, we will explore, in more detail, these deep memories and deep policies.

The 'deep historical memory' behind the Tanzimat syndrome

The term *Tanzimat*, which means arranging things in a new and better order, refers to a series of modernising reforms in the Ottoman Empire, which were set in motion in 1839 by the promulgation of the Imperial Decree of Gulhane. The Gulhane Decree was later supplemented in 1856 by the declaration of another major statement, called the Reform Decree. The backbone of the Tanzimat reforms was to provide the Ottoman subjects with modern citizenship rights and to create a state based on the rule of law. These basic citizenship rights included equality before law, irrespective of one's social status and religion; supremacy of law over the acts and decisions of the political authority; security of life, property and honour of all citizens; regulation of taxation and putting an end to the arbitrary confiscations of property. The Reform Decree of 1856 brought special new rights and privileges to the Christian subjects of the Empire, including freedom of prayer, the right to establish their own educational institutions, the right to enter into the military service, and equal taxation.

One particular expectation of the palace in launching this reform programme was to regain the allegiance of the Empire's Christian subjects (mostly Greeks and Armenians) and thereby to contain their separatist tendencies. Another expectation was to stop the great powers of Europe from interfering in the internal affairs of the Ottoman Empire. Indeed, the European states, particularly Britain and Russia, had long been active in mobilising the Christians against the Ottoman state, and they were putting demands on the palace to grant the Christians economic, political and cultural liberties and advantages. By engaging itself in the Tanzimat reforms, the Ottoman centre was hoping to satisfy some of the demands of the European great powers and thereby to put an end to their provocation and support of the Ottoman Christians towards separatism.

This is not the place to judge the value, wisdom or success of the Tanzimat reforms. However, even a cursory look at Ottoman history after the initiation of the Tanzimat reforms in 1839 reveals a constant process of imperial collapse, which was brought about by the successful independence movements of the Christian and non-Turkish peoples supported by this or that European power. As a result, between 1839 and 1908, the Empire lost its entire east-central European lands. The Balkan and North African territories were gone between 1908 and 1918, during the Balkan Wars, the Italian invasion of Ottoman North Africa, and World War One. Finally, during the Allied occupation of the Empire between 1918 and 1922, the defunct Treaty of Sèvres detached large chunks of Anatolia from the Empire, which had already been reduced to a symbolic entity.

One reason for the reverse effect of the Tanzimat's society-empowering reforms was that they remained suspended in the air as the Ottoman imperial centre could not develop a new institutional model of centre–periphery relations and it could not define a new imperial ideology which might have contained community demands under the roof of a revitalised Empire. Under these circumstances, granting modern national, religious and legal rights to the peripheral communities, in accordance with Russian and Western European demands, resulted in nothing but the destruction of the traditional centre–periphery relations and the rapid weakening of the centre's hold over the periphery. In many cases, the imperial centre had to engage in state-strengthening reforms just to be able to contain the divisive consequences of the previously undertaken society-empowering reforms.

This historical record taught the Ottoman statesmen and the Republican founding fathers two lessons. One was that giving rights and freedoms to a people would not make them more loyal to the state; on the contrary, this would even supply them with more opportunities to organise a stronger assault on the state. The second lesson was that the real intention behind the European demands of respect for human rights was to divide the Turkish nation and weaken the Turkish state. The combination of these two lessons, which are so deeply engraved in the historical memory of the Turkish state and society, and which makes up the main axis of the mentality of contemporary Turkish conservatism and isolationism, we call the Tanzimat syndrome.

Perhaps the best exemplification of the Tanzimat syndrome can be found in the words of Sultan Abdulhamid (r. 1876–1909), who had eliminated the Young Ottomans to consolidate his powers and who lost his throne to the Young Turks. In his political memoirs, Sultan Abdulhamid writes:

> The reform demands of the great powers never end. They know nothing about our country, yet they still play the role of the all-knowing counselor . . . Though they disagree among themselves as to what our problems are and how we are going to deal with those problems, there are two points which they all agree on: First, to create the impression in our public opinion that all reforms are done because of their recommendations and pressures, and thereby to put us down in the eyes of our own nation; and second, to enhance the position of the Christians in our country, and to make them come forward with even more excessive demands from us. This reform thing is a dirty trick. They should take off their hands from our business. The reforms they are recommending cannot possibly be taken seriously and implemented without doing serious harm to the interests of our nation. If we proceed in our own way I am sure that we will develop more slowly but more smoothly. (Sultan Abdulhamid 1984: 110–11)

Another illustration of the Tanzimat syndrome comes from Recep Peker, a prominent bureaucrat, prime minister, and ideologue of the Turkish one-party regime from the 1920s through the 1940s. In his *Lectures on the Revolution*, which he offered at Ankara University in the 1930s, Peker sharply criticised the Ottoman constitutional regime as an unwarranted imitation of the western model. He argued that the Ottomans had borrowed the western conception of freedom, which was not suitable to the local conditions and traditions. According to Peker, Islamic reactionaries and Christian separatists exploited freedom to achieve their ominous goals:

> The destructive elements found many supportive opportunities in the atmosphere of constitutional monarchy. In this air of freedom, and in the name of freedom, a fool named Dervis Vahdeti began publishing a newspaper called *Volkan* and founded a party called The Mohammadan Union (*Ittihad-i Muhammedi*) . . . Such a newspaper would have done great damage even today, if we had allowed its publication. Back then, however, the Empire was tolerating such newspapers in the name of freedom, and when legal measures were being taken to stop such unwanted developments, a chorus was starting to shout that freedoms were being violated. Again using this freedom, a deputy of Greek origin could say 'My exterior is Ottoman, but my interior is Greek' in the Assembly of Deputies, and the Ottoman Assembly showed no reaction to this in the name of freedom. (Peker 1984: 33)

The 'deep policy' imperatives of the Tanzimat syndrome: delegitimisation of rights and freedoms

The 'deep policy' imperatives of the Tanzimat syndrome can be formulated as follows:

1. Declare as illegitimate all demands for minority rights, particularly those that are put forward by ethnic and religious groups.
2. Declare as illegitimate all demands for group rights, including those that are put forward by social classes and regional communities.
3. Declare as illegitimate all demands for rights, including basic human rights.

The best policy alternative, implied by the Tanzimat syndrome, has been to deny the very existence of the ethnic and religious minorities, and to try to assimilate them into the mainstream national culture by all means at the disposal of the state. However, if the state had to recognise the existence of a minority, and if assimilation policies did not bring about the total transformation of a group, then it would become essential to resist, as much as possible, their demands for recognition and cultural rights. It was believed that it was the western powers who would galvanise the minorities to come forward with more and more demands for rights and freedoms. Hence, granting any rights to the minorities would make them less, rather than more, loyal to the state. More rights and freedoms would simply give birth to more and stronger secessionist movements among the minorities, and the western powers would not hesitate to give them their ideological, political and sometimes military support. In the end, the minorities would end up founding their own independent state, which would be nothing more than a puppet state under the protection of one or more western powers.

A more general, and certainly more significant, policy prescription of the Tanzimat syndrome is a delegitimisation of the very idea of rights, including individual rights, as it was believed that rights would endow the individuals with a larger space of action, and individuals would use that larger action space to engage in anti-state activities. Therefore, the state had to resist granting even the basic rights to individuals, in order not to weaken the authority of the state over society. The state, perceiving the world through the lenses of the Tanzimat syndrome, perceived a zero-sum game between state and society, between state authority and societal rights, the latter being either collective or individual rights. Hence, the state perceived itself as a Leviathan and demanded absolute submission from social groups and individuals. Rights simply did not fit into this Hobbesian picture, and all kinds of rights were perceived as challenges, big or small, to the authority, and more than that, to the very existence of the state.

Indicators of the Tanzimat syndrome in the Turkish public opinion: public attitudes towards basic rights and freedoms[1]

One way of measuring how deep the beliefs and attitudes that are characterised under the Tanzimat syndrome have sunk into the political culture of the Turkish public is to observe the public's attitudes towards individual and collective rights and freedoms. The data in Tables 9.1 and 9.2 are chosen to illustrate those attitudes. The first remark to be made regarding the data in these tables is that almost everybody expressed an opinion on the issue of rights and freedoms; those who chose not to give an answer remained around 1 per cent for Table 9.1 and 4 per cent for Table 9.2. In Table 9.1, the respondents are offered a number of basic rights and asked if they think a given right must always exist, regardless of the context and conditions, or if they think the right in question can be restricted under certain circumstances. It should be noted that, at this stage, the circumstances under which a given right can be restricted are not specified. It turned out that the public were most sensitive for two rights, namely, 'equality

Table 9.1:   Indicators of the Tanzimat syndrome in Turkish public opinion: public attitudes towards basic rights and freedoms (expressed in absolute terms)

	Must exist at all times and circumstances	Can be restricted in certain times and circumstances	No opinion/ no response	Total
Equality before law	91	7	1	100
Freedom of conscience and religion	90	8	1	100
Freedom of communication	85	13	2	100
Right not to be subjected to torture	83	16	1	100
Freedom of expression	74	25	1	100
Right to use one's mother tongue	74	25	1	100

Table 9.2:   Indicators of the Tanzimat syndrome in Turkish public opinion: public attitudes towards basic rights and freedoms (expressed conditionally when national interest, public safety or social order is at stake)

	Tend to agree	Tend to disagree	No opinion/ no response	Total
We do NOT have to tolerate those opinions that are completely opposed to the opinions of the majority	56	39	4	100
When the interests of the nation are under serious threat, human rights CAN be restricted	50	46	4	100
When the newspapers publish news and articles that are opposed to the interests of the nation, they SHOULD NOT be closed down	47	51	3	100
Radical and extremist groups should NOT be allowed to make rallies and demonstrations, even if those rallies and demonstrations pose no threat to the public order	46	50	4	100

before law' and 'freedom of conscience and religion': 90 per cent of the people said that those two rights must not be restricted under any circumstances. Then came two other rights, 'freedom of communication' and 'freedom from torture and ill-treatment'. For these rights, the sensitivity dropped slightly, by 5 percentage points, and around 85 per cent of the people interviewed said that these two rights must be upheld at all times. The last two rights, about which the respondents turned out to be least sensitive, were 'freedom of expression' and 'the right to use one's mother tongue'. Hence, only about 75 per cent of the people were of the opinion that no restrictions should be imposed on these two rights.

If we leave aside the first two rights, 'equality before law' and 'freedom of conscience and religion', about which there is almost unanimous agreement that they should in no way be restricted, the picture is not so bright when it comes to the remaining four rights. Hence, 13 per cent of the people believe that, when conditions call for it, individuals can be prevented from communicating freely. Yet another 16 per cent think that, if necessary, a person can be tortured. The picture becomes even darker when the respondents expressed their opinions regarding freedom of expression and freedom to use one's mother tongue. Hence, on both occasions, a very sizeable minority, close to 25 per cent, opined that there may be occasions in which the authorities can prevent a person from saying what he wants to say and, even more gravely, that the state can prohibit a person from using his own language.

The cultural penetration of the Tanzimat syndrome is more visible in Table 9.2. Here, the respondents are again offered a series of rights and asked whether they would agree that the authorities should restrict these rights when national interest, public safety, or social order is at risk. In other words, unlike in the previous set of questions, now the types of restrictions are made clear and specified. The results are admittedly much more gloomy compared to those in Table 9.1. Hence, on all counts, close to 50 per cent of the respondents said that the state can suppress basic rights and freedoms when such highly esteemed community norms and values as national interest, public safety and social order are at serious risk.

Taken together, these two tables give us important clues of the extent to which nationalist conservatism's perception of rights as illegitimate has been adopted by the general public. First of all, sizeable minorities in the Turkish public do not think that basic rights and freedoms are inalienable and inseparable attributes and that they are embedded in the very definition of being a human being. Secondly, and echoing the Hobbesian spirit of the Tanzimat syndrome, the Turkish public seems to be ready to trade freedom and rights for order and security.

The 'deep historical memory' behind the Sèvres syndrome

The Mondros armistice of 30 October 1918 marked the final defeat of the Ottoman Empire in World War One. By that time, the CUP cabinet had already resigned on 8 October and the triumvirate of Enver, Cemal and Talat Pashas were about to flee the country (they would do so on 7 November). The Mondros treaty provided for a total and unconditional surrender of the Ottoman Empire. The Ottoman navy and armies, including the armies still operating in the eastern front, were to be demobilised, and all communication and transportation facilities and food and coal supplies were to pass to the control of the Allied powers. The Straits were to be opened to the passage of the Allied warships. The treaty included special provisions for the Armenian population of the Empire, such as the releasing of all Armenians held in the Ottoman prisons whatever their crimes were. The Allies reserved for themselves the right to occupy any strategic area of the Empire, and particularly the six Armenian-populated eastern provinces, in case of disorder (Kili 1982: 5–8; Lewis 1968: 239–42; Shaw and Shaw 1977: 327–8).

With the exception of Mosul in Iraq, which would be occupied by the British soon after the Mondros armistice, the Arab-populated Iraqi, Syrian, Lebanese and Palestinian provinces of the Ottoman Empire had already fallen to the British or French forces right before the conclusion of the Mondros armistice. Kirkuk had fallen in May 1918; Nablus, Haifa, Acre, Damascus, Aleppo, Homs, Alexandretta and Beirut had been occupied in September–October 1918. Thus, by the time the Mondros treaty had been concluded, the territory of the Ottoman Empire had already been reduced to Anatolia (including eastern Thrace and Istanbul).

The Turks formed the majority in western and central regions of Anatolia, with sizeable Greek minorities living in Istanbul and the Aegean. Eastern Anatolia was home to the Armenians remaining after the expulsion of 1915, the Kurds, and the Turks. Calculations based on the 1914 census show that, out of the 11 million people living in Anatolia (excluding eastern Thrace and Istanbul), 85 per cent were Muslims (Turks and Kurds), 9 per cent were Greeks, 5 per cent were Armenians, and 0.8 per cent were Jewish and other non-Muslims. In eastern Thrace, the total population was approximately 630 000, of which 57 per cent were Muslims, 35 per cent were Greeks, 3 per cent were Armenians, and 4 per cent were Jewish and other non-Muslims. Finally, the population of Istanbul was divided between the Muslims (60 per cent), the Greeks (25 per cent), and the Armenians, Jews and other non-Muslims (15 per cent) (Kili 1982: 72).

In the year that followed the Mondros treaty, Istanbul and parts of Anatolia, and particularly those regions with sizeable Armenian and Greek minorities, also came under the occupation of the Allied powers and the Allied-supported armed forces of Greece. On 13 November 1918, the Allied warships anchored in the port of Istanbul, though the official occupation of the city did not yet begin. In December 1918 the French occupied the southeastern Anatolian province of Adana (Cilicia). At about the same time, the British forces entered Antep, Birecik, Maras and Urfa in the southeast, Batum and Kars in the northeast, and Samsun on the Black Sea coast of Anatolia. On 16 March 1919 Istanbul was officially taken under Allied occupation. Beginning from 28 March 1919 the Italian forces landed at the western Mediterranean city of Antalya and its environs. Finally, on 15 May 1915, accompanied by the Allied warships, the Greek forces began occupying the city of Izmir and the Aegean region.

The new situation created by the occupations was formalised in the Treaty of Sèvres, signed by the Ottoman Empire and the Entente powers on 10 August 1920. According to the Sèvres Treaty, the Arabian peninsula and Mesopotamia (Iraq) were ceded to Great Britain; Syria and the southeastern Anatolian provinces of Antep, Mardin and Urfa were taken by France; eastern Thrace, and Izmir and its environs were surrendered to Greece; and western Anatolia except Izmir was designated as the economic dominion of Italy. The Sèvres Treaty also stipulated that an independent Armenian state under American mandate would be created in northeastern Anatolia, and an autonomous Kurdistan would be established in southeastern Anatolia. According to the terms of the treaty, all the non-Muslim subjects of the Ottoman Empire who had been previously expatriated would be allowed to return to their homelands and their initial wealth and property would be returned to them. Istanbul was left as the Ottoman capital and the seat of the sultan, but the Straits were taken under the control of an international commission. The Ottoman government was denied the right to have armed forces other than a gendarmerie for internal security purposes. The Ottoman finances were to be regulated by a permanent Allied commission and part of the Ottoman revenues was to be reserved for payments of reparations to the Allies (Kili 1982: 84–6; Shaw and Shaw 1977: 356).

The circumstances created by the treaties of Mondros and Sèvres, and especially the prospect of the foundation of Armenian and Greek states in Anatolia, led many Turks in the occupation zones to found Defence of Rights Committees and to start an armed resistance movement. Thus, in the course of November–December 1918 three such committees were formed: the Committee for the Defence of Ottoman Rights (*Mudafaa-i Hukuk-u Osmaniye Cemiyeti*) in Izmir, the Committee for the Defence of Thrace (*Trakya Pasaeli Cemiyeti*) in Thrace, and the Committee for the Defence of Rights of the Eastern Provinces (*Vilayat-i Sarkiyye Mudafaa-i Hukuk Cemiyeti*) in Istanbul. The Defence of Rights Committees were accompanied by urban and rural guerrilla wars against the occupation forces. The Kemalists entered the stage after these initial organisations and forms of nationalist resistance had already taken root. What Mustafa Kemal Pasha and the Kemalist revolutionaries did was, first, to organise the various Defence of Rights Committees into a centralised resistance organisation called the Committee for the Defence of Rights of Anatolia and Rumeli. Another contribution of Mustafa Kemal Pasha and the Kemalists to the nationalist cause was to replace the irregular guerrilla forces by a regular army called the National Forces (*Kuvva-i Milliye*). In 1922 the national resistance movement ended in victory, and many of the territorial losses of the Sèvres Treaty were reversed under the Lausanne Treaty of 1923. The Lausanne Treaty also implied the western recognition of the Kemalist state as the new political authority of Turkey, replacing the defunct government of the Ottoman sultan.

The 'deep policy' imperatives of the Sèvres syndrome: isolationism and westernisation without the West

The following formulae are the 'deep policy' imperatives of the Sèvres syndrome:

1. Isolationism: Do not enter into economic, political or cultural pacts and alliances with the western world. Never trust the western states and always watch your back.
2. Westernisation without the West: westernise/modernise the state, the military, the economy and the society without getting engaged in economic, political or cultural pacts and alliances with the western world.

The basic assumption underlying the Sèvres syndrome was that the Europeans perceive the Turks as the illegitimate invaders and occupiers of the European-Christian lands and as the oppressors of the European-Christian peoples. Therefore, the syndrome went on, the Europeans have always tried to sweep the Turks away from the ancestral European-Christian territories and to restore those lands back to their rightful owners, the Armenians and the Greeks in the past and now the Kurds. This historic 'missionary struggle' of Europe had started with the Crusades in the middle ages and culminated in the Sèvres Treaty of 1920 ending World War One, under the terms of which Turkey was carved up between western powers and the Christian minorities collaborating with them. Scrape every European and you will find a Crusader behind it! The Sèvres Treaty, and with it the Crusader mission of driving the Turks away from Anatolia, became defunct as a result of the Turkish national resistance.

However, Europeans, and the Christian minorities inside Turkey, have never given up the Crusader's mission. Even today, the European Union's seemingly innocent demands for individual and minority rights are nothing but concealed attempts to revive the terms of the Sèvres Treaty, and they simply want to get by peaceful means what they could not achieve by force of arms eight decades ago.

Indicators of the Sèvres syndrome in the Turkish public opinion: public attitudes towards Europe and the West[2]

The data from the public opinion survey, which was conducted in November 2003 as part of my Euroscepticism project, offer ample evidence on the way to measure the impact of the Sèvres syndrome on the political beliefs and attitudes of the Turkish public. Part of this evidence is shown in Tables 9.3, 9.4 and 9.5. The basic assumption of the Sèvres syndrome was that the Europeans perceive the Turks as the illegitimate invaders and occupiers of the European-Christian lands and as the oppressors of the European-Christian peoples. Therefore, the syndrome went on, the Europeans have always tried to sweep the Turks away from the ancestral European-Christian territories and to restore those lands back to their rightful owners, the Armenians and the Greeks in the past and now the Kurds. According to the data in Tables 9.3 and 9.4, this assumption is well received by the Turkish public. Hence, as shown in Table 9.3, a net majority of the public (54 per cent) think that European states are now trying to divide and rule Turkey, just as in the past they tried to divide and rule the Ottoman Empire.

Moreover, a close look at the data in Table 9.4 shows that a sizeable proportion of the Turkish public (approximately 40 per cent) is of the opinion that Europeans, today, continue to be motivated by the 'Crusader's

Table 9.3:   Indicators of the Sèvres syndrome in Turkish public opinion: Europe's historical intentions towards Turkey

	Some people think that European states are now trying to divide and rule Turkey, just as in the past they tried to divide and rule the Ottoman Empire. Do you agree with this opinion?
Tend to agree	54
Tend not to agree	33
No opinion/no response	13
Total	100

Table 9.4:   Indicators of the Sèvres syndrome in Turkish public opinion: public beliefs on the Crusades, capitulations and the Sèvres Treaty

	Some people think that a Crusader's spirit shapes the attitudes of the Europeans towards Turkey. Do you agree with this opinion?	*Some people think that the reforms that have been made for Turkey's accession to the European Union are no different from the capitulations in the ancient times. Do you agree with this opinion?*	*Some people think that the reforms that the EU wants Turkey to make are no different from the concessions that the European great powers once demanded from the Ottomans in the Sèvres Treaty. Do you agree with this opinion?*
Tend to agree	46	41	36
Tend not to agree	27	27	27
No opinion/ no response	28	32	37
Total	100	100	100

Table 9.5:   Indicators of the Sèvres syndrome in Turkish public opinion: public attitudes towards the idea of 'Westernisation without the West'

	Some people think that Turkey would have been in a better situation today if she had followed her own, rather than Western, values and traditions. Do you agree with this opinion?
Tend to agree	63
Tend not to agree	26
No opinion/no response	11
Total	100

spirit' in their dealings with Turkey, that they relentlessly try to recapture the capitulations of the middle ages and to degrade Turkey to an economic colony, and that they still attempt to resuscitate the Sèvres Treaty of 1920. It is notable that those who do not share these ideas remained only at 27 per cent, as opposed to the 40 per cent approval rate, and one-third of the respondents expressed no opinion on the issue of the Crusades, capitulations and Sèvres. Finally, based on the date in Table 9.5, we will try to find some evidence for one 'deep policy' imperative of the Sèvres syndrome, namely, 'westernisation without the West'. 'Westernisation without the West' would imply an inward-looking model of development without following the economic, political or cultural models of the West.

As we can see in Table 9.5, this policy imperative has gained wide recognition in the Turkish public opinion. In fact, a clear majority of the people interviewed (63 per cent) said that Turkey would have been better off today if she had followed her own, rather than Europe's, values and traditions. Only about 25 per cent of the respondents opposed that idea, while 11 per cent chose not to express any opinion regarding the issue.

The strategic turn of Islamic conservatism towards Europe[3]

The outcome of the 3 November 2002 general elections in Turkey was an 'expected surprise' for the observers of Turkish politics. It was 'expected' because the general ranking of the parties in relation to one another had been estimated by many people. It was, on the other hand, a surprise, because no one could predict with any precision the high performance of JDP and the near annihilation of the parties of the former prime minister Bulent Ecevit (the Democratic Left Party), and of the former foreign minister Ismail Cem (the New Turkey Party). Similarly, contrary to the estimations by many analysts, the secularist-social democratic Republican People's Party (RPP) could not manage to make a big showing, despite its last-minute recruitment of Kemal Dervis, the much-acclaimed former economy minister, into its ranks.

The JDP turned out to be the undisputable victor of the elections, with 34 per cent of the votes and 66 per cent (363 out of 550) of the parliamentary seats. It was followed, by a large margin, by the RPP, which won 20 per cent of the votes and 34 per cent of the seats (178 out of 550). No other party managed to top the national threshold of 10 per cent. As a result, slightly more than 45 per cent of the voters, nearly half of the electorate, remained unrepresented in the new parliament. Seventy per cent of the voters voted for the right-wing parties and 30 per cent for the left-wing parties. The 70 per cent right-wing votes were divided between the self-declared conservative-democratic right of the JDP (34 per cent), the radical (Turkish ethno-nationalist or Islamist) right of the Nationalist Action Party and the Felicity Party and others (22 per cent), and the centre-right of the True Path Party and the Motherland Party and others (15 per cent). The 30 per cent left-wing votes, on the other hand, were divided between the centre-left of the Republican People's Party and the Democratic Left Party and others (22 per cent) and the radical left of the Democratic People's Party and others (7 per cent). Finally, 77 per cent of the electorate chose parties which had declared themselves as 'Eurosupporters', whereas 23 per cent of the electorate preferred the 'Eurosceptic' parties of the left and the right.

The first remark to be made regarding the profile of the JDP supporters is that 60 per cent of them thought that their primary identity was
'Muslim', while the national average was only 35 per cent. In a similar
vein, 40 per cent of the JDP supporters identified themselves primarily
in national terms (as 'Turks' or 'citizens of the Republic of Turkey'), while
the national average was 60 per cent. It is therefore clear that the JDP supporters perceived themselves as being 'more Muslim' and 'less Turkish'
than the average Turkish citizen. Secondly, the JDP supporters turned out
to be less educated than the average respondent, and much less educated
than the RPP supporters: 54 per cent of the JDP voters received only five
years of elementary school education, while the national average was
42 per cent; 33 per cent of the JDP supporters went to middle or high
school, while the national average is 40 per cent. Finally only about 8 per
cent of JDP supporters were university graduates whereas the national
average is 12 per cent. All in all, the JDP has a constituency of which 60 per
cent identified themselves as being primarily Muslim and which was less
educated than the average citizen.

A brief look at the JDP voters' attitudes towards Europe and Turkey's
membership in the EU reveals that they cannot be labelled as Euro-
rejectionists but they manifest significantly more Eurosceptic tendencies
when compared with the national average and with the voters of the
opposition party, the RPP. Hence, in a hypothetical referendum on
Turkey's membership in the EU, the JDP supporters would vote YES by a
ratio of 56 per cent. This was significantly below the national average of 64
per cent and far below the RPP figure of 82 per cent. Similarly, when asked
whether their lives would change for the better in the case of EU membership, the YES rate among the JDP supporters, at 34 per cent, though it was
slightly above their NO rate of 30 per cent, still fell far below the national
average of 42 per cent and the RPP average of 53 per cent. When it comes
to the expected harm from EU membership, 78 per cent of the JDP supporters were reported to have said that the most important disadvantage of
EU membership for Turkey would be a corruption of national and religious
values. This emphatic sensitivity of the JDP supporters on the issue of the
would-be negative impact of Europeanisation on Turkish national and religious values, reaching a total of 78 per cent, far exceeded the national average of 64 per cent and the RPP average of only 46 per cent.

A clear majority of the general respondents turned out not to believe
in the sincerity of the EU in admitting Turkey as a full member. This overall Eurosceptic tendency became much more emphatic among the supporters of the JDP. Thus, around 60 per cent of the respondents said that
the Europeans did not understand Turkey and the Turks, that the EU was

not sincere in accepting Turkey as a full member, and that the Union imposed on Turkey conditions that it did not impose on the other candidate states. Among the JDP supporters, the ratio of those who shared a similar scepticism towards Europe and the EU rose to about 70 per cent. In a similar vein, close to 50 per cent of the average respondents believed that the EU would not accept Turkey as a full member, even if Turkey fulfilled all the preconditions required for membership. This ratio too was found to be around 60 per cent among the potential voters of the JDP. Finally, when asked the ultimate question, i.e. whether they perceived the EU as a 'Christian club' or not, the overwhelming majority of the JDP supporters, close to 75 per cent, said YES. This was significantly higher than the average of 54 per cent and much higher than the RPP average of 46 per cent. It seems that, as they primarily identify themselves as 'Muslim', using a religious category, they perceive Europe also in religious terms and define it as being Christian before everything else.

In a striking opposition to its constituency's Eurosceptic attitudes, the leadership of the JDP, right from the day they won the elections, committed themselves to the cause of bringing Turkey into the EU. Hence, the JDP turned out to be a party with the most Eurosceptic and isolationist constituency and the most Euro-supportive and integrationist leadership. Given this dramatic discrepancy between the tendencies of the party's base and leadership, it would not be a big surprise if clashes and tensions occur between the generally conservative, inward-looking and isolationist constituency and the self-declaredly liberal, outward-looking, integrationist leadership of the JDP. In the years since coming to power, the JDP leadership, to its credit, was admittedly more inclined to bringing its own constituency forward into the sphere of European values rather than yielding to an easier and populist method of playing on the nationalist and Islamic sentiments of its supporters for covering up mistakes and mismanagement.

Admittedly, the pro-EU attitudes of the JDP elites had started as a tactical choice, as a matter of finding European protection against the suppressive policies of the Turkish secularist establishment. However, this tactical choice seems to have been evolving into a strategic one. This strategic choice also has to do with the defeat of Turkish political Islam, which has been traditionally represented in the political arena by Necmettin Erbakan and by the so-called 'National Doctrine' parties he led, through the shock waves of the 'postmodern' military intervention of 28 February 1997. Hence, anti-Kemalist revanchism, top-down transformation of the society along Islamic lines, using democracy as no more than an instrument to be able to come to power, this quintessentially political project has proved to be futile. Erdogan, who was a radical Islamist in the pre-28 February period, once said that democracy was but a train and that one should get down from the train at the right station. The same Erdogan now says that he and his party reject any project of 'social engineering', that is to say using political power to change the society according to the precepts of a certain ideology, including the Islamist one. He also, now, vehemently denies that his party is Islamist or even that it is a religiously based institution. In a quest for a more appropriate appellation that would better reflect the party's new orientation away from political Islam and towards the centre, the party ideologists came up with the rather euphemistic term 'conservative democratic'. What can be said about the ex-Islamists' strategic choice for the EU and how different is it from the earlier tactical rapprochement towards the EU? The strategic choice seems to involve the following dimensions: (a) delinking from political Islam, ideologically as well as institutionally; and (b) Europeanising the public sphere for it to accommodate the performances of Islamic identity, particularly by passing legislation that would allow Muslim women wearing a headscarf to have a legitimate presence in the universities and government institutions.

Here the claim is the compatibility of Muslim identity and European modernity. In this respect, Kemalist nationalist understanding of modernity is too restrictive, too exclusive for the desired integration of Islamic identity and modernity. Hence, a new, more liberal, more inclusionary version of modernity, one could say a more 'postmodern' definition of modernity, such as the one that is upheld by the European Union, would offer a much better ground for that integration to take place. The Kemalist understanding of modernity is, paradoxically, too modernist, too much attached to an earlier, French revolutionary, nineteenth-century definition of modernity to allow the manifestations and performances of Islamic identity in the public sphere. On the other hand, the current European understanding of modernity is, again paradoxically, much less 'modernist' than Turkey's. Therefore, a Europeanised public sphere in Turkey would more easily tolerate the free display of Muslim identity. Two forces will resist this project, however.

1. Euroscepticism and nationalist isolationism in Turkey: Nationalist isolationists will not leave the battleground without, at least, a fierce last battle. Nationalists will particularly be willing to mobilise the public opinion against the government, whenever the latter attempts to touch upon nationally sensitive issues such as the Cyprus question and minority rights.
2. Turcoscepticism and rejectionism of Turkey in Europe: European rejectionists of Turkey, such as Giscard d'Estaing and Helmut Kohl, sticking

to theses of 'cultural/civilisational incompatibility between Turkey and Europe' (which is reminiscent of the infamous 'clash of civilisations' thesis of Samuel Huntington) will make it harder for Turkey to get integrated into European Union, alienating many Muslim supporters of the JDP, while at the same time playing into the hands of Turkish nationalist isolationists.

Concluding remarks: what future for Turkey and its conservatisms?

The armed Kurdish secessionist movement that has gained force in the 1980s has reintroduced the concept of group rights into Turkish politics. The Kurds were followed by other ethnic and religious groups, notably by the minority Islamic sect of the Alevites, in putting forward demands for political, cultural and economic rights and privileges for themselves. In this way, the concept of group rights re-entered Turkish political discourse with a force unseen since the last years of the Ottoman Empire. The 'individual', which was discovered in the optimistic years of the 1980s, was buried again under the blanket of the communitarian demands of ethnic and religious groups. As expected, ethnic separatism stirred the Tanzimat and Sèvres syndromes and fostered nationalist isolationism. Turkey's integration with Europe, which has leaped forward since the Helsinki summit of 1999, helped build a social and political coalition of integrationism. The reflection of integrationism in the domestic arena has been the transformation of the state structure and political regime in line with the norms and values of the European Union. For the moment, this project of integrationism and political Europeanisation is represented by the JDP.

The success of the conservative democratic project for Europeanising Turkey depends essentially on an external and uncontrollable factor, namely, the EU policy towards Turkey. Squeezed between Turkish Euroscepticism and European Turcoscepticism, the JDP project may very well fail. If it fails, then Islamism, as a political ideology, will surely come back. Kurdish secessionism would most probably follow suit, as Kurds would lose their hopes of expanding their community rights in a democratic Turkey. As a result, Turkish politics would again revert to the battlefield, much the same as in the 1990s, of Islamism, Kurdish nationalism and Turkish isolationism. If Turkey's integration with the EU makes a leap forward with the opening of the accession negotiations in the autumn of 2005, then the expected short-term consequence of this would be felt, at the political front, in the form of the consolidation of a more democratic and liberal atmosphere. In such an atmosphere, it would be easier for the JDP to build a wide-ranging consensus for the purpose of integrating Muslim identity into the liberalised Turkish public sphere. That would satisfy the party's more religious constituency and provide the party leadership with enough ideological ammunition to fight against, and detach themselves from, their Islamist critics. In this manner, the JDP could pass a critical threshold in its journey towards the secular centre of Turkish politics, and this would surely make a significant contribution to the stabilisation and consolidation of the democratic regime in Turkey.

The most optimistic scenario for the solution of Turkey's ideological problems regarding democracy and freedom would be the opening and smooth progression of the accession negotiations with the European Union. The most important ideological effect of the inclusionary attitude of the EU towards Turkey would be to alleviate the Tanzimat and Sèvres syndromes, which traditionally represented the lenses through which nationalist conservatives, both the elites and their followers among the masses, viewed Europe and Turkey's relations with it. The prospect of EU membership would placate nationalist conservatism's deep-rooted claims that Europeans have never given up the Crusader's cause of crushing the Turkish state and driving the Turks out of Istanbul and Anatolia. The promise of being admitted to the EU would be taken by most Turks as the West's affirmation of the legitimate existence of Turkey within its existing borders. Under these circumstances, it would be easier for the integrationists to argue that there is no hidden agenda behind the EU's demands from Turkey to recognise the cultural rights of the Kurds and other ethnic and religious minorities. These circumstances would supply a fertile ground for the solution of the most pressing group rights problems, particularly of the Kurds and the Alevites, without violating the territorial unity and national integrity of Turkey. It can be expected that the settlement of the group rights issues would then open the way for a historically new stage in the ideological domain, in which the rights discourse would be centred around the individual.

In the more pessimistic scenario of the obstruction or indefinite suspension of the accession negotiations, by the coming to power of the Turcosceptic Christian Democratic parties in France, Germany and elsewhere in Europe, for instance, the Tanzimat and Sèvres syndromes, nationalist conservatism, and isolationism would be enhanced. Under these circumstances, integrationists would suffer irreparable damage to their credibility and they would be left with very little to say in defending the project of the Europeanisation of Turkish politics and society. As a result, the political regime would most probably drift back towards being the playground of incommensurable radicalisms, as it was in the 1990s, represented by political Islam, Turkish nationalism and Kurdish nationalism, the 'patriotic' Mafia gangs would wage wars against one another for the sharing of political rents, and the military would take back the political ground they have lost to the civilians during the 'short-lived' democratic experiment of 2000–5.

Notes

1. The data that are used in this section are drawn from TESEV-Bogazici 2002.
2. The data that are used in this section are drawn from OSIAF-Bogazici 2003.
3. All the data in this section, except for the electoral data, are drawn from TESEV-Bogazici 2002.

References

Bayar, Celal (1991) *Bir Darbenin Anatomisi [The Anatomy of a Coup D'Etat]* (Istanbul: Emre Yayinlari. Prepared for publication by Ismet Bozdag).

Cakirtas, Osman (1994a) *Osmanli Tarihi 1 (Siyasi) [Ottoman History 1 (Political)]* (Ankara: Koza Yayincilik).

Cakirtas, Osman (1994b) *Osmanli Tarihi 2 (Kultur ve Medeniyet) [Ottoman History 2 (Culture and Civilization)]* (Ankara: Koza Yayincilik).

Karaosmanoglu, Ali L. (1991) 'The International Context of Democratic Transition in Turkey', in Geoffrey Pridham (ed.), *Encouraging Democracy: the International Context of Regime Transition in Southern Europe* (Leicester: Leicester University Press), pp. 159–74.

Kili, Suna (1982) *Turk Devrim Tarihi [The History of the Turkish Revolution]* (Istanbul: Tekin Yayinevi).

Lewis, Bernard (1968) *The Emergence of Modern Turkey* (Oxford: Oxford University Press).

OSIAF-Bogazici (2003) 'Euroscepticism in Turkey: Manifestations at the Elite and Popular Levels'. Research project supported by a joint grant from the OSIAF (Open Society Institute Assistance Fund) and Bogazici University Research Fund. Date of completion: July 2004. Project director: Hakan Yilmaz. The opinion survey was conducted in November 2003, over a nationwide random sample of 2250 people.

Peker, Recep (1984) *Inkilap Dersleri [Lectures on the Turkish Revolution]* (Istanbul: Iletisim Yayinlari, first published in 1935).

Shaw, Stanford J. and Shaw, Ezel Kural (1977) *History of the Ottoman Empire and Modern Turkey. Volume II: Reform, Revolution, and Republic: the Rise of Modern Turkey, 1808–1975* (Cambridge and New York: Cambridge University Press).

Sultan Abdulhamid (1984) *Siyasi Hatiratim [My Political Memoirs]* (Dorduncu Baski: Birinci Baski 1974; Istanbul: Dergah Yayinlari).

TESEV-Bogazici (2002) 'Turkish Public Opinion Regarding the European Union'. Research project supported by a joint grant of TESEV (the Turkish Economic and Social Studies Foundation) and Bogazici University Research Fund. Date of completion: January 2002. Project directors: Ali Carkoglu, Refik Erzan, Kemal Kirisci, Hakan Yilmaz. The opinion survey was conducted in May 2002, over a nationwide random sample of 3060 people.

10
Europe in the Mirror of the Mediterranean[1]

Kalypso Nicolaïdis and Dimitri Nicolaïdis

The Mediterranean is both Europe's mirror and its extension, too close to ignore, too far to embrace. It is the cradle of its 'civilisation' and its demographic future, but also its poor southern neighbour and the source of its discontents. It is One with it and yet the Other – Arab, Muslim – at its doorstep. The Mediterranean is a space of intertwined histories and presents, a space of intense mingling and conflict. For some, it is a beautiful idea, for others a horrible headache. In the political or institutional realm, there is almost no evidence of it. From its beginning, the European Union has tried to define the nature of its relations with this space of imprecise contours, formerly the chosen territory of colonial expansion for its more powerful members. A decade ago, freed from the constraints of the Cold War, it gave birth to a new idea, the 'Euro-Mediterranean Partnership' (EMP). Fearing the winds of globalisation and feeling the pull of EU attraction, states of the southern Mediterranean, even while belonging to other geopolitical groups such as the Maghreb, the Machrek, the Middle-East and, of course, the 'Arab world', allowed themselves to be seduced by the idea.

If today the Mediterranean is the privileged terrain of the notorious 'clash of civilizations',[2] we should turn this representation on its head and see the Euro-Med project as a springboard for a countervailing 'convergence of civilisations'. Without this minimal convergence of norms and values, the EMP has little chance of showing results. Indeed, the EU increasingly sees itself as 'a power of another kind' where this claim to difference is to be tested above all in its immediate neighbourhood. In 1995, the EMP was represented as part of its development policy; today we can interpret it as an expression of the EU's normative power and in that sense a response to the aforementioned clash of civilisations. And yet, a decade after the inception of the EMP, the cleavage between the northern and southern shores of *mare nostrum*, that between its Western and Arab-Muslim worlds is deeper than ever, and the civilisational rhetoric has hardened.[3]

To understand, correctly, the limits of the Barcelona Process, it is appropriate to examine not only cultural factors but also the politics of power relations. If the EMP has failed to reduce the economic, political, social and cultural rifts separating Europe from the Arab world, it is partly because of the unexpected explosion of extraordinary events that have deepened the gulf between the two shores. Europe, first, has incontestably changed since 1995. The beginning of the twenty-first century is synonymous for Europe with reformulation and questions about its own identity and boundaries. The laborious process of adopting a European constitution after the enlargement to the East – which extended the borders of the EU all the way to Russia – has made Europeans aware that Europe's extension could stop once it had reached the limits of a 'European territory' that remains to be defined. Whence the appearance of a correlative theme of this territorial expansion, that of a 'Wider Europe', which, via concentric circles, extends its influence towards its immediate neighbours. Europe is once again the centre of *a* world, its continental world.

At the same time, Europe can less than ever claim to be the centre of *the* word, a world order transformed to its core by the aftermath of 11 September 2001. The attacks on the World Trade Center and the Pentagon have indeed shaken the geopolitical configuration of the Middle East and the Mediterranean, provoking an American intervention inspired more than ever by Messianism, which has constrained Europeans to position themselves *in relation to* United States policy. Thus divided and marginalised, Europeans were able at best only to react to the project of restructuring the 'Greater Middle East' – and this was despite growing resentment in Arab public opinion about a Europe incapable of relieving Palestinian suffering and countering the marginalisation of the Palestinian authority.[4] At worst, Europeans seized upon the 'Islamist threat' as a pretext for closing their eyes to the hardening of authoritarian regimes that suddenly found new life in the context of the 'struggle against terrorism'.

The frame of 'the West versus Islam' came to override even the timid prior attempts at jointly managed change, be it in North Africa or in the Middle East. And when the US set forth its vision for a Greater Middle East, the EMP – after all a much more consensual, albeit EU-centred precedent – did not figure in the picture.

To be sure, notwithstanding declarations on 'the superiority of Western civilisation' from the likes of Silvio Berlusconi, Europe's leaders on the whole sought to resist the extreme version of a dualistic discourse. But there is no denying the spillover effects in Europe of this era of new wars, notably in the media and in other public forums, thus incrementally justifying a closure *vis-à-vis* Southern Mediterranean peoples. Finally, these geopolitical developments have only served to entrench a long-term evolution within Europe itself which has known an undeniable swing to the right that has encouraged the tendency to withdraw into ourselves and to reject the Other. Exclusionary discourses and practices toward the 'other side', both in the geographical and cultural sense, spill over from domestic to regional politics – evidenced by the triumph of security-minded reasoning in the management of immigration policies as well as by the reactivation of the territorial conflict between Spain and Morocco over some tiny islands; or, further, the unexpected side-effects in the Muslim world of the debate about the banning of the Muslim headscarf in French schools; or another, even more virulent, about Turkey's entry into the EU where opposition was led not only by most right-wing parties, but also by many on the left. It is indeed the 'place of Islam' in Europe that is at stake here, and even if Europeans think of themselves as more familiar with the Arab-Muslim cultural realities than their American counterparts, the logic of clash produces the same kind of effects on both side of the Atlantic.

Can we explain the failures of the EMP συμπλυ by the conjuncture of events? Are there not more fundamental causes? To answer this question, we must return to the founding act of a process characterised from the beginning by tension between, on one side, what was coming out of EU foreign policy – a process therefore conceived and directed by European institutions – and, on the other side, what constituted a new vision for 'community building' in the region, combining a multilateral approach modelled on the OSCE (Organisation for Security and Cooperation in Europe), with an integrationist approach based on identity discourse. In two words, Euro-Med versus EuroMed.

This tension progressively became opposition between a power logic and an identity and cultural logic. If the impasse in which the EMP currently finds itself is the result of divisions that affect the region at different levels, is it not partly because the EMP is now seen as a means for the EU to use its normative power? How to fix it so that countries south of the Mediterranean make the project their own when it is increasingly considered by Europeans as an integral part of their – relatively civilised – strategy for self-affirmation on the world stage? It is true that the creation of 'security communities' based on mutual confidence is not necessarily incompatible with asymmetrical power relations.[5] However, we need to look at the question in a different way from the political and institutional one if we think that, despite the weakness of traditions, and tools for cooperation, it is worth building links between peoples living in the same region.

This is why we will attempt to show to what extent the 'civilisational grid' is the source of the impasse in which the Barcelona Process finds itself today. Indeed, from a Eurocentric point of view, the EMP can be understood either as a privileged interface between Europe and the Arab-Muslim world, which would facilitate 'convergence' or 'dialogue' between civilisations; or as an integration process that would encourage the emergence of common values and norms – the very ones the European Union is not only supposed to incarnate but also to export to the rest of the world. Yet these representations both largely assume away the project of building a Mediterranean region in favour of a 'Wider Europe'. On the one hand, by consolidating its own borders, the EU takes the risk of solidifying an imaginary civilisational divide; on the other, as it absorbs these peripheral spaces into its own project, it deprives the EuroMediterranean idea of its specificity and its autonomy.

We think it is possible to transcend this alternative and we suggest concrete ways of doing so. We wish to defend the adoption of a *postcolonial agenda* for the Mediterranean that is neither a utopia nor an alternative to the EMP, but rather a return to its original multilateral spirit, which can be expressed by the construction of a true community. With this objective, the Mediterranean must be absolutely at the heart of the project and EuroMediterranean institutions relocated as far as possible from Brussels, encouraging the states of the region to participate in a far-reaching exercise of mutual recognition while aiding the empowerment of civil societies through transnational practices and procedures planned for the third phase of the EMP. It is only under these conditions that the idea of a deterritorialised EuroMediterranean region can make its way.

This we believe can only be achieved by 'bringing the Mediterranean back in' and recentring the EuroMed institutions away from the EU of Brussels, by co-opting the states of the region into a far-reaching exercise of mutual recognition while aiding the empowerment of civil societies through transnational practices and procedures planned for the third basket of the EMP. It is only under these conditions that the idea of a deterritorialised EuroMediterranean region can be given true substance.

A Eurocentric process

The Euro-Mediterranean partnership is undeniably the creation of the European Union, which gave itself ambitious and original means to act outside of its borders. That this process has tended to be increasingly Eurocentric is not astonishing in as much as, from the beginning of the EMP, there was tension between the desire to launch a true European Union foreign policy – especially in the direction of the Arab world – and the temptation to base the process on the idea of regional integration consisting in sharing with its immediate neighbours certain internal practices of the EU. But it is also fair to recognise that the two initial ways of framing the EMP – EU foreign policy versus regional security partnership – were 'not incompatible', since at that stage, the notion of 'partnership' – 'special' or 'strategic' partnership – started to be used by the EU in other contexts (Russia, Turkey . . .) to simply connote a privileged status in the pecking order of the EU's external relations. The fact that such a partnership can be an intermediary stage in the construction of a more ambitious 'Euro-Mediterranean community', distinct from the European Union itself, is perhaps an implicit given in the discourse about the EMP. But, if taken seriously, it does make the founding tension much more intractable. How can the EMP remain both an 'external' relation and a self-centred process? In reality the Barcelona Process is marked by the contradiction between a post-colonial rhetoric and neo-colonial practices.[6] Before beginning to transcend this contradiction, it is appropriate to update its core.

The Euro-Mediterranean partnership: a multilateral process or a European affair?

To illustrate this tension, one can show with Figure 10 that, in contrast to a process purely defined as EU foreign policy and to the so-called Global Mediterranean Policy of the previous decade, the EMP represented an evolution in two directions – at least in theory. On the one hand, it heralded a *multilateralisation* of relationship between participants, as reflected in its institutional set up. On the other hand, it introduced practices that could potentially lead to *deeper integration*, moving on *inter alia* from a special trade status with the EU to a security charter.

A diagnosis about the last ten years would consist in assessing whether and to what extent the EMP has moved along either dimension. In the longer term, only the combination of the two – the transcendence of the Eurocentric character of the process at the same time as the deepening of integration between members and non-members of the EU – can eventually lead to the construction of a EuroMed Community. Here is the paradox: shifting from a purely functional regional foreign policy to an enterprise in region building involves a whole array of practices and representations – which pertain to all four categories identified here – while at the same time the two remain opposite ideal types.

Mode of relationship Depth of integration	EU-centred relations vs. . . .	Multilateral relations
Cooperation vs. . . .	EU regional foreign policy *Euro-Med: 'Creating a separate Mediterranean region'* GMP/70s-Mercosur **EMP?**	'Partnership' as regional multilateralism *Euro-Med as a Mediterranean OSCE with formal equality between members*
Deeper integration	'Partnership' as regional mentoring *Euro-Med as part of Euro-neighbourhood (sub-regional integration as precondition)* Pre-Enlargement → Balkans Pact Non-Enlargement → Wider Europe	Community building or region-building *EuroMed: Constructing a EuroMediterranean Community together*

Figure 10:   Dilemmas and tensions in the EMP

In order to explain why in effect there is a structural need to combine various approaches to the EMP we must first come back to basic geographical intuitions and dilemmas. The EMP differs from any other theatre where European power is exercised because it alone combines the property of neither being a separate region with which the EU connects more or less closely (like Mercosur or ASEAN), nor a region destined to be integrated to the EU itself and encouraged to build horizontal ties as a pre-requisite to EU accession (like the Visegrad group or the Balkans).

If, before the accession of Greece, Spain and Portugal into the European Community, it seemed still possible for Europe to build different types of relations with the countries around the Mediterranean, the dilemma was not then as evident as today: is the EU goal trying to create a region *together* with the Mediterranean . . . or to promote the creation of a Mediterranean region *separate* from itself? To create a regional whole with Mediterranean countries was illogical in the respect that the EU was made up of a majority of non-Mediterranean countries; and to promote the creation of a Mediterranean region separate from the EU was unrealistic, since neither the countries of the northern shore nor those of the southern shore defined themselves primarily as 'Mediterranean' – the former being 'European', the latter 'Arab' or 'Muslim'. And if this separate region had to be made up uniquely of countries from the southern shore, how could they by themselves form a 'Mediterranean region'?

In spite of – or perhaps because of – this ambiguity, the EMP borrows from both these geographical frames, which, in turn, connote differently the notion of 'partnership', according to the policy the EU means to conduct with respect to the EMP, as Figure 10 illustrates. On the one hand, with respect to *regional multilateralism*, the idea is to build together a EuroMed region (including the European Union but not defined by it), the notion of 'partnership' being then synonymous with equal relations – at least formally equal – between members and non-members of the EU inside a group including the twenty-seven countries of the EU and the Mediterranean. From this point of view, the EMP is inspired by the Helsinki process and by the OSCE, to which it gave birth – in the beginning an asymmetrical process aiming to promote reforms on one side of the border separating the two camps during the Cold War, but which progressively evolved towards an association of formally equal countries. Indeed, the originality of the EMP process lies in its ability to bring together countries of the South and North in a dialogue about a shared political space. This vision of things sets up the normative framework for building a 'regional security partnership', founded on respect and thus mutual confidence: *EuroMed* is full of post-colonial rhetoric.

On the other hand, *regional mentoring* is about encouraging South–South collaboration through the Euro-Med, and thus the idea of 'partnership' is above all an expression of EU pragmatism. This propensity to present itself as a referent to the outside world whenever region building is the issue leads the EU to consider it easier and more productive to work with a group of countries than with individual states, whether with the goal of integrating these countries (the Visegrad group in the 1990s, South-East Europe today), or simply with the idea of creating privileged links to give more weight to Europe in international affairs (the EU accords with Mercosur or with ASEAN). From this point of view, the EMP can present itself as a multilateral process between equal partners, but it remains largely centred on the EU, conceived and financed by the EU, which also defines the methods, the goals, and the different stages of the process: the Euro-Med would then correspond to neo-colonial practices wrapped up in a post-colonial discourse.

On the other hand, *regional mentoring* is about encouraging South–South collaboration through the Euro-Med, and thus the idea of 'partnership' is above all an expression of EU pragmatism, a neighbourhood version of the EU's general propensity to offer itself as an anchor for region building outside its shores, whereby it is easier and more productive for the EU to deal with groups of countries than with individual countries, whether with the ultimate aim of integrating these countries in the EU (the Visegrad group in the 1990s, South-East Europe today), or simply with the idea of creating privileged links to give more weight to Europe in international affairs (EU–Mercosur or EU–ASEAN agreements). From this point of view, the EMP can present itself as a multilateral process between equal partners, but it remains largely centred on the EU, conceived and financed by the EU, which also defines the methods, the goals, and the different stages of the process: the Euro-Med should indeed be read as neo-colonial practices wrapped in a post-colonial discourse.

In this perspective, it is interesting to note that if elsewhere the EU was able to be a model for regional integration without having initiated such processes, the EMP proceeds from a different logic. Even though partner states from the Arab world, while sharing a strong common identity, do not show real cohesion nor have they up to the present deployed real policies of regional or sub-regional integration, the EU is using all its possible leverage to develop horizontal cooperation between Mediterranean non-member states, as it is doing in South-East European states (with the difference that the latter seek to become members). The recent decision by the European Commission to take *cumulated* added value into account to define the origin of products from non-member Mediterranean countries is a good example of pressure *from the outside* to deepen regional economic integration.

In the case of the Balkans, however, functional cooperation was accompanied by a collective desire to reshape the identity of the region in a less connotative sense, by getting rid of the identity mark 'Balkans' for the more neutral 'South-East Europe'. This effort to modernise a collective identity could have had diverse motivations, including that of courting the EU, but still the region was the originator of this initiative. From the European point of view, this ideological underpinning has an instrumental function and is destined to be subsumed under the EU banner. The invention by Brussels of the concept 'Wider Europe' in the run-up to enlargement was destined to transpose this pre-accession thinking to non-accession countries and thus unsurprisingly conveys through its very label the idea of a centre–periphery relationship.

Finally, what is at stake with the EMP is the need to find a just middle between two traditionally opposed demands: efficiency and legitimacy. More multilateralism would encourage the second, but it would also mean that greater deference would be given to the EU partners' resistance to interference in their internal affairs. On the other hand, if the EU's preponderant position in questions of conception, organisation and financing of the Barcelona Process can be interpreted as neo-colonialism, it allows also for mobilising more resources and developing policies of conditionality, which represent an efficient tool for manufacturing ties that bind, even against the will of certain players.

The EU as a 'normative power': still a power in the Mediterranean?

To consider the European Union as a 'normative power' is perhaps a way of overcoming the efficiency/legitimacy dilemma in presenting the influence of the EU as both more concrete, more legitimate, and distinct from that of the United States. For it is true that Europeans have a problem with the idea of power. They care about it but are unable or unwilling to project it bluntly. The US may or may not be a reluctant superpower but the EU is certainly a reluctant power *tout court*. This is why analysts and politicians have come up with various labels for the Union, reflecting this ambivalence, mitigating the bluntness of the assertion: civilian power of course,[7] as well as quiet power, middle power, emancipatory power, postnational power and now normative power. The labels are not simply exultations of Joseph Nye's soft as opposed to hard power. Nor are they lofty concepts to accommodate the psychology of weakness, as Robert Kagan would have it.[8] Rather, European unease with power is part and parcel of a compelling narrative still in the making: that of a Union of nation-states slowly and painfully constructing together the instrument of their collective post-colonial atonement. This is at least one way of telling the story, about a power tamed to serve collective rather than individual state interest. With a normative version of civilian power we appeal to an idea of the EU itself as a model that is increasingly willing to give itself the tools to export such construction beyond Europe's southern shores.[9]

In congruence with the right to intervene, a recent, albeit contested, part of the repertory of international relations, the notion of 'normative power' goes beyond the simple ambition of making partners share habits and methods of cooperation. It presupposes, also, a commitment to taming the capacity of states to do harm within and not only outside their borders, and an urge to export a substantive political agenda (like, for example, the abolition of the death penalty). However, behind this logic there is first of all the distinction between members and non-members: the community might be inclusive but the EU is the one that defines normative appropriateness. One can ask to what extent this other kind of power is compatible with the emergence of a common feeling of belonging and what purpose it is meant to serve.

Fundamentally, normative power can only be applied credibly under a key condition: real consistency between actions and prescriptions *vis-à-vis* the outside world and those deployed at home. Yet, EU policies aimed at promoting democracy often, and increasingly, conflict with security demands not only due to the short-term conflicts and instability that generally come with democratic transitions. In the region, this instability is compounded by the fear that elected Muslim groups will lock the (democratic) door behind them. What one could call the Algerian dilemma in reference to the civil war of the 1990s and the relaxed attitude of Europeans regarding military power in Algeria is the black hole of normative power: democracy, but at what price? From this point of view, if the exercise of normative power to empower local players is not neo-colonial, what do we say when the latter are deprived of their capacity to define autonomously the content of their actions and for instance when activists in the region do not share the secular aspect of European political pluralism?

Beyond the incapacity of member states to agree on values and interests that should be priorities (policy reforms? regional stability? poverty reduction? . . .), the notion of normative power reaches its limits as soon as the will to export a package of normalised procedures enters into contradiction with the choice to allow partner countries to develop their own political spaces, in which case convergence with the EU is less controllable. This dilemma is perfectly illustrated by EU ambivalence towards the current reform process in Turkey.

The EU's failure to apply consistently over time principles of democracy promotion is due in part to the lack of agreement between member states over the desirable tradeoffs they are willing to make among different goals and the values underpinning these goals (e.g. political reform versus stability or poverty reduction). But the failure is also due to the contradiction inherent in the idea of normative power itself, between exporting a given set of procedural norms and allowing for the emergence of new political spaces in partner countries, which are necessary for a long-term convergence with the EU. The EU's great ambivalence when faced with current Turkish reforms is a case in point.

The rhetoric of normative power thus appears as it is: an instrument of EU foreign policy more than a common basis for creating ties between neighbours. It was at the Valencia Summit (April 2002) only a few months after 11 September 2001 that European decision-makers took note of the need to place the emphasis on the *cultural* dimension of the process so as to counterbalance the power logic at work in the region. If indeed normative power can design the contours of a community, it cannot by itself define the content. That more or less powerful or influential players exist within a regional community is undeniable, but the community cannot be credible if there is not at least formal equality between members. A community will not tolerate being divided into subjects and objects of power: it was on this fundamental question that the founders of the European Community argued during the negotiations of 1957, that is, the extent to which the new arrangements were to institutionalise non-hegemonic politics in Europe through the formal equality between member states. Still, there is no point in abstracting from the asymmetrical nature of power relations in the Mediterranean – this would be naive and even dangerous. Rather, it is better to articulate and distinguish between, on the one hand, the benign practice of power by the EU and, on the other, practices related to community building founded on appeals to common belonging and the sharing of identities. It is towards the latter that we must now turn.

The 'EuroMediterranean' beyond civilisations

Is noting the increasingly pronounced Eurocentrism in the Barcelona Process the same as saying that a dualist vision of the region – the EU versus its partners – is progressively dominant or that the notion of EuroMediterranean community is already moot, absorbed into a 'Wider Europe' whose integrating project seems sometimes to verge on hegemony? In any case, is it not pointless to want the contours of an 'us' in a framework that is above all a diplomatic exercise? The whole problem comes from the fact that, from the beginning, the partners avoided coming to an understanding on the meaning of 'partnership' and were not inclined to invest enough of their material, political or symbolic capital to give body to the project.

A regional reality in the Mediterranean can be collectively constructed even if those formally in charge lack the will, the capacity or the imagination to do so. From this point of view, the creation of a EuroMediterranean Foundation for dialogue between cultures and civilisations is emblematic. Is this not the first real EuroMediterranean institution, created not to manage economic aid or questions of security but to empower the unlikely domain of culture? Its avowed goal – 'to encourage a culture of peace and arrive at mutual understanding, draw people together, repel threats to peace, and reinforce exchanges between civilizations'[10] – is evidence of an awareness within the EU of the need to bring more identity content to the EuroMediterranean project by facilitating exchanges at the civil society level. It would obviously be naive to think that such a Foundation could by itself create a feeling of belonging, a sense of we-ness, to the region. Nevertheless, it serves to reflect the various presuppositions of the partners involved and the undercurrents shared among intellectuals and activists. But at least it serves to make explicit and amplify the expectations of partners, intellectuals and activists co-opted in its operations. It is thus all the more necessary to inventory the ambiguities and biases taken at the beginning of this project. What kind of political and material autonomy ought to be accorded this new transversal institution? What conception of a 'Euro-Mediterranean region' does it put forward?

Even if the 'guiding principles of dialogue between cultures and civilisations' recall the stereotyped 'common history' sought after by European institutions, it also emphasises the goal of better understanding the Other so that, rather than changing him, one learns to coexist peacefully with him in a world in which our differences would be better recognised and, as a consequence, better respected. The 'us versus them' rhetoric is apparent already in the dichotomy of 'dialogue of civilisations', which presupposes the presence of two sides, in this case the West on one side, the Arab-Muslim world on the other.

'The "dialogue of civilisations"' one reads in a highly incisive report to the European Commission, 'derives from the polemical, not to say warmongering, concept of the *"clash of civilisations"*, and while it may be intended as a counterblast, it unfortunately shares the same logic in spite of itself by giving credence to the idea that the whole question is thrashed out between "blocs" distinguished by quasi-ontological differences.'[11] We need to transcend the civilisation paradigm to give substance to the idea of a deterritorialised Mediterranean identity by reinforcing the concrete attempts to bolster the human networks that form the portrait of a EuroMediterranean cultural community.

'Wider Europe' versus *'mare nostrum'*

Thus, the discourse that permeates the EuroMed project has consistently oscillated between two kinds of thinking, dualist and monist. The first presupposes the recognition of a fundamental cultural separation between the northern and southern shores of the Mediterranean and considers the EMP as an institutional bridge – from 'clash' to 'dialogue' – encouraging the creation of a 'zone of peace and stability'. The second insists on the common destiny of all partners of the EuroMed, in such a way as to transcend the intrinsically unequal nature of the relationship and thus to create the conditions for a more integrated 'secure community' to emerge. Perhaps better still than the European Union itself, the

Mediterranean can rely on solid cultural representations and practices to underpin, even superficially, such an argument. At the same time, there are enough 'realities on the ground' – from the status of women to the place of religion in social and political spheres, as well as the nature of state–society relations – to feed the dualist thinking. Perhaps sadly for idealists who dream of constructing a Mediterranean region, essentialist understandings of identity, be they European or Mediterranean, are bound to falter on the altar of modern socio-political realities.[12]

This dilemma remains fundamental if one states the problem in terms of a political project. Must the Mediterranean be considered as a line of demarcation, an interface between two cultural spheres, Europe and the Arab-Muslim world – in other terms, as the managed periphery of a 'Wider Europe'? Or must it be retransformed into *'mare nostrum'*, propagating its concentric waves always further towards the outside of a circle including twenty-seven, now thirty-six countries? An impossible choice, between colonial nostalgia and an integrative utopia.

Still, the important identity questions here do not so much concern stabilised representations but political processes that, in the long term, at the level of nation building or region building, contribute to the redesign or even the creation of collective identities or, rather, identity-frames that give meaning to 'secondary belongings'. In the framework of relations between Europe and countries on the other shore of the Mediterranean, the very idea of the Euro-Med region can be a new geographical frame – and, more implicitly, identity frame – thus a way of ideologically leveraging the exercise of normative power. So, if this innovative concept can lead the involved countries into reconsidering the way in which, until now, they represent to themselves their geopolitical environment, it could also help in the redefinition of their 'significant others'. While unsurprisingly the concept has had little impact on most EU countries, has it led the southern countries (for whom the relationship with EU countries is more central) to revise these perceptions and patterns of exclusion and 'othering'? Have we reached the stage where these countries have adopted the EuroMediterranean region as their new space of reference? While admitting that this transmutation can occur, is it compatible with the idea, dominant within many European circles, of the Mediterranean seen as an interface?

Part of the answer depends on the compatibility between this new transnational framework and the perception that each country has of its place in the region. If the compatibility is weak, the integrative potential of the EMP will also be weak; the same is true that a weak national identity contested from the inside will provoke mistrust *vis-à-vis* everything that can appear as an attempt at identity manipulation – such as the superposed concept of 'Euro-Med region'. The case of Israel illustrates rather well the dilemma any nation with poorly established identity references must face: 'The option of moving towards a different regional order exacerbates Israel's domestic identity conflicts, which, in turn, put a strain on engaging consistently in Euro-Mediterranean region-building. On the other hand, postponing crucial policy decisions increases societal cohesion, at least among Israel's Jewish majority, yet without solving Israel's crucial identity questions.'[13] Not only did the collapse of the peace process give new life to the vision of a nation struggling in a hostile environment for its survival, this identity crisis reinforced 'Israel's particularistic self-definition, and accentuates Israel's cognitive boundaries between "the Jewish State" and "the other".' Promoting regional integration totally loses its meaning when one realises that the perception Israelis have of themselves in their geopolitical environment corresponds largely to that of Ehud Barak who, in his time, compared Israel to a 'villa in the jungle'. Reticence is obviously reciprocal. Israel's participation in the EMP represents for Arab partners a serious obstacle to the construction of an inclusive region as long as Israel seeks to guarantee its security only through the unilateral use of force. The fact that Israel is largely seen as a European graft onto an Arab-Muslim root, like a prolonging of European colonisation, heightens Arab suspicion of European intentions in the region. Can this be the basis for conveying an alternative message to the US?

Most important, reticence *vis-à-vis* the EMP is also linked to the fear of seeing it as an attempt to divide the Arab world by excluding non-Mediterranean Arab countries. The gulf that exists between the old rhetoric about Arab unity and the absence of any real regional or sub-regional inclusion among the countries of the Maghreb or the Machrek only emphasises the difficulty for these countries to negotiate with the EU from a position of strength. In this sense, the expressed fears of European neo-colonialism through the EMP are less a reflection of Europe's attempt to counterbalance the exercise of American power, than the expression of divisions within the Arab world and of structural Arab dependence towards Europe.

In short, we must recognise that the EMP unavoidably creates new exclusionary boundaries: *vis-à-vis* the EU for an aspiring member like Turkey or for a self-perceived Western ally like Israel; *vis-à-vis* Europe's 'new neighbourhood' for non-Mediterranean Arab countries, which are socially and culturally linked to their neighbours, like Iraq or Mauritania. Furthermore, the fact that these borders are not stable, that they can move at decisive moments – when countries such as Malta or Cyprus, for example, pass abruptly from the status of non-members to that of members – contributes, paradoxically, to muddy the image of a potentially inclusive EuroMed region. If tomorrow the EU allows Turkey to join the club, followed by the inclusion of all the Balkan states, EuroMediterranean partners that are not members of the EU will be only Arab countries – with the additional very particular case of Israel – and the *face à face* between the northern and the southern shores of the Mediterranean may come to freeze the perception of a divide between civilisational worlds. If, on the other hand, Turkey is ultimately excluded, the *face à face* will even more blatantly be about 'Islam and the West'.

Is there then a real inclusive space that can counterbalance this logic of exclusion? As has been said, the notion of normative power can have an inclusive dimension, but only in an instrumental way; it is not sufficient to define a project – only through the restricted notion of exporting norms. If the EMP fails to take into account the manner in which the exercise of normative power interferes inevitably with identity questions that characterise nations or communities circling the Mediterranean, it risks ending up exacerbating rather than calming tensions throughout the region. When a political process touches fundamental questions linked to the way in which a nation defines itself, its promoters cannot just simply ask: 'What do we have in common that brings us together?' Rather, they must ask themselves to what extent, beyond the diversity of national projects, they share experiences that can be exploited, less as a means to an illusive sense of shared identity than as the basis for engaging in common projects for the future.

These shared experiences correspond in particular to the relatively recent appearance in the region of modern nation-states, themselves exclusive by nature, which, without any political transition, superimposed themselves on old networks of interpersonal sociability and thus ended heterogeneous societies which, until then, had resisted all attempts at cohesion. If *mare nostrum* evokes shared identities and overlapping communities, it can also refer to similar traumatic experiences linked to state building and to the process of homogenisation that accompanied it and that never fails to leave scars . . . absorbable on condition that the gradual work of mutual recognition is undertaken. If proof was necessary for this kind of awareness, the recent failure of the referendum for the reunification of Cyprus in April 2004 showed that the use by the EU and the UN of all the potential of normative power was far from sufficient for definitively mitigating an identity crisis with deep roots in colonial and post-colonial inheritance.

Exclusive memories, common experiences, interlocking societies

When trying to understand any process of community or region building, recourse to history obviously cannot substitute for an analysis of contemporary phenomena of political and social convergence. Still, a return to the past allows one to see the diverse, multiple and complex origins of Mediterranean communities – or for that matter European ones – and the differences that divide them. The modalities of nation building through which non-EU member Mediterranean countries like the Balkan countries have passed, offer many similarities from one country or one region to the other, illustrating what one could call a Mediterranean version of the process of homogenisation and exclusion in which European states played an essential catalyst role and through which they themselves passed in the nineteenth century.[14] If this process ended essentially during the first half of the twentieth century, it went on much longer in regions where coexistence between communities remained problematical (ex-Yugoslavia in the 1990s, the Middle East and the emblematic Palestinian question, Cyprus before and after the partition of 1974, etc.).

As a result, even more so than in Europe, today's most meaningful identity reference for a large majority of people in the region is their national identity. The nation-state remains the natural frame for the social and political life of most individuals living in either old or recent states. The multiculturalism of proto-national times is gone, and transnational community building cannot simply rest references to the past, on *souvenirs*. To the degree that, as it is commonly recognised, national identities are the product of conflicts about the same recurrent issue – drawing a line between the ins and the outs, citizens and aliens – national imagined communities, to use Benedict Anderson's expression, have unceasingly cultivated the collective memory of these tragic splits, albeit while denying their dark side. Each collective memory proposes its own national saga, cherishing irreducible identity references whose function follows the evolution of changing national realities.

If the main purpose of a 'dialogue between cultures and civilizations' is to unearth the roots of the many conflicts around the Mediterranean, then the partners must have the courage to revisit their past and the divisive memories therein. This effort must be made in a spirit that contributes to reconfiguring each community's identity in reference to its 'significant others', whereby instead of creating new transnational identities, collectivities learn to incorporate each other's identities in their own narrative. Indeed, this goal of founding a community on the basis of shared identities, rather than the construction of a common identity, ought to characterise the EU project itself.[15] The possible emergence of a single shared European identity is perhaps even more of a utopia than that of a Mediterranean one. Instead, and in both cases, a community can only be progressively built through the mutual confrontation and accommodation of unique and overlapping identities.

The collective appropriation of memories, as the antidote to the instrumental use of a cold, stereotyped but legitimising past, can help people recognise to what extent national sagas can be similar around the Mediterranean – and thus hedge the irreducible nature of national myths on which modern states have been built.[16] We could venture that greater awareness of the heterogeneity of their national community, would, in the long run, increase the self-confidence of these populations and strengthen the often fragile legitimacy of their state. In addition, the generalised recognition that exclusionary processes have long been a very common phenomenon, linked to the construction of modern nation-states, would in turn greatly facilitate the official acknowledgement of past 'crimes' committed by or on behalf of the state, as well as by communities against one another. This process, once engaged, would be able to contribute to the rediscovery, beyond the borders, of 'twin' or transnational communities and thus to create – or maybe recreate – a sense of shared experience, which is crucial to the kind of compatibility that ultimately underpins security communities.[17] Why then is it so difficult to engage in such a process of remembering and, as a result, of reconciliation?

The irony for the EMP is that the historical references that could underpin a sense of shared experience are in the countries of the Mediterranean basin *impossible references*: the collapse of the Ottoman Empire and the colonisation of the Arab world by the European powers. While intimately connected with the creation of modern nation-states in the region, these references can not be openly used in a political context.[18] Indeed, it is largely in opposition to these two realities (the Ottoman Empire and European colonisation) that nation-states of the Mediterranean basin (the northwest excluded) were built, both concretely and symbolically. How can a Serb recognise the fact that he still belongs, at the dawn of the twenty-first century, to an Ottoman cultural universe? How can a Tunisian or a Syrian accept the idea that it was the Turks and, even more, the French who initiated the creation of countries today named Tunisia or Syria? Mediterranean peoples need to learn that if they confront similar problems and perhaps share similar dreams today, this is to a great extent the result of a common past. This past that offers meaning does not date back to Phoenician or Arab trade, the mythical era of *mare nostrum* and its lingua franca, but to the recent past of the Ottoman era and the colonial era. In turn, European ex-powers must recognise more explicitly the fact that the relations they maintain with their neighbours in the South today are largely conditioned by the colonial heritage. This includes not only structural changes introduced during the colonial period and the decolonisation phase, whose effects are felt today, but also transformations that have affected their own societies as a result of migratory waves coming from the Mediterranean basin. Rebuilding ties among the people of the EuroMediterranean space requires uncovering this repressed knowledge and using these new interpretations of the past as levers to transform the present. We will come back in closing to concrete ideas on how to pursue such an agenda.

On the other hand, recognising that the multicultural components are in some way written into the national DNA, for the process of identifying the Other, is a step towards building a pluralistic secure community. Europeans, in particular, have a duty to engage in such a programme. If they want to appear credible at the moment they seek to make progress in regional integration, they must create dynamic links rather than use threats.

In the end, the two shores of the Mediterranean will understand each other all the better to the extent that their so-called partnership is about mutual enrichment from the confrontation of differences predicated on a sense of core compatibility, a sense that respective historical experiences make it possible to *listen* to one another. The detour through the history and memories of others is the key for each community to rediscover its own complexity and multiple heritages. Lack of recognition often results in social or political violence. On the other hand, recognising that the multicultural components are in some way written into the national DNA, and that the uniqueness of each community does not preclude the feeling of responsibility in the struggle of others with their own self-identification, all represent steps towards the building of a pluralistic security community. Europeans bear a particular responsibility to engage in such a journey. If they want to appear credible in their quest for regional integration, they must systematically favour positive linkages to threats and must not spare any symbolic or recognising gestures.

From that point of view, there is much to learn from a country 'between West and East' whose historic founder refused the idea of the impossible classic alternative faced by the peoples of the Muslim world: accepting Occidental values at the risk of losing its identity or refusing modernity to preserve its integrity. Modern Turkey, for Ataturk, had in fact contributed, just like other nations, to the construction of what he called 'contemporary civilisation' and thus made modernisation acceptable to its people.[19] In a certain way, the current attempt by the Erdogan

government to create a synthesis between Islam and modernity prolongs this post-civilisational vision, something that ought to inspire the
'normalisers' of Europe. EU blueprint drafters must learn to learn from
their neighbours.

Civilisation rhetoric, even when softened by the idea of a dialogue
between the West and Islam, reinforces perceptions against the reality,
for the South as for the North, is one of porous and profoundly intercon-
nected societies, in which the phenomena of convergence and accultur-
ation do not go in just one direction.

On one side, interdependent phenomena – such as urbanisation, generalised education, or the emergence of the middle classes – have been
the vectors for the penetration of values and Occidental lifestyles into
southern societies of the Mediterranean; on the other side, Mediterranean
culture – through music, dance, architecture, or even cuisine and fashion – has deeply penetrated Northern Europe, which was far from the
case not so very long ago. As for immigration, it has of course profoundly
transformed social norms and behaviours within European societies. As
the Experts' Report mentioned earlier says:

> It is precisely when 'civilizations' are so much in contact with each
> other that they start to blend, that the potential difference between
> them becomes problematic. This is not, then, so much a process of
> one civilisation forging ahead and the other lagging behind, but rather
> internal upheavals within each one, which, if they are on a large enough
> scale or last long enough, rapidly start to create a new area of civilisa-
> tion, a process which repeats itself in an ongoing cycle. Nowhere is
> there more of a difference between 'civilisations' than within these
> areas. As soon as one leaves behind the ideological register of general
> categorisations, one discovers the profusion of differences, distinc-
> tions and oppositions of which every society is made up.

In this sense, the double process of penetration and influence, from North
to South and from South to North, has already given a certain coherence
to the EuroMediterranean region, understood not as a limited physical
space but as a new dimension of the European construction with its own
dynamic. Throughout the region, as in Italo Calvino's *Invisible Cities*,
interpersonal networks, cultural exchanges and comparative advantages
come to draw crisscrossing lines under which hard borders between
'them' and 'us' eventually end up blurred.[20] In fact, seen from Europe,
'they' are not reducible to neighbours from over there, they have become
our 'next-door neighbours', uncomfortably familiar.

From this point of view, when the EU's efforts to promote changes in the countries south of the Mediterranean are presented as a simple explortation of universal values, older formulas come to mind – like the 'civilising mission' – and give an undeniably neo-imperialist flavour to the enterprise. Whatever European attempts to avoid falling into an Americanstyle hierarchical approach to cultural realities in the world might be, their reciprocal concept of universalism is in reality rather similar. As much as the notion of 'civilisation', it is therefore the notion of 'universalism' that should be questioned altogether, as did Edward W. Said, for whom it was not an absolute ideal for peoples or communities to attain but rather emerging through horizontal relationships between peoples and their interdependent writing of their respective narratives. Universalism thus understood becomes a means for transgressing existing boundaries and dominant power relations, since, based on this reading, power relations transcend geo-strategic realities and depend instead on the movement of people, the transnational nature of beliefs, or the de-territorialisation of conflicts.[21]

For the adoption of a post-colonial agenda

We need a truly post-colonial political agenda for the EuroMed project. To call for the adoption of such an agenda presupposes both recognising the weight of the colonial heritage in the relations that formerly colonised countries on the southern shore maintain with the former European colonial powers and inventing a new way of cooperating to build together a regional space that transcends this heritage. This of course is not easy. The EU, on its side, is caught between accusations of neo-colonialism when its conditionalities are too intrusive and perceptions of ineffectiveness as it lacks the full panoply of instruments for action available to its member states. Meanwhile, most partner countries' governments preside over systems that are structurally the product of colonial times and cannot claim to represent their people.

Perhaps the EU's current enlargement to the former satellite states of the Soviet Union contains the promise of a renewed approach on the part of countries which themselves are highly sensitive to the travails of hegemony. In short, a post-colonial agenda constitutes a call for taking seriously both the positive and negative potentials implied by the notion of normative power. It must lead us, first, to propose concrete measures to give the EMP a new face that empowers each party and, second, to consider the nature of relations between states and communities within the EuroMediterranean space.

Moving the Mediterranean back into the centre of the Euro-Mediterranean partnership

At the heart of the colonial relationship lie patterns of dependence and domination both between the metropolis and its periphery and within the colonised territory itself. It is against this colonial paradigm that the Euro-Med process was originally conceived symbolically according to principles of regional multilateralism and formal equality between states; though it is difficult to deny that the relationship thus established between the two shores of the Mediterranean remains a relation between object and subject. It follows that, in the long term, the process of community building in the region necessitates putting into practice, with imagination, the original principle of multilateralism in its true post-colonial version. In this regard, at least three complementary principles should be respected.

First, the need to answer repeated demands by players involved in the EuroMed project to accede to true co-ownership of the process could be correctly met with a much greater institutional autonomy in the EMP and through effective recentring away from Brussels. Certainly there are good reasons for running the EMP from Brussels. This is where the money and other 'hard' resources emanate from and where mechanisms of accountability have been founded. The EMP remains, for whatever it's worth, a contract between democratic and non-democratic states, in which the latter allow themselves to be 'bribed' in exchange for a certain degree of outside interference in their internal affairs through the exercise of the financial and normative power of the EU. In short, the principle of formal equality between partners cannot radically mitigate structural power asymmetries. But it can be progressively translated into a shift from the EMP as an EU 'policy' to the EMP as a partially *autonomous* reality from the EU itself, both institutionally and in terms of missions.

For that, its centre of gravity in Brussels would have to give way to common institutional forums situated around the Mediterranean. To date, the Euro-Mediterranean Foundation is the only such forum, perhaps because policy-makers think of culture as an innocuous subject. In the short term, it might be conceivable to decentralise implementing agencies in particular that have to do with the Mediterranean itself, such as sustainable development, tourism, or preservation of the patrimony.

Beyond these, and in the political field, such recentring, from decentralised implementation to formulation of policies, will depend on the maturation of the EMP more generally and on the domestic political agenda supporting it. To start with, much greater visibility should be given to the Euro-Mediterranean Parliamentary Assembly created in

2003 whose first session was held in Athens in March 2004, and whose original mission might not be strictly legislative but rather the promotion of democratic practices throughout the Euro-Mediterranean area. Eventually, the EMP should be supported by a jointly staffed secretariat and involve greater participation in the running of meetings and decision-making procedures of state administrations from the South. Why not adopt for the EMP the same rotating presidency that has so well served the EU? In the EU context, the holding of the presidency on a periodical basis may have been the greatest contributor to the *Europeanisation* of national administrations. This practice, which is characterised by dynamic learning-by-doing and 'baptism of fire', not only forces national bureaucracies to internalise the administrative cultures of their counterpart for the sake of successful bargaining, but also creates enormous incentives for the greater transparency of their own proceedings and better connections among their own disparate involvement with the EU. Obviously, the likely dynamic effects of a rotating presidency might very well be different in the EuroMed where authoritarian regimes do not encourage individual initiative or autonomy in segments of the state apparatus. Nevertheless, it is conceivable that at least similar effects of 'healthy' bureaucratic competition may deliver incremental increases in transparency and accountability in the South, which, albeit insufficient to qualify a regime as democratic nevertheless constitute essential components of democratic reform. As for EU member states such rotation specific to the EuroMed would mean that their presidency would not be hostage to other EU developments and would also contribute to focusing their efforts on the region. If socialisation of domestic bureaucratic elites constitutes a basic avenue for political change in the region, a rotating EuroMed presidency could have a significant effect. Nothing could better symbolise the idea of co-ownership of the partnership.

This approach would obviously raise a number of questions: What would an autonomous institutional set up actually look like? Given the financial implications, which authority would have ultimate control? What kind of relationship would exist between the different decision-making levels? What would be the conditions for the access to the facilities offered by these EMP institutions? How would its efficiency be assessed and personnel renewal ensured? Finally, while there is little doubt that governments from the South would be happy with more control, should we assume that they also want more responsibility? If there are fundamental structural limits to the confidence it is possible to have in authoritarian regimes successfully carrying out this process of transnational community building, how would these limits be managed?

The second principle that can guide such a 'recentring' towards the Mediterranean in our post-national agenda underscores the necessity for greater autonomy of the social sphere *vis-à-vis* the state. This principle is to make *empowerment* of groups and individuals the benchmark of EMP action, a principle which moreover represents a reversal of colonial patterns of subjugation of societies.

The example of the EU itself shows well that community building is not only about formal institutions. One of the earliest neo-functionalist insights about European integration was to underscore how *informal* integration – that links people separated by borders but whose collaboration allows them to promote common objectives – serves to support and deepen integration led by state policies. Of course the first implications to be drawn from this argument – knowing that cross-border links would lead to a transfer of loyalty onto the supranational level, as well as to spillover from one domain of integration to another – have yet to materialise. Still, European integration and the cost of adjustments it has necessitated over the years on the part of different social categories would doubtless not have been tenable without cross-border mobilisation of a multitude of groups (from women to human rights activists and of course unions, minorities, or even consumer associations), whose capacity for influence within each state has grown, thanks to the EU.

It could seem less pertinent to apply this logic in the framework of the EMP, where demands by civil society are addressed to the state rather than to supranational institutions. At the same time, precisely the lack of democratic legitimacy of the state, combined with generalised suspicion of externally imposed schemes, makes a bottom-up approach to transnationalism all the more necessary in the EMP context. This implies starting with, and giving greater prominence to, the so-called third basket, which deals with culture and civil society, singling it out for the kind of increased autonomy from the EU advocated above and magnifying its synergies with other areas. In short, it is not impossible to imagine that with the EMP, contrary to the EU, the *horizontal* opening of societies towards one another can precede, rather than result from, the *vertical* liberalisation of state–society relations.

One of the direct consequences of 11 September 2001 is the politicisation of culture by making it a subsidiary of the clash – or dialogue – of civilisations – and thus to have pointed out the need to no longer consider the cultural sphere as a minor dimension of the Barcelona Process. This in any case was conveyed by the Valencia Summit six months after 11 September through the inclusion of a new justice and home affairs component in the third 'basket' – thus promising to further ensure that political and cultural issues are dealt with in conjunction, both as part of a long-term region-building project. Shouldn't this logic be carried even further? As the group of Experts cited above said, we should 'allow the dialogue between peoples and cultures to inform the whole of Euro-Mediterranean relations and to give it that special quality which can humanise the impact of globalisation and the play of international relations within it'. Already, dense social networks exist in the Mediterranean which can be mobilised, including in the economic realm, where one of the core issues is to help in the connected development of Southern metropolis as hubs for the managed inclusion of these economies within the global economy. At the popular level, such transnational empowerment could be enhanced and symbolised by the support for the multiplication of EuroMed agora offering an open, transparent and publicised arena for meetings connecting civil societies and politicians from the region, which would start publicising this common framework.

Empowerment, in short, is not only about what the EU should do. It is also about how the populations across these states can empower each other. Ultimately, the value of such empowerment will be measured by the extent to which it is translated into the emergence of a Mediterranean citizenship (in the socio-political rather than legal sense), where citizenship is understood as being grounded in, and a means of, generating the key values of belonging, rights and participation.[22] All these values suggest hard won equality between citizens, unlike between colonised subjects: whether it is about equal capacity to identify with the collective space, to benefit from collective solidarity, or, especially, to intervene at least theoretically in the creation of laws. The day citizens from participating states become aware of this equality benchmark *among* their society and start protesting about it can be counted as the turning point when such a citizenship has started to emerge. In the meantime, the European Commission can take small steps to create the beginning of such a dynamic. In order to reinforce infra-state participation, some have proposed that delegations of the Commission in partner countries organise workshops within civil society. To the extent that this type of activity risks displeasing authorities of countries in the South, it could at least allow the differentiation of governments based on their capacity to increase political participation in civil society in regard to both internal and transnational plans (national action plans negotiated with certain neighbouring countries could function in this fashion for example).

However, the simultaneous adoption of complementary principles of autonomy and of empowerment of players must not mean the disengagement of states from the process – on the contrary.

In fact, the viability of these principles is predicated on the promotion of a third principle, *the ethics of responsibility* to guide the actions of the EU and of states in this turbulent region. In the first place, an ethic of responsibility presupposes that we know how to distinguish between, on the one hand, the process of community building strictly speaking and, on the other hand, the other kinds of policies established by the EU aimed at countries of the southern shore of the Mediterranean that continue – and for good reason – to function explicitly in the subject/object mode. Why not give a larger margin of manoeuvre to the EU so that the long process of building a EuroMediterranean region does not prevent the use of its coercive strength to apply pressure and to incite partner states from the South to adopt reforms aimed at, for example, promoting democracy, the rule of law and citizen participation, accompanying the American presence both critically and constructively? By default, the process will remain hostage to contradictory forces. It is thus, for example, for the use of conditionality, which, according to Gillespie, must only be used exceptionally, to signal to populations of partner countries that the EU is ready to take a position in favour of democratic values.

Such a separation between spheres – the EU on one side and the EMP on the other – must reinforce in turn the capacity of EU member states to act on their own initiative in the region, in the framework of bilateral actions in which a state-to-state relationship is sometimes more pertinent and keeps the Barcelona Process from being a pretext for inaction. In short, genuine region building on one side could enhance the leverage of both the EU and member states towards countries of the South. In addition, member states ought to exercise power and influence in parallel and in concert with the EU. The EU cannot substitute for national diplomacy, especially for countries like France, Britain, Greece and Italy. To be sure, it may be most desirable to see these countries act and speak in the region 'in the name of the EU', lending their own ties to EU normative powerhood, but such obligations of diplomatic mutuality should remain fluid in the current political context. The EU should practise in its foreign policy realm what it preaches for others: learn to live with its internal differences and exploit its member states' comparative advantages.[23] Often, individual member states can go much further in the purely political dimension of the relationship: France must continue to have its 'Arab policy' while Sweden can be relied upon to lend all its weight to multilateral projects such as the Anna Lindh Foundation in Alexandria.

A shared culture, a deterritorialised region

We believe that in the end it is unlikely that a regional identity can be consciously built only with political and institutional means, but these can contribute to the creation of conditions in which other constitutive factors can emerge. It is difficult to imagine building a region starting from scratch, but this is not the case in the Mediterranean. It exists in the imagination of many and represents in itself a source of shared meanings that must be exploited.[24] When we ask about these shared meanings, it seems crucial, however, to escape once and for all the trappings of the nation-state construct. Indeed, while there are fascinating debates on the determinant grounds for the construction of national identities – essentialist *versus* functionalist, historical or political, etc. – one thing is sure: the sense of belonging in nation-states is rooted in territory. We believe that the promise of the EuroMediterranean idea lies precisely in this proposition: the construction of a non-territorialised region.

The EuroMed must not aspire to be yet another 'bounded identity community', whose limits need to be defined as in today's EU. Rather, it should be thought of as a process and an idea that, from the bottom-up, contribute in creating we-ness in an area of the world referred to as the EuroMediterranean region, but whose reality radiates well beyond the shores of this sea itself. Such a perspective is embedded in a broader call to move beyond territory in our understanding of international relations, not in the name of some unstoppable phenomenon of globalisation, but simply because there are many types of boundaries that matter, which cannot simply be superimposed.[25] In the words of Adler and Crawford, 'the new literature on regionalism no longer conceptualizes regions in terms of geographical contiguity, but rather in terms of purposeful social, political, cultural, and economic interaction among states which often (but not always) inhabit the same geographical space.'[26] This is especially true for the Mediterranean, where many informal contacts exist between people who share this space as a reference but not necessarily as a place to live in. Region building, if it is to escape the territorial logic, must be based on elements other than the state, such as informal networks of cooperation, value dialogue, and transnational networks of information and communication. All these elements link groups and individuals who live in different socio-political environments but who nevertheless have something to share. We advocated above partially taking the cultural realm out of state hands precisely because, in the Mediterranean context, this realm has a strong potential for helping to transcend territorial logic and for creating a new kind of polycentric and borderless institutionalised community.

Otherwise stated, to use the Mediterranean as a common reference for building a collective project is not the same as building a 'Mediterranean identity', inevitably exclusive of the non-Mediterranean. Indeed, how could people from all the EU member states, from Dublin to Krakow, be engaged in the building of a EuroMediterranean region on the basis of a territorially defined identity? Instead, the shared motivation for this project must lie in the sense that the EuroMed area is one where identities have long been intertwined and increasing mutually shaped. Thus, have not European countries all become Mediterranean through immigration, whose effects are amplified by historical ties? If countries like Germany or the United Kingdom have been long present in the Mediterranean, others, such as Holland or Denmark, are becoming in turn increasingly multicultural and 'Mediterraneanised'. Of course, all EU member states do not need to feel as concerned or as involved in the EMP process. And yet, precisely because north-eastern EU members hold the least territorial vision of the Euro-Med, such as it exists, it is they who could give real substance to the non-'EU centric' nature of the Euro-Med. So, while for Italy, recentring means moving the Brussels institutions to Naples, it means, for a Swede, moving Brussels to Alexandria. Beyond this, Warsaw would perhaps be more in phase with the universal nature of the Mediterranean challenge, precisely because it considers the Euro-Med to be a political transition founded on cultural bases that transcend a particular space.

EU policy aimed at encouraging sub-regional groupings goes in this direction, in particular when such groupings are not founded on geographical proximity, as two free-trade agreements illustrate, the one signed in Agadir in 2001 between Morocco, Tunisia, Egypt and Jordan, the other in April 2004 between Morocco and Turkey. Although these groupings concern the economic sphere, they echo other evolutions in social and/or political fields. In the sociological realm, internal divisions within each of the countries are much deeper than international divisions. It is thus easier to find actual or potential 'intermediaries' among the educated upper middle class northern or southern countries, sharing the same values and lifestyles and perhaps more willing to share their differences. A Turk from the Aegean Sea would doubtless have more affinity with an Italian from Mezzogiorno than with another Turk from East Anatolia. If the latter emigrated to Hamburg, he would perhaps feel less at ease in his new environment than a compatriot from Istanbul on a business trip to Munich. Such transnational patterns of identification constitute the essential components of progressive consolidation of a Mediterranean region.

More important still, this transnational cultural approach to the process of community building is the most promising response to the dualist frame – Arab/Muslims versus Euro/Christians. First, it promotes the value of multiple but overlapping cultures, transnational communities, and phenomena of ancient and modern nomadism. Second, it is the best counterpoint to structural inequality between the North and the South, since it targets and seeks to empower individuals directly. Let us take for example the Sephardic Jews who live in Israel. While early supporters of Likud policies in the regional context, their domestic status as a socially and economically dominated group and their continued attachment to their 'Oriental' homelands and cultures, gives them a potential role in bringing together people across states who have much to share in terms of past experiences, ways of life or even ways of referring to tradition and religion. In the same vein, networks of immigrants, especially beginning with the second generation, already contribute to reducing the cultural separation between their countries of origin and their host countries, and they could be empowered to do it more systematically and more broadly. Descendants of refugees, victims at different times of deportations or ethnic purifications – whether they are Greeks from Asia Minor, Turks from Macedonia, Muslim Bosnians from Banja Luka, Serbs from Osijek, Palestinians from Haifa, or Jews from Iraq – must be encouraged to reconsider revisiting the way they perceive 'the other' by confronting their mutual memories and experiences, thus potentially becoming new 'go-betweens' in their local micro-cosmos. It goes without saying that the Balkan countries (not yet members of the EMP) ought to be included as soon as possible in this process of community building.

Concretely, the Foundation for Dialogue between Cultures, recently created, is well positioned to support practices promoting this kind of collective learning process. As the first and only institution created in the framework of the EMP, it is poised to serve as a regional catalyst for a movement of multifaceted recognition of overlapping identities in the region, both through the empowerment of civil society actors and through state channels. Indeed the principle of *mutuality* or *mutual recognition*, which interprets and gives concrete expression to the search for compatibility among our differences, is crucial to the legitimacy of the entire learning process.

In this spirit, one possible early initiative that could be taken by the Foundation could be called 'the project on shared memories'. It would consist in revealing current expressions of the past as reflections of communities' shared roots, in particular, by collecting individual and collective testimonies from those who experienced the schisms and conflicts that accompanied the consolidation of nations in the region. Such testimonies would constitute the basis for analysing similar historical realities across nations and therefore for highlighting the existence of transnational Mediterranean experiences. They could then be broadcasted to the populations of these regions, along with the shaping and diffusion of a new discourse on the part of academics, intellectuals, school teachers and artists, who then could start giving substance to the emerging notion that Mediterranean peoples are linked by shared traumas, fractures and denials, and that they may be able to transcend them by confronting them together.

We must stress, however, that we do not see such 'memory work' – *travail de mémoire* – advance in the EuroMed framework, as bypassing the state. On the contrary. States in the region have a crucial role to play here as agents of recognition, that is by giving official recognition to the hardships inflicted on dominated communities by dominating states and communities. In many cases, symbolic acts and institutions at the state level give visibility and legitimacy to sub-state interactions. Such considerations are crucial if a regional process of mutual recognition is to be translated into political capital for the sake of further integration in EMP functional fields, such as security, economics and the environment. Recognition by governments that sub-national communities may also be part of transnational communities will in turn go a long way to support the notion that these communities matter in the relationship between Europe and the Mediterranean as a whole. In both spaces, transversal identity patterns overlap with national identities and other infra- or supra-national identities.

In sum, the relationship goes both ways: the consolidation of dense networks among transnational cultural communities gives substance to state-to-state, region-to-region relationships, and, in turn, the involvement of states in the 'management of meaning' gives *gravitas* to the process itself. Indeed, the spirit of mutual recognition ought not to be limited to the treatment of culture, but should, in the context of democracy promotion, for example, evolve towards the question of the values that underlie political reform. Shared historical narrative can in turn help make visible the shared aspirations of the people doing the sharing and help replace political values – such as liberalism, pluralism and even democracy – in a proper comparative historical context for the societies concerned, while blending them with local cultural realities. In Gillespie's words: 'liberalism should be promoted to the extent of pursuing a joint commitment to effective pluralist structures, not as a preordained and comprehensive set of common values around which Euro-Mediterranean convergence must take place. In practical terms this would involve a common search for types of political reform and institutional structures capable of embracing both religious and secular liberal values.'[27]

Short of such a blending of values, democracy in this region risks failing for lack of 'democrats'.[28] Why would Mediterranean societies still living under authoritarian regimes be exempt from the same growing pains of modernity as other societies before them, with all the inevitable regressions and dynamics of correlative resistance? Why would external institutions that are supposed to nurture this spirit of modernity and empower local groups that defend it not reflect these groups' very own reckoning with religion, history and politics?

What does all this mean for the European Union itself? We have tried to show that the EuroMed must not be seen as an extension of the EU model to its neighbours, but rather an alternative or complementary project of community building. The EU must effectively accept the idea that it is not necessarily a laboratory for the Mediterranean region and that the EuroMed pertains to a different logic.

Is that the whole story? Such an affirmation presupposes that the essential character of the EU be uncontested, whether it is or is not the pure product of territorial logic. The rejection of the European Constitution by populations voting in referendums, a continual scepticism in relation to the democratic deficit in the EU, and the collective introspection provoked by the 'Turkish question' show us, on the contrary, that the EU is struggling with the challenge that building a true political community represents. One may actually argue that, in essence, the EU is an association of the peoples of Europe, a *demoï-cracy* in the making, a federal union of nation states, rather than a federal state.[29] The principles of constitutional tolerance and mutual recognition between states are at the heart of the European project also.

Of course, a significant fraction of public and elite opinion in the EU is far from having embraced such a vision. Alternative statist paradigms of integration, embraced by sovereignists or supranationalists, are in fact still dominant. But the new Constitution in many ways was a step in the self-representation as *demoï-cracy*, compatible with understanding the EU as an exercise in the sharing of identities rather than in the merger into a single European identity. Such an exercise of course should be open to the world and socialise Europeans into recognising 'the other', whether fellow European or non-European. It should lead to acceptance of the principle of mutual inclusiveness in each other's policy, not only *vis-à-vis* other Europeans, such as the EU practices today, but also *vis-à-vis* partners, such as those from the EuroMed. We are far from living in such a world.

In the meantime, and only to stimulate reflection, we may for once try to inverse the EU's self-aggrandising proposition of serving as a model for the rest of the world. What if one day the EuroMed process were to serve, in a subtle fashion, as a laboratory for the EU, endowed with new forms of mutual recognition adapted to contexts subject to conflict? What if it could be a laboratory for the honing of overlapping identities, binding together groups and individuals? What if one day, finally, beyond Europe and the EU, the experience of the EuroMed became the source of inspiration for a new kind of truly universal transnational politics?

The reader will pardon us if we conclude very concretely with an idea we hold dear. Why not literally build a capital for the Mediterranean region that would symbolically incarnate, in the eyes of a wide public, the idea of a EuroMed community in the process of becoming? Why not situate such a capital *in* the Mediterranean itself (but neither in Malta nor in Cyprus, because, since their accession to the EU, the two islands have lost their 'intermediary' status)? In fact, why not deterritorialise completely the capital by placing it on . . . a ship? And why not share this ship among the many intertwined communities of the region by making it journey around the Mediterranean, casting anchor in a new port every six months or every year? Why not make it the expression of human and social roots in the region by organising a big pan-EuroMed festival each time it changes ports, exhibiting artistic and cultural creations of all peoples and communities who recognise themselves in it? Why could it not serve, between these biannual events, as a Mediterranean agora, both for some of the many official or semi-official meetings the EMP would hold and for more spontaneous citizen events? What more beautiful symbol for this Mediterranean region that may one day exist, beyond the territorial logic that has caused its political decadence in recent centuries.

Notes

1. We would like to thank Penny Allen for her assistance.
2. Samuel P. Huntington, *The Clash of Civilizations and the Remaking of the World Order* (New York: Simon and Schuster, 1996); appeared in French with the title *Le Choc des civilisations* (Paris: Odile Jacob, 1997). Read the critical analysis proposed by Dario Battistella, 'Recherche ennemi désespérément . . . Réponse à Samuel Huntington à propos d'un affrontement à venir entre l'Occident et l'Islam', *Confluences Méditerranées*, 12, Autumn 1994, republished in no.40, Winter 2001–2.

3. See Georges Corm, *Orient-Occident, la fracture imaginaire* (Paris: La Découverte, 2002).
4. See Eric Philippart, 'The Euro-Mediterranean Partnership: a Critical Evaluation of an Ambitious Scheme', *European Foreign Affairs Review*, 8, 2003, pp. 201–20.
5. See Emanuel Adler, 'Imagined (Security) Communities: Cognitive Regions in International Relations', *Millennium*, 26(2), 1997, pp. 249–77; and Emanuel Adler and Michael Barnett (dir.), *Security Communities* (Cambridge: Cambridge University Press, 1998).
6. Emanuel Adler and Beverly Crawford, ' "Normative power" and the European Practice of Region Building: the Case of the Euro-Mediterranean Partnership', introduction of *The Convergence of Civilizations*.
7. Richard Whitman, *From Civilian Power to Superpower? The International Identity of the European Union* (London and New York: Macmillan/St. Martin's Press, 1998).
8. Robert Kagan, *Of Paradise and Power: America and Europe in the New World Order* (New York: Knopf, 2002).
9. Kalypso Nicolaïdis and Robert Howse, ' "This is my EUtopia . . .": Narrative as Power', *Journal of Common Market Studies*, 40(4), 2002, pp. 767–92.
10. EuroMed report no. 59, European Community, May 2003.
11. EuroMed report no. 68, European Community, December 2003. The 'Group of Experts', author of this report entitled 'Le Dialogue entre les peoples et les cultures dans l'espace Euro-Méditerranéen', submitted to the then-President of the European Commission, Romano Prodi, was co-presided by Assia Alaoui Bensalah and Jean Daniel, and composed of the following people: Malek Chebel, Juan Diez Nicolas, Umberto Eco, Shmuel N. Eisenstadt, George Joffé, Ahmed Kamal Aboulmagd, Bichara Khader, Adnan Wafic Kassar, Pedrag Matvejevic, Rostane Mehdi, Fatima Mernissi, Tariq Ramadan, Faruk Sen, Faouzi Skali, Simone Susskind-Weinberger and Tullia Zevi.
12. See Jean-François Bayart, *L'Illusion identitaire* (Paris: Fayard, 1996); and Michael Wintle (ed.), *Culture and Identity in Europe: Perceptions of Divergence and Unity in Past and Present* (Aldershot: Avebury, 1996).
13. See Raffaella A. Del Sarto, 'Israel's Contested Identity and the Mediterranean', *Mediterranean Politics*, 8(1), Spring, 2003, pp. 27–58.
14. See Dimitri Nicolaïdis, 'Penser l'identité nationale', *Les Temps Modernes*, no. 548, March 1992, pp. 19–51.
15. See Kalypso Nicolaïdis, 'Demos et Demoî: fonder la Constitution', *Lignes* (NS), 13, February, 2004, pp. 88–109; and ' "We, the Peoples of Europe . . ." ', *Foreign Affairs*, 83(6), November–December 2004, pp. 97–110.
16. See 'Mémoires en miroir. Autour d'une Méditerranée plurielle', monograph in *La Pensée de midi*, 3, Winter 2000; and Maria Todorova (dir.), *Balkan Identities: Nation and Memory* (London: Hurst, 2004).
17. See for an example of this the admirable initiative of a group of forty-seven women from ex-Yugoslavia and Albania who made a trip in the Spring of 2002 along the new borders separating their countries, an initiative related in the bilingual work (French/English) of Ghislaine Glasson Deschaumes and Svetlana Slapsak (dir.), *Femmes des Balkans pour la paix. Itinéraires d'une action militante à travers les frontières*, Transeuropéénnes/Réseaux pour la culture en Europe, 2002.
18. See Dimitri Nicolaïdis, 'Méditerranées, des mémoires en souffrance', *Rive. Revue de politique et de culture méditerranéennes*, 3, 1997, pp. 12–18; and

Georges Corm, *L'Europe et l'Orient. De la balkanisation à la libanisation. Histoire d'une modernité inaccomplie* (Paris: LaDécouverte, 1989).

19. See Metin Heper, 'Turkey "Between East and West"', *The Convergence of Civilizations*.
20. See Jocelyne Cesari (dir.), *La Méditerranée des réseaux. Marchands, entrepreneurs et migrants entre l'Europe et le Maghreb* (Maisonneuve and Larose, 2002).
21. Edward W. Said, *Culture et impérialisme,* (Paris: Fayard, 2000) (first edition in English: 1993). See also Thierry Hentsch, *L'Orient imaginaire. La vision politique occidentale de l'Est méditerranéen* (Paris: Editions de minuit, 1988); Bertrand Badie, *La Fin des territores,* (Paris: Fayard, 1995); and Sophie Bessis, *L'Occident et les autres. Histoire d'une suprematie* (Paris: La Decouverte, 2001).
22. Richard Bellamy, Dario Castiglione and Emilio Santoro, *Lineages of European Citizenship: Rights, Belonging, and Participation in Eleven Nation-States* (New York: Palgrave Macmillan, 2004).
23. Kalypso Nicolaïdis, 'Living with our Differences', in Nikos Kotzias and Petros Liacouras (dir.), *EU–US Relations: Repairing the Transatlantic Rift* (Basingstoke: Palgrave Macmillan, 2004).
24. Michelle Pace, *The Politics of Regional Identity: Meddling with the Mediterranean* (London: Routledge, 2005).
25. See John G. Ruggie, 'Territoriality and Beyond: Problematizing Modernity in International Relations', *International Organization*, 47(1), 1993, pp. 139–74.
26. Adler and Crawford '"Normative power" and the European practice of Region Building'.
27. See Richard Gillespie, 'A Political Agenda for Region-Building? The EMP and Democracy Promotion in North Africa', in *The Convergence of Civilisations*.
28. Ghassan Salame (dir.), *Démocratie sans démocrates. Politiques d'ouverture dans le monde arabe et islamique* (Paris: Fayard, 1994).
29. See footnote 14 and also Kalypso Nicolaïdis, 'La France doit changer d'UEtopie', *Le Monde*, 27 May 2005, p. 15.

Part IV
Geopolitical Fears and Institutional Responses

11
Europe, America and the 'Greater' Middle East

Martyn Bond

Introduction

If you took out a new subscription to the prestigious American journal *Foreign Relations* in the latter half of 2004, the publishers would offer you a free copy of Huntington's classic *Clash of Civilizations*. On the one hand that may say something about falling demand and a savvy way to dispose of remaindered copies, but on the other it may also demonstrate a conscious gesture of support for the thesis contained in the book. After all, several strands of American thought and many economic interests come together in defining external opposition around the world of Islam and internal loyalty attached to Christian belief and observance. In America, neo-conservatives, oil interests and the Christian right have found an alliance, if not completely in their philosophical underpinnings, at least in their foreign policy recommendations.

The G8 initiative

In June 2004 the G8 meeting at Sea Island, Georgia, endorsed a document offering *Partnership for Progress and a Common Future with the Region of the Broader Middle East and North Africa*. It offered partnership 'based on genuine cooperation with the region's governments, as well as business and civil society representatives, to strengthen freedom, democracy, and prosperity for all'. The initiative was born of compromise between the broad aims of American foreign policy in the region and the continuing concerns of the Europeans, for whom the Mediterranean and the Middle East are their own backyard.

The document spelled out the principles on which the initiative itself was based: peace and stability as essentials; the resolution of conflicts – especially the Israeli–Palestinian conflict – as an important element of progress in the region; political and administrative reforms to play a significant role in resolving conflicts; the restoration of peace and stability specifically in Iraq; such reforms resting on the countries of the region, not imposed from outside; respect for diversity and local conditions; involvement of the business sector and civil society as well as governments; and recognition that this initiative implied a long-term effort, a generational commitment.

The Partnership launched at Sea Island acknowledged previous work carried out in the Euro-Mediterranean Partnership (Barcelona Process), the US Middle East Partnership Initiative and the somewhat less important Japan–Arab Dialogue. It planned to focus on three areas: political, social and cultural, and economic. The document is full of laudable activities, such as a micro-financing facility, encouragement for literacy, support for business, entrepreneurship and vocational training, a new Private Enterprise Development Facility at the IFC, a task-force on investment, efforts to broaden participation in public and political life, to support free and transparent elections, to encourage parliamentary exchanges, to expand women's role in society, to pursue judicial reform, to encourage an independent judiciary and independent media, good governance and anti-corruption efforts, to strengthen civil society, to reform education systems, to enhance digital access, to facilitate remittances from overseas, to help create fair, secure and well-functioning property rights, to promote intra-regional and global trade involving the whole region, even to hold regular ministerial meetings.

It is a long list, illustrating the all-embracing nature of the initiative, and the principles on which it rests are unexceptional. They belong to the mainstream of international development, even though they smack perhaps of a greater degree of conditionality and intervention than some of the Arab governments concerned would like. A year previously – but that was before the war in Iraq – the proposals when still in draft form met fierce criticism from Arab governments for their implied imposition of democracy and good governance on a western model. After the invasion of Iraq the caravan has moved on and the final document uses less strong language. All the parties – including the Americans – are more anxious to cooperate.

The overarching political forum for the initiative is welcomed as an opportunity for 'discussion' and 'learning together'. The 'rich cultural history of the region' is acknowledged and the overt conditionality of earlier is no longer so apparent. And the sum involved – $100 million in the first instance – while not generous given the number of countries and the populations involved, is not insignificant.

The G8 between Washington and Brussels

One of the problems with initiatives such as this, which rightly reflect G8 priorities, is uncertainty about how far they can be applied in practice since they require the willing cooperation of other governments and, in this case, other actors from within the targeted societies. In the current climate all initiatives from America are seen in the dual focus of Iraq and the Israeli–Palestinian conflict. Uncertainty about the prospects for the much trumpeted road map for resolving the Israeli–Palestinian issue that accompanied the invasion of Iraq cast doubts on the motivation for what by all appearances was and is a laudable initiative. Past experience of western involvement in the region, with its overwhelming concern for securing oil supplies and reserves, led to what at best could be described as uncertainty about the nature of the western governments' real interests in this initiative.

But to speak of 'western' interests may already be to pre-judge the issue and the initiative. There are useful and practical distinctions to be drawn between the interests of America and of European states in the region. Although major European states subscribed to this initiative alongside the USA, their motivation and their track record are appreciated by leaders in the region somewhat differently.

Sometimes referred to as 'Europe's uncertain pursuit of Middle East reform', the European Union has at least got a track record of consistent involvement in the Mediterranean region that goes back for a respectable period of time. It reaches back well into colonial history two or more generations ago when French migration to North Africa and British imperial interests in the Suez Canal meant that for France and Britain above all what happened around the old Roman *mare nostrum* was considered in their respective capitals as of vital importance. Even after the painful unravelling of that history with the repatriation of the *pieds noirs* and the debacle of Suez in the mid-1950s, cultural as well as economic and political interest in the region remained high. Essentially the interest of Europeans in the region is currently to extend the zone of stability they have secured in Europe itself by helping to solve – or at worst to keep at bay – the social, demographic, environmental and cultural issues that afflict the region. After all, the region is Europe's backyard or soft underbelly, depending on your choice of image, and problems have to be solved there if the Europeans want to stop them from spreading to Europe itself.

The European track record

As the European states organised themselves during the latter half of the last century so their concern for the region became formalised. They developed a common policy towards the region culminating in the Barcelona Agreement in 1995. Since then the European Union has poured considerable sums into cooperation with the Mediterranean states, with 1.243 billion euros earmarked for 2005/2006. Algeria was to receive 106 million, Egypt 243 million, Jordan 110 million, Lebanon 70 million, Morocco 275 million, Syria 80 million and Tunisia 144 million euros. Over and above these sums, which make the financial support for the G8 initiative seem rather meagre by comparison, the region as a whole is to receive a further 215 million euros. As outgoing External Relations Commissioner Chris Patten put it, 'This decision illustrates the extent of our political commitment to the Euro-Mediterranean Partnership; we put our money where our mouth is. We are determined to continue developing the Barcelona Process to foster democratic stability, security and sustainable development throughout the Euro-Med region, against a background of increasing interdependency between the EU and its Southern neighbours.'

This increasing interdependency is real. The figures for several of the states around the southern shore of the Mediterranean show an export dependency on the EU of close to 70 per cent. The EU in turn is dependent on Algeria and Libya for 30 per cent of its energy needs in gas and oil. These economic statistics are just the tip of the iceberg for a range of human contacts that they necessitate and the mutual understanding that flows from them. Educational exchanges, formal cultural links and joint research activities are also extensive and add to the complexity of the texture of the relationship between the EU and its partner states in the Mediterranean basin.

But it is not just the distinction between the much more serious financial involvement of the Europeans when compared with American efforts in the region that matters. Nor is it just the long roots of European involvement which contrast with the more recent commitment of the US to the region. There are even more fundamental differences in the way Washington and Brussels define the region, and through their differing definitions envisage different policies towards the countries involved.

Disparate definitions

The preferred US terminology is the 'Greater Middle East'. For the US administration this includes not only the Mediterranean states but stretches as far as Afghanistan, the former Soviet states, Iran, Iraq, the Gulf states and Saudi Arabia. Widening the Middle East to this extent lends the definition a threatening coloration. It throws up the issue of oil supplies, the threat of terrorism and the problem of failed or failing states. Seen in this perspective, the definition calls for a security component to be dominant in any policy response. It opens the door for intervention to assure stability and security, to further values and interests. These are American priorities.

For the Europeans, on the other hand, the preferred definitions divide the Mediterranean states (plus Jordan) from the states beyond. The EU is keen to focus on issues such as demography, migration, environment, transport, economic and social development, education and cultural relations – essentially a soft-security agenda without obvious military implications. Experience has shown that this agenda can be pursued within the Mediterranean dialogue despite the running sore of Israeli–Palestinian relations. And relations with Arab and other states beyond this circle can be treated in a different manner, often on an individual state-to-state or state-to-EU basis, where the differentiation, which the EU insists is necessary in relations with the disparate states of America's 'Greater Middle East', can better be assured.

Clearly the US approach plays down the civilian aspects which the EU is keen to play up, while the EU plays down the security and especially the military implications of relations in the area. Policy recommendations flowing from these different analyses have a quite different emphasis.

The EU concentrates on economic development, essentially through the MEDA programme, complemented by the individual member states' additional financial efforts in respect of particular states around the Mediterranean with which they individually have close or good relations. It implies considerable latitude for partners to adapt assistance to local conditions and to manage development at varying speeds, in some cases with a very long-term perspective.

The US approach is altogether more in a hurry. It aims at speedier internal adaptation to global pressures, if necessary with radical alterations to the administrative and economic culture of the states concerned. Within the Greater Middle East, that clearly includes regime change and does not exclude the possibility of pre-emptive action.

Both the US and the EU are concerned to see secure and stable states as partners in the region – large or small – but the Europeans are prepared to play a longer game in what they see as a slow process of development. This development includes the modernisation of Islam, at least in its social impact on Muslim societies, and its impact within EU society. But the US seems impatient to go further and encourage a fast transition to modernity defined as democratic government and a capitalist economy, recognisable features in US eyes of all developed states in the modern world.

Sticks, carrots and opportunities

The EU and the US have different sticks and carrots to offer in order to achieve their aims in relation to states of the Mediterranean and the Greater Middle East. For the special case of Turkey, the EU offers the prospect of accession. For Palestine it offers massive financial assistance targeted as relief for refugees and associated support. For Algeria and Libya it offers economic partnership as the closest developed market for their oil and gas. The US, on the other hand, can concentrate its aid in bilateral support, essentially for Israel and for Egypt. It can also project its potential force from a position of local strength, especially naval strength in the Mediterranean and through its military agreements with both Turkey, Israel and several other states in the region.

In terms of Kagan's classic thesis, the Americans are from Mars and the Europeans are from Venus. The contrast of the two shows up clearly in the Middle East. The US is identified with hard power, the EU with soft power.

But there is not only a difference of style and of instruments of policy between the two sides of the Atlantic. There are also real and enduring differences of interest and of opinion which divide the USA and the EU in the region, and which underlie the unease with which many Europeans view the actions of their powerful ally in the Middle East. The key document which brought this into the open was the Venice Declaration of the European Community twenty years ago concerning the Israeli–Palestinian conflict, with its evident partiality towards the Palestinian position.

Now that Yassir Arafat has died and there is new leadership in the Palestinian authority, now that the power of Likud in the Knesset has had to seek support from the opposition to put through its plans for Gaza and the Occupied Territories, now that George Bush has been re-elected and may be under less obligation than before to the Jewish lobby in the US, there may be a window of opportunity for making progress on the stalled road map for solving this bitter and long-standing problem. Certainly making progress here would defuse much of the anti-American and anti-western feeling that easily fuels extremism in the region. Reaching a settlement might even reverse the process and develop good will for those who manage to broker a just and lasting peace.

Abiding distinctions

But there will remain some basic facts within both the EU and the US which will not go away and which will continue to press the US and the EU to differing analyses of events in the region.

The EU is home to over six million migrants from the Mediterranean basin, while there are at least as many Jews living in the United States as there are in Israel. The EU is a physical neighbour to the states of the Mediterranean and the Middle East – more so now that Cyprus and Malta have recently become members and that negotiations are shortly to open with Turkey. America lies several thousand miles away across the Atlantic. There is no denying the facts of geography.

And when we seriously review historical links, then the role of Islam within European development appears in a considerably brighter light. Notions of tolerance and rational scientific exploration – which we attribute normally to the eighteenth-century Enlightenment and the fourteenth- and fifteenth-century Renaissance – have roots hundreds of years earlier in the golden age of Islamic Spain. Christian and Islamic strands within and around Europe have always been closely interwoven. That is simply not the case with the United States.

It is not easy for America as the overwhelming superpower to acknowledge that the European experience of the Middle East and the Mediterranean may be more rich and subtle, and may lead to better policy recommendations than their more recent perception. In their defence they can argue that the European 'softly, softly' approach has not delivered what it promised. The Arab states are the least democratised of any region in the world, and on several social indicators they show worse progress than any other region over recent years. Above all – in the view of the mind-set that widens the definition of the area to the Greater Middle East – the region is a source of terrorism, and after 9/11 America is not prepared to countenance any normal relations with states that harbour or encourage terrorism.

This divergence of approach shows most clearly in the differing policies of America on the one hand and Britain, France and Germany on the other vis-à-vis Iran. While the Europeans are keen to pursue 'positive engagement' with Iran even to the point of assisting the development of nuclear power, America classifies the country, along with North Korea, as part of the notorious 'axis of evil'.

Unanswered questions

There are myriad questions thrown up not only by the relationship of the EU and the US to each other but also their individual relationships with the Mediterranean and the Middle East, let alone the Greater Middle East as the G8 now define it. A brief introductory talk or a short article cannot do justice to them all. But some issues and some questions are so basic that they need repeating if only to offer beacons among the shifting sands of day-to-day events and the policy adjustments which follow them. It was Dr Johnson who once wisely wrote, 'Mankind needs reminding more than it needs informing.'

First there is the close interdependence of the developed West with the energy supplies from the region. The West would not enjoy the economic standard of living that it does without the oil and gas of the Middle East regularly supplied at whatever price can be struck between supplier and consumers. Hence energy reserves as well as current supplies are a vital interest for the West, and a fair price is in the interests of all partners. What the West will do to preserve what it sees as a vital interest is a sharply divisive question, especially in Europe, as reaction to the invasion of Iraq has shown.

Second, the economic disparities between the West and the region are gross, as is the distribution of wealth within most of the region's states. The region still has far to go to develop both economically and – more contentiously – in social terms. This is reflected in innumerable statistics, from GDP to infant mortality, and implies a long haul towards economic development goals and subsequent social change. While the West favours this development and is prepared – in Chris Patten's words – 'to put our money where our mouth is', it is not always welcome to elites in the region who see their position potentially challenged by democratic and social developments that will mean they have to share wealth and power more widely.

Third, there are demographic facts which cannot be denied. The youth/ age ratio across the Mediterranean has been inverted within two generations. Now there are twice as many young North Africans as there are young southern Europeans, and nearly three times as many aged southern Europeans as there are aged North Africans. It is a situation that is likely to persist for at least two or three further generations, and any overview of European–Mediterranean relations – and in particular immigration policy – has to bear this in mind. While the population of the United States is on average slightly younger than in Europe, the ratio is not dissimilar; America and North Africa, however, are separated by more than the Straits of Gibraltar.

Fourth, there is an environmental stress within the Mediterranean basin of which those living there are well aware, but which is far from America's shores. As an example, 94 per cent of the water within the Mediterranean basin is located on the northern side and only 6 per cent on the southern. Given the population growth implied by the age disparities above, this seriously strains the capacity of several states to develop economically.

Fifth, the wave of fundamentalism in faith – Jewish, Muslim and Christian – raises as many risks as it creates opportunities. Some far-sighted faith communities are encouraging dialogue with their neighbours, seeking common ground for all the 'Children of the Book'. Others are erecting higher and higher barriers between believers with the argument that theirs must be the one true faith. Here the battle for the hearts and minds of the people could still go either way. Civilisations do not need to clash simply because they contain extremists; they grow and develop by containing their extremists.

Conclusions

Back in the world of current policy towards the region, what can we expect?

On the very day the G8 initiative was announced, an EU Commissioner was speaking in Cairo at an international event where he commented that he feared the G8 effort could duplicate what was already being undertaken by the EU. He added that the initiative appeared to him to 'lack a clearly thought out plan'.

Shortly afterwards another Commissioner in Brussels declared that he feared there were misunderstandings between the G8 partners about this initiative, and a senior EU Commission official offered the understated but dismissive remark: 'We will continue to work alongside it.'

None of these were auspicious welcomes for a much trumpeted international developmental initiative, but it is understandable that the EU Commission, with a well-funded programme already running, might look askance at such potential duplication. What those comments missed, however, was the new definition that America wanted – still wants – to impose on the West's vision of the region.

America's priority is seen through the prism first of anti-terrorism and secondly of secure energy supplies. The EU has lived with terror of different sorts – IRA, ETA, Red Brigades, Baader Meinhof – for generations and 9/11 did not change European views of the outside world, nor European views of the Arab states from which those particular terrorists came. The EU's priorities still centre on extending stability and security first to the smaller region of its immediate neighbours around the Mediterranean, and then widening the circle. Classic instruments of development appear largely sufficient for this, and any additional activity in relation to security and anti-terrorism are simply that, additional activities. They are not seen as a reason to roll up the old map and devise an extensive and necessarily thin policy for a new region that would stretch from the Western Sahara to the Punjab.

12
Expansion towards the South: an Alternative Scenario for a Partnership in Crisis[1]

Jean-Robert Henry

The intensification of crises and conflicts in the Middle East makes the issue of peaceful management of the Mediterranean space more pertinent than ever. In recent years, attempts to meet this challenge have multiplied.

After proposing in 2003 the creation of a free-trade zone between this region and the United States, President Bush concentrated on the Greater Middle East Proposal, which underwent several changes. Launched as an improvisation, the proposal was reworked by the G8 to make it more acceptable to Arab countries and their European partners.

On the European side, there is continual talk of the need to re-start and make more dynamic the Euro-Mediterranean partnership. Beginning at the end of 2002, Romano Prodi strove to promote in the press and with some of his partners a 'philosophy of friendly neighbours', which would regulate relations between Europe and all of its eastern and southern borders, from Russia to Morocco. Europe would 'share everything except institutions' with these neighbours (which thus excludes a common political space). The concept was approved by European institutions but with numerous changes. Now the idea is 'safe' neighbours rather than 'friendly' neighbours.

The French leaders preferred to explore the idea of an 'exceptional partnership' with countries of the Maghreb, which would consist of reinforcing links established in the Barcelona Process, without going so far as to offer the possibility of EU membership.

In this regard, the '5 + 5'[2] Tunis summit in December 2004 was more of a symbolic success than a concrete one. It brought together ten heads of state or of government, along with the three main leaders of European foreign policy at the time (Romano Prodi, Chris Patten and Javier Solena). But the achievements were not up to expectations announced by the newspaper *Le Monde*, which headlined on page 1: 'Europe-Maghreb: the

Other Expansion?' The summit turned a deaf ear to the crucial question of open cross-border movements.

Whether it is a question of 'neighbours' or of 'reinforced cooperation', the formula remains ambiguous – or, rather, prolongs the ambiguity often pointed out in the Barcelona Process, which is summarised in two complementary questions: When the Euro-Mediterranean partnership states that it intends to promote solidarity and common destiny, what does it really mean? Can we favour the free circulation of goods, ideas and values in the Euro-Mediterranean space while restraining that of human beings?

The European project, despite its weaknesses, is doubtless the greatest advance towards peaceful management of international relations in half a century; though the development of a period of peace, prosperity and democratic well-being also has consequences – not always beneficial – on its surroundings. We have seen this in the Balkan crisis. Aside from the occasional divergences between European powers, that crisis threw into relief both the desirable and the undermining effects the European dynamic exercises had on outer-limit regions seeking to join the European Union. The increasingly greater contrast between the peace reigning in the new Europe and the development of conflicts on its margins calls into question the European project: up to what point are these conflicts encouraged by the European process?

Of course the issue of rich and poor as 'neighbours' is being addressed in similar terms regarding other places on the planet. However, in the Mediterranean space, the problem is aggravated by the fact that the European process brings with it a *specific contradictory dynamic*, which tends to make the Mediterranean both a peripheral part of Europe and an identity and cultural border.

On the one hand, Europe seeks to expand and to organise its influence, especially economic and cultural, by creating a vast Euro-Mediterranean region in which the area south of the Mediterranean would become a peripheral market and entry point for Europe, but, on the other hand, while the economy opens the European space onto the world, the construction of Europe makes the Mediterranean into a border: the extension of the European project with its political, security and identity criteria produces closure in the Mediterranean, a cultural, social and human border faced with the Islam-Mediterranean world increasingly considered as a radical 'other'. The establishing of this Mediterranean European border creates and accentuates differences with the southern side. Despite the universalism professed by the European Commission, a confused ethnic and religious vision of European identity tends by default to prevail, defining, in relation to the South and the Muslim world, a whiter and more Christian Europe than ever before. Fears of Islam, of terrorism, of demographic pressures, and of insecurity, all blamed on Arabs, increase the mental distancing from societies on the other side of the Mediterranean, while they have never been so close to us in their cultural practices because of links related to immigration, and because of the 'desire for Europe' they experience.

On the whole, the double effect of the European dynamic translates into a contradictory process of inclusion–exclusion of the South by the North, which carries with it huge inter-societal tensions between the North and the South of the Mediterranean.

From 'Euro-Mediterranean partnership' to the false new arrival of 'neighbours'

Faced with the risk of aggravated tensions in the Mediterranean region, answers provided by the Barcelona Process are not equal to the challenges. The relational space instituted in 1995 by this Euro-Mediterranean partnership at the initiative of the Europeans is both a space-border and a peripheral regionalism, a different level between a region defining itself as European and an external periphery from which Europe protects itself by placing it within its zone of influence. Contrary to the Euro-Arab dialogue of the 1970s, the Barcelona Process does not define an 'inter-region' (to use Edgar Pisani's formula) that would bring together roughly equal parties. Nor is it a new regional organisation, but rather a 'multilateral framework for negotiation' between two unequal groups of partners.

Above all, the partnership instituted by the European Union generally consecrates a divorce between economic and human spaces. It draws together the economies and seeks to integrate those on the other side of the Mediterranean into the European space (this is the project of the free-trade zone). But it keeps the people at a distance; it excludes them from integrating for reasons as varied as they are implicit: they are too poor, too prolific, they belong to another religion, to another 'culture', they are not geographically or ethnically European. Out of fear they will invade us, European borders with the South have been reinforced to limit human circulation. Let us remember that this closure of the European human space by the Schengen system is relatively recent, as the evolution of fluxes between Algeria and France testify: before 1985, more than a million Algerians came to France every year. The figure dropped, ten years later, to 50 000, but has gone up slowly in recent years towards a goal of 300 000 people.

The human dimension of the Euro-Mediterranean partnership remains dominated by 'the two I's and the D' that Fathallah Oualalou, the Moroccan professor and governmental minister denounced: immigration, Islamism, and drugs. This is indeed how the inclusion–exclusion process translates, at least for those in the North: European attachment to an abstract Mediterranean affiliation as a source of European identity enters into tension with the idea of a stricter-than-ever border as a result of migratory fluxes. To get past this contradiction and reduce the effects of the divorce between economic and human space, we are counting on cultural dialogue and the capacities of 'civil society'. Unfortunately these two resources are uncertain.

In as much as the postulate of cultural difference is often over-valued to justify rifts in the Mediterranean human space, the role of cultural dialogue is over-worked: the laboured reference to medieval Andalusia refers to a dialogue model of relations between cultures supposedly irreducibly or essentially different, without taking into account phenomena of cultural mixing, osmosis or elimination, particularly noticeable in the Franco-Maghreb space. The insipid and conventional soup served up in dozens of conferences about Mediterranean identity, solidarity and humanism aims to exalt a virtual Mediterranean, at the expense of constituting a true common human space, which necessarily implies widespread human mobility such as has occurred in Europe.

As for civil society, we ask much more of it than it can deliver. Public powers pass on to NGOs social and cooperative missions that they should be doing themselves, and actors in civil society find themselves invested, via humanitarian cooperation, with the Promethean task of staving off real inequalities and symbolic rifts between the two shores of the Mediterranean. Like virtual humanism, the humanitarian serves here as a pretext for the absence of true human solidarity: without human mobility and reciprocal exchanges, there will be no true Mediterranean civil society on the European model.

The dysfunctions and impasses of such a system have become obvious even to responsible institutions. In March 2002, just before the European conference of Valencia, the European Commission described, in alarmist terms, the importance of the Mediterranean risk for Europe:

> In the first half of the twenty-first century, Europe should have the major objective of keeping the Mediterranean region from becoming a fault line.

But this was followed by weak and vague references to culture:

> This region must on the contrary be a source of dynamism, creativity, and exchange, all fruits of secular cultural diversity.

The same split between geopolitical diagnosis and toned-down cultural treatment inspired one of the only concrete decisions at the Valencia conference, later confirmed in Naples: the creation of the Anna Lindh Euro-Mediterranean Foundation for cultural dialogue, which would have a three-year budget of ten million euros. That is the price of a single assault force, which leaves one sceptical about the capacity of this Foundation to work in depth for a transformation of Mediterranean mentalities.

For two years now there has been less talk in the partnership of 'culture' in the abstract sense and more about common values, human rights, and 'good governance' to bring together Mediterranean societies. The need to take more notice of the human dimension of the partnership has prudently been recognised.

The formula 'friendly neighbours' was proposed by Romano Prodi and seconded by the European Council as a means of better managing peaceful relations between the European Union and its eastern and southern neighbours. This is not a new idea, as it was already suggested in 1995 in the Barcelona Declaration on the Euro-Mediterranean partnership. But it was enlarged to include countries traditionally thought of as the East in our vision of the world.

This rhetoric about neighbours – which seeks to bridge the fracture created by the Mediterranean – reveals an ethno-cultural vision of Europe. It mobilises a family-like metaphor, which borrows from common-use language, to mark the difference between neighbours and the European family. Yet 'family' is still an unspoken category in the texts, made implicit by recourse to the idea of 'neighbour': if 'they' are 'neighbours', 'we' refers then to the 'family'. To say, like Romano Prodi, that 'with neighbours, we will share everything but institutions', this denies their vocation to belong fully to the European 'family', that is, the same human space as us: Europe must remain 'endogamous'.[3]

Romano Prodi's most explicit discourse about the 'philosophy of friendly neighbours' was what he said at the Alexandrine Library on 13 October 2003. After throwing out the clash-of-civilisations myth and affirming that Europeans want no new wall, he argued for a 'politics of proximity' likely to guarantee a 'soft security' between Europe and its 'circle of friends'. The human dimension was not absent (the goal of free movement of peoples was mentioned), but it was treated as a side-effect of the development of economic and cultural relations. With the mission assigned to the consulting group on the dialogue of peoples and cultures, as with the creation of the Anna Lindh Euro-Mediterranean Foundation for inter-cultural dialogue, the President of the European Commission strongly called upon cultural dialogue to put an end to misunderstandings and to promote throughout the Mediterranean the values on which European integration is based. The Mediterranean itself did not escape this culturalist approach: it was designated as the 'cradle of European civilisation' and as a 'crossroads of exchange and dialogue', which means that it would be considered both inside and outside of Europe.

Romano Prodi's reflection was deepened in a fruitful and non-conformist way by the seventeen Experts of the consultative group, to whom the President of the Commission entrusted the mission of looking at the dialogue of peoples and cultures in the Mediterranean. Without questioning the 'philosophy of friendly neighbours' nor adopting another expression, these sages (an old-fashioned word, but nicer than 'experts') produced a fine and substantial analysis of the complex cultural stakes at work in the Mediterranean space. Denouncing essentialist visions of the dialogue of cultures as coming from the same logic as the clash of cultures, they noted that the problem in the Mediterranean is much more about learning how to manage cultural proximity than cultural difference. They proposed to restore all human dimension to culture by fixing concrete objectives anchored in institutional actions. There are, of course, ambiguities and contradictions in this text written by several people, representatives from the North and the South – the report accepted the postulate of 'two halves of the Mediterranean' even though referring to 'a common civilisation' – but, on the whole, the report shows how the management of cultural diversity in the Mediterranean relies on the same analyses and calls for the same solutions as those that have successfully prevailed in Europe.

The manner in which European political institutions adopted the 'philosophy of friendly neighbours' is unfortunately much more reductive than the open reflection of the sages.

In its conclusions of June 2003 on 'Enlarged Europe: New Neighbours', the European Council did not speak of a single politics of proximity but of an 'array of politics' regarding European neighbours not concerned with eventual membership (for the Euro-Mediterranean partnership, this no longer concerns Cyprus, Malta and Turkey). The goal is to 'create a space of prosperity and shared values' with neighbours but, all the more, to assure a 'safe management' of Europe's borders.

In June 2004 new texts from the European Council confirmed this security orientation. They refer to 'promoting on the borders of the Mediterranean basin an ensemble of well-governed countries with which we can have close relations based on cooperation'. The human dimension is hardly mentioned. Europeans do not seem at all in a hurry to invite their new 'friends' home. Will 'friendly neighbours' turn out to be a 'false friend' for the people of the South?

As seen in policies, 'friendly neighbours' increasingly takes on the face of a fiefdom proposed by Europe to societies on its periphery. It intends to impose on them a series of values, norms and reforms, in exchange for some aid. *We want our neighbours to be like us, with us but not in our homes: let us resemble each other without being together.* This 'levelling' of neighbours – at the least cost and without the possibility of an uncertain 'shared prosperity' – is a humiliating and hardly seductive deal for the beneficiaries. It emphasises a larger than ever separation between the strong intra-European solidarity and the much weaker and stingy solidarity that Europe has with the outside world.

In any case, the Euro-Mediterranean partnership's attachment to the larger perspective of 'neighbours' does not suffice for exiting the impasse – that is, the disjunction between economic and human space. This divorce can never be a viable long-term formula nor a credible future for our partners. It is incapable of reducing economic and social imbalances in the Mediterranean. We will not be able, in the name of totally over-estimated cultural differences, to long stabilise the border between poor and wealthy with a security management, while limiting the free movement of peoples of the South towards the North.

In the South, the near and familiar prosperity of Europe and numerous phenomena of cultural osmosis invite a permanent comparison with the lifestyles in the North. The growing separation between the two shores can only accentuate frustrations, radicalise claims, sap the value systems of the South, and encourage by every means their 'desire for Europe', which has already pushed to their deaths several thousand clandestine emigrants – more victims than the Intifada or the Manhattan towers. When we consider it, the human and symbolic cost of the Euro-Mediterranean system's dysfunctions is thus enormous, despite the good conscience of Europeans.

Further, the growth in virtual communication between the two shores, thanks to new technologies such as the Internet, does not calm frustrations and tensions. Instead, it heightens them by creating a virtual human space, which makes the lack of a veritable space of human mobility felt even more keenly. Societies on the other side of the Mediterranean, notably those in the Maghreb, live our history and our debates (such as the matter of the headscarf in France) in real time; they are outside our windows, but our door is closed. How much longer will the lock hold, and at what price?

Towards a renewed utopia

The relation to the other side of the Mediterranean weighs heavily, in the North and in the South, on the future of these societies, and it is not excluded from the formulation of Europe's destiny. More than any other external relation, proximity with the Arab-Muslim world poses a dilemma for Europe. It invites the choice between two fundamentally different models of the European project: either construct a fortress of prosperity, a sort of grand continental Switzerland withdrawn into its human, economic and cultural patrimony, protected from the influx of southern populations and imagined threats from the Muslim East by supposedly insurmountable barriers; or else return to the notion of a 'Europe without borders',[4] which foresaw another way of organising the world that would truly integrate these countries in a common prosperity with Europe.

The first model seems to correspond to the current trend; it incarnates notably the Schengen system. However, it is the second that, in reconnecting with the 1960s debate about the global village and in joining today the partisans of 'a different globalisation', appears the more apt to manage the future of the Mediterranean space. It consists of *thinking about Europe less as a withdrawal into the continent but as an open and dynamic regionalism; and less as an identity goal than as a utopia heralding a universalist process.* This is what has been attempted with the enlargement of Europe towards the East. Why not pursue towards the South this process of progressive enlargement of a peaceful, prosperous space, one of solidarity and of *wanting to live together*, without imperial intentions, a space that already includes one-seventh of the world's countries? Will Europe be slowed in this path by the feeling that cultural differences are an insurmountable obstacle to greater solidarity with its close southern neighbours, or will it give in to the Swiss reflex of standing firm on its prosperity?

The European project's strength is to have put the politics of possibility and small steps in the service of an ambitious utopia formulated in the 1920s around the 'European spirit'. Yet it is this founding utopia that is lacking in the Barcelona Process as in the philosophy of neighbours: they offer nothing in regard to the organisation of the human space, no other future than the weak idea of 'neighbours', without inter-mixing, while asserting the existence of irreducible cultural differences to be managed. This implicit philosophy of a moderate apartheid in the Mediterranean cannot be the common destiny for the societies concerned; it has only served to reaffirm the human boundary between Europe and its South rather than make its crossing more flexible.

Instead of thinking of the Mediterranean only as a suburb of Europe, managed by an unequal partnership annexed onto the European Union system, why not take the historical risk of converting this unsatisfactory coupling into a veritable Euro-Mediterranean Union? This would be a crucial move for Europe that would reconfigure its regional role as a global responsibility.

Rather than the vague 'regional organisation of Europe and the Mediterranean' advocated by former President Giscard d'Estaing in October 2002, the Euro-Mediterranean enlargement can become a realistic utopia that merits being explored in order to rethink our common belonging to the same Mediterranean human space. It wouldn't be to 'Europeanise' the South but rather to 're-Mediterraneanise' Europe, to reconcile it with its Mediterranean roots, while ceasing to view Arabs and Muslims as usurpers of the ancient heritage of Europeans.

Necessarily progressive, a scenario to convert the European Union into the Euro-Mediterranean Union would of course require stages: first would be to make of the Mediterranean a space of human *mobility* – as before Schengen – and of mutual respect; in the medium term, a common space of *civility* would be appropriate, that is, with the same human and social rights; finally, one must not exclude – differing with Romano Prodi – an evolution towards a political space of common *citizenship*.

These perspectives of human reopening towards the South are not unrealistic. They join what certain economists propose today for managing the complementary needs of societies south and north of the Mediterranean in regard to the evolution of their demographics and their working populations, while profiting from a 'window of demographic opportunity'.[5] Managing this concrete problem implies that Europeans would succeed in dropping the mental barriers of their xenophobia. This is a genuine revolution to achieve, one that electoral preoccupations do not encourage. Yet Europeans need to admit that understanding their interests well would mean strongly aiding societies on the other side of the Mediterranean to join them, following the model of what was done for Spain and Portugal. Without the availability of European structural funds, no veritable space of solidarity could possibly be built; a space likely to bring together, strongly, people and their standard of living, and to support the democratic transition in countries such as Morocco.[6] So, without a return to free movement of people encouraging back and forth travel, local development of certain regions south of the Mediterranean risks destabilisation as a result of permanent emigration.

The progressiveness of a true Euro-Mediterranean project must also reinforce Maghreb–European links at a time when events in the Middle East and the invasive role of the United States in this region seem to be slowing the development of a global Euro-Mediterranean logic. This was a direction the European Parliament had pursued by rediscovering sub-regional realities in the Mediterranean. In the western basin, the over-lapping of societies on the cultural, religious and human levels is stronger than anywhere else on the Euro-Mediterranean scene. For France and Algeria, for example, the framework of connections established with each other, even though evolving, remains exceptionally strong. This relationship without equivalent within Europe can help rekindle imaginative relations turned more towards people than towards goods or abstract cultures in this part of the Mediterranean. We must be inventive in finding formulas apt to manage in a concerted way this *common human space* that the Mediterranean is, especially in its western reaches. Dominique de Villepin, former French Minister of Foreign Affairs, spoke at the end of 2002 of a to-be-delineated status between 'member' and 'associate', sec-onding what Mohammed VI had proposed some time before.[7] The extremely strong relationship with the Maghreb, which continues to develop astride the Mediterranean border with Europe, calls for creative institutional solutions in all cases.

Whatever the path might be, the Euro-Mediterranean utopia can give meaning to possible measures that are today within reach, such as the expansion of the Council of Europe to include the Mediterranean, the development of priority actions for youth (beginning with the extension of the Erasmus exchange programme to include the Mediterranean), or, of course, a more favourable reception to requests for membership on the part of Turkey and Morocco.

However, the Euro-Mediterranean utopia can also be a way of better fashioning the European project in universalism. Today, it is a fertile model for a realised regional space of peace, prosperity, solidarity and democratic well-being. But it can also, on condition of avoiding any withdrawal inward, take on the political management of the globalisation process by progressively enlarging the space of hope that Europe has been able to create. The 'need to live together' is today global and is there-fore a European project, seen and perceived by many as a universality. It is first in the Mediterranean that Europe can put in place its vision of international solidarity by answering the challenge of humanising globalisation. The Mediterranean is the place where it is most important today to actively combat the pernicious ideology of the 'clash of cultures' and to counter an antagonistic vision of relations with the Arab-Muslim world. This world, for various reasons, is in crisis, destabilised, humiliated by the West's behaviour towards it. It will not long be possible to contain by force reactions in the Arab world that will reach into our suburbs if the Muslim presence in a stingy Europe is increasingly stigmatised.

Since its creation, the EU has continued to hesitate between looking inward, protected by its relations with the United States, and maintaining its ambition to promote a pacified world. The tension between these two visions of Europe was expressed more clearly than ever in regard to events in Iraq.

Today, the international stakes are rising because of mistakes made by the American administration and because of the environmental challenge. The strictly continental dimension of problems pales before the urgency of world challenges, and it is likely that Europe must learn to manage two levels at once. It has all the qualities needed to respond with audacity to problems of the Mediterranean region. The multiple crises in the Middle East have offered the spectacle of joint American and European powerlessness. In reality, while America has wasted its power in the Iraqi affair, Europe is a victim of its feeling of powerlessness. It has had trouble admitting that it may have become the most credible player in the region. Without the trappings of an imperial strategy, it exercises a dominant economic influence. Further, its image remains generally positive in the Arab world. Finally, the flexibility of its variable doctrines – in particular via the system of 'small groups' – allows for specific initiatives in questions of sub-regional cooperation. For all sorts of reasons – providing it wants to play – the ball is in its court.

Notes

1. Translated by Penny Allen
2. A group composed, on the Maghreb side, of Tunisia, Algeria, Libya, Morocco and Mauritania, and, on the European side, Italy, France, Portugal, Spain and Malta.
3. See Ramdane Babadji, 'Face au Sud, l'Europe serait-elle endogame?', *La Cohabitation culturelle en Europe, Hermès*, 23–4 (Paris: Editions du CNRS, 1999). It is interesting to compare this family metaphor with the one used in the colonial period, when the 'mother country' was supposed to gather colonisers and colonised into the same family.
4. From the title of François Perroux's book, *L'Europe sans rivages*, published in 1954.

5. See the introduction by Jean-Louis Reiffers to the report *Méditerranée: vingt ans pour réussir* (Economica, 2001). The question of the window of demographic opportunity has been analysed in various recent articles by Philippe Fargues.
6. J. L. Reiffers, ibid.
7. H. R. E. Mohammed Ben El Hassan Alaoui, 'Le maroc et l'Union européenne à l'aube du XXIe siècle', in *Marier le Maghreb à L'Union européenne. Revue Panoramiques*, third trim. 1999.

13
The Euro-Mediterranean Partnership: Reformulating a Process[1]

Thierry Fabre

The Euro-Mediterranean partnership, or Barcelona Process, which gathered together the Ministers of Foreign Affairs of twenty-seven so-called partner countries in the Catalan capital in November 1995, was established in a unique geopolitical context that at least four elements made possible:

- The post-Gulf War, and the awareness on the part of European countries that after the shock of a largely Occidental military intervention, under the leadership of the United States, it was important to send a friendly signal in the direction of the Arab world and to take an initiative likely to encourage rapprochement.
- The expansion to the East: after the fall of the Berlin Wall, Europe was changing its geopolitical configuration; it was defining its future in a continental perspective with the principal objective of reincorporating its two halves divided since just after World War Two. A European initiative to the South, in the Mediterranean, appeared indispensable, at least to the Mediterranean countries of the European Community.
- The civil war in Algeria: after the interruption of the second round of legislative elections, Algeria entered into an exceptional period of political and military chaos. The fear of an Islamist power led Europe, and especially France, to seek a political initiative in the Mediterranean.
- The Madrid conference: with the joint impetus of the United States and Russia, a process of negotiation was officially underway in the Middle East, between the Israelis and the Palestinians. This process would continue with other initiatives, based on the Oslo accords. It was up to Europe, one of the regions most affected by this geopolitical configuration, to launch an initiative.

This initiative was the Barcelona Process, clearly a European idea, in which the United States sought without success to participate. The countries to the South and the East of the Mediterranean, which on the whole felt marginalised by Europe's enlargement to the East, responded favourably to the European Commission's request to launch the partnership.

The geopolitical conditions prevailing at the time of the Euro-Mediterranean partnership's birth largely explain the impasse in which the multilateral agreement remains more than ten years after its launch in November 1995.

It is not our intention here to evaluate the record of the Euro-Mediterranean partnership by looking at its three components – political and strategic; economic; and social, cultural and human – but to attempt to understand the blockages and impasses of an institutional agreement that for the most part does not appear to realise its ambitions.

The Euro-Mediterranean has always appeared to be an asymmetrical and subordinate process: asymmetrical especially between a Europe that has a coherent form and partner countries that separately negotiate bilateral partnership accords. In this arrangement, the North finances, decides and sets requirements, while the South adapts, gets up to speed, and tries to escape the multiple constraints weighing on it. We have thus a vertical vision (North/South), quasi-hierarchical and in any case hegemonic, that rules in a partnership without true partners. To better understand this dissymmetry, it would suffice to turn the map upside down for a moment and imagine Europe accepting conditions comparable to those it imposes on countries to the south and east of the Mediterranean. Such a reversal of perspective could have a useful mirror effect on our understanding and on greater reciprocity in relations between Europe and the Mediterranean.

It is true that international relations generally operate according to power relations: we therefore should not be surprised by such dissymmetry, which is accepted in any case with perfect awareness by the Europeans who establish the rules of the game. Still, if power relations are the determinant, they are not always decisive, especially in a project in which there is the pretence of together defining, for the long term, a world region with shared interests: the Euro-Mediterranean.

How then to achieve a sincere membership on the part of so-called 'partner' countries? They adapt to constraints, face up to realities, but they do not share a common historical project. The Euro-Mediterranean partnership looks rather like an illusion, like a way of holding off confrontation without really seeking to transcend it. Between neo-colonialism and post-colonialism, Europe is staging a play with the South, a play in which it is the only veritable actor, the partners on the other shore just extras.

The Barcelona Process resembles more and more an impasse than an endless process. Indeed, what is the future of the Euro-Mediterranean partnership? Where is it supposed to end up? What are its true goals?

With Eastern countries, the vision was at least clear: to create the conditions for a possible membership in the European Union. From the fall of the Berlin Wall, in 1989, up until today, the European Union has gone from fifteen to twenty-five members and the membership process of new member countries remains unfinished.

What is happening with our Mediterranean partners? Cyprus and Malta have become members of the EU, and Turkey has begun the official negotiating process despite strong resistance and predictable future blockages.

One major problem to appear is that the goal of the Euro-Mediterranean partnership is the process itself. It leads to nothing other than its own perpetuation. This absence of a political perspective in the Euro-Mediterranean partnership leads into an impasse. What is the point of belonging, if not just for pragmatic reasons, to mobilise funds, to seize market opportunities, to gain advantages? But all that does not add up to a political project; it amounts instead to an arrangement of convenience that does not map out a strategic orientation, even less an historic one, for the countries concerned.

The Barcelona Process is not only asymmetric, it is also subordinate to a geopolitical framework and context: the process of Israeli–Palestinian peace or, in the larger view, Israeli–Arab.

The Euro-Mediterranean partnership was in fact born in the wake of the Madrid conference and the Oslo accords. However, this moment passed several years ago, and the peace process turned into a war process. In these conditions is autonomy possible for the Barcelona Process during the Israeli–Palestinian conflict? It seems unlikely. One can imagine a kind of limited autonomy, in the same way that one spoke in the past of limited sovereignty for Eastern European countries in relation to the Soviet empire.

The political heart of this region of the world is situated where the question of war and peace is being decided. The Israeli–Palestinian conflict creates a shock wave throughout the Mediterranean and in a number of European societies where tensions and sometimes confrontations exist between Jews and Arabs. These interpenetrations and interactions between different levels of conflict feed into a chaotic situation which has gone, essentially, out of control. The Israeli–Palestinian and the larger Israeli–Arab confrontations exist within the limits of the Barcelona Process's political reach, which maintains an open framework for discussion but which, nevertheless, does not allow the European Union to act on the international scene.

Thus the impasse of the Euro-Mediterranean partnership, which sometimes is improvisationally configured economically or in relations between sub-regions, as being between Europe and the Maghreb; but the Israeli–Palestinian conflict subordinates the Barcelona Process with the intensity of its confrontations. This is the key to understanding the impasses in which the partnership finds itself today, more than ten years after its launch.

The other strategic variable is related to the role of the United States in the region. The Americans are not in favour of building a regional Euro-Mediterranean group, in which they would most certainly be marginalised. So they propose an array of initiatives as a counterweight to any possible regional development: for example, the policy of free-trade agreements negotiated directly with certain partner countries such as Morocco and Tunisia; or a series of security agreements related to the war against terrorism conducted by the Americans. The United States finds ways to work with authoritarian regimes, which are then presented as guarantors of 'liberty and democracy'.

This questioning of the Euro-Mediterranean partnership by the United States appears clearly when they try to impose a strategic framework such as the 'Greater Middle East', which takes no account of a regional configuration such as the Euro-Mediterranean, and which aims to build strategic partners directly linked to American security priorities.

This divergence in regional approaches between the United States and the European Union is all the more complex, given the disaccords within the European Union on the subject. Differences of opinion related to the war in Iraq – especially between the United Kingdom, Italy or Poland on one side, and France, Belgium or Germany on the other – testify to the multiple unknowns in the matter and emphasise the current impossibility of defining a coherent position for the European Union in the Mediterranean in face of American strategy. The Euro-Mediterranean partnership is not disassociated from fluctuations in the Euro-Atlantic partnership, and it remains subordinate to them to a certain degree.

Given the situation, what are the possibilities for the Barcelona Process today?

Three main trends appear: a stuck-in-the-sand process, a contested process, and a reformulated process. All appear to indicate, in the current political configuration within the European Union and with partner countries, that the Barcelona Process is indeed stuck in the sand, as is Euro-Arab dialogue. It looks like an institutional machine running on empty for lack of a political impetus. There is a structural incapacity for exiting impasses.

The dissymmetry of the partnership has not been corrected, and there is today no credible initiative for establishing a veritable reciprocity between partners and for defining a common agenda. As it is, the Euro-Mediterranean partnership risks being transformed into a partnership without partners. The European Union refuses to recognise its hegemonic posture. Sure of its rights, values and its economic and commercial dynamic, the EU imposes its choices. Thus the Euro-Mediterranean partnership is much more a European Union foreign policy than a truly common project. As Raymond Aron correctly pointed out, 'hegemony is an unstable form of equilibrium'. Transcending this hegemonic posture is an indispensable condition for exiting the impasse.

The partnership's goals have not been clearly defined. In the political domain, there is no possibility of membership for so-called partner countries. In the economic situation, a simple free-trade zone planned for 2010 is not a project for co-development or shared prosperity. There are persistent misunderstandings between countries on the two shores of the Mediterranean. Expectations, from one shore to the other and from one country to another, are divergent, and no political dynamic has been created to surmount obstacles inherent in a multilateral process of this amplitude. Misunderstandings between those who aspire to more security, migration control, or control of terrorism, on the European side, and those who want organisational economic projects, active solidarity, and facility of movement, on the southern and eastern shores of the Mediterranean, have only multiplied since the launch of the Barcelona Process.

What can be undertaken together? Improvised accords with limited interests or a strategic partnership that engages in the future? The lack of decision-making about partnership goals is far from comforting as far as credibility is concerned. As for the double subordination of the Euro-Mediterranean partnership, in relation to the Israeli–Palestinian conflict and to American policy in the Middle East, the stranglehold is not loosening.

Despite several attempts to relaunch the 'road map to peace', the situation remains blocked between Israel and Palestine. The colonisation of territory continues and the withdrawal from Gaza does not seem to promise a definitive peace. It is difficult to see how, given all this, the Barcelona Process can escape the intensity of a conflict that has lasted now for half a century. Can the political will manifested by the United

States and France, with United Nations Resolution 1559 regarding Syrian occupation of Lebanon, be as efficient in regard to the UN resolutions not respected by Israel? This is a key for the future of the Barcelona Process and certainly a unique role for Europe in the region. But is such a difference with American policy imaginable in a Europe with twenty-five members, where most new member countries do not feel very concerned by the future of the Mediterranean? The weight of American policy in the region does not seem to be counterbalanced by European Union foreign policy, which lacks cohesion and consistency.

The Barcelona Process is widely contested, from both above and below. The United States is trying to make another political-strategic framework prevail, the 'Greater Middle East', in which the Mediterranean is not a region related to Europe. As for the European Union itself, it is in the process of diluting the uniqueness of the Euro-Mediterranean partnership in a vast array of the politics of neighbours. Of course, the EU has proposed to include the Mediterranean partners in the politics of neighbours (according to the conclusions of the Ministers of Foreign Affairs meeting in Dublin in May 2004). However, this 'politics of neighbours' is still vague, and does not define in any way a strategic priority for the EU in the Mediterranean. The indecision is growing, which has the effect of rendering fragile the Barcelona Process.

The Process is contested as well by other players. This is the case particularly with Islamist movements, for whom the Mediterranean process is a new version of colonialism, a way of integrating Israel into a regional whole, and a means of diluting Arab and Islamic identity. Opposition to the Mediterranean reference is resolute and declared by most Islamist movements, who see also in the Euro-Mediterranean partnership an international project that reassures authoritarian forces now in power. This is a point of convergence with democratic movements that often vigorously contest the passivity of European authorities in the face of political repression and threats to public freedoms.

The rhetoric of human rights, willingly invoked by the European Union, is rarely followed by action. As if of our colonial heritage, one must not defend universal principles. This European political cautiousness, so different from the intense reactions in eastern countries and in the Soviet world during the 1980s, explains for a large part the loss of European political and leadership credibility. The partnership, contrary to the terms of the accords signed with various countries, in the end shows itself scarcely a protector of human rights.

Given this, to say the least, mixed record of the Euro-Mediterranean partnership, more than ten years after its launch, it can be saved only by a true reformulation. There are strategic issues that touch the heart of politics, that is, the question of war or peace. We are approaching a moment of truth, when the masks fall, when the make-believe slips away, when we will have to 'pay up'.

Confronted with this challenge of war or peace, the Euro-Mediterranean partnership cannot be celebrated, but truly and deeply reformulated: a political reformulation, such as at the level of heads of state who met in Barcelona in the autumn of 2005, whose job was to set the direction and choose a new future. A common historical project between Europe and the Mediterranean must be given a form built on relations of confidence.

There is a need for an economic reformulation that aims to exit from the simple idea of a free-trade zone and opt instead for the creation of a zone of shared co-prosperity. Why not invent, for example, structural policies for the Euro-Mediterranean space, modelled on what has been accomplished within the European Union for undeveloped regions? Possibly, a human reformulation, to transcend the destructive mechanisms of borders. This would help to encourage Euro-Mediterranean mobility and to distinguish such mobility from immigration movements. Why not create, for example, a Euro-Mediterranean agency for exchanges, which would have the goal of encouraging links, from society to society?

An intellectual and cultural reformulation is above all needed. It would begin by creating a true epistemological change allowing an end to opposition between 'them' and 'us'. This would give new meaning to the Euro-Mediterranean partnership, both as an orientation and as a priority.

The time has come to be done with Orientalism, this invention of a radically different 'other'. What we most need is a common world that connects without confusion and allows an exit from the vertical and hierarchical vision between the North and the South of the Mediterranean. This intellectual and cultural reformulation would give us the means of imagining together our common future. The great challenge of our political generation is to construct Europe not without the Mediterranean but with the Mediterranean. Human and social sciences will perhaps show the way.

Note

1. Translated by Penny Allen.

Index

Abbaside caliphate   102
Abdulhamid, Sultan   141, 145
absolutist socialism   122
açabiya (primitive forces)   114, 119
Acre   150
Adana   151
Adler, E.   165
Aegean   150–1
Afghanistan   43, 200
Africa   41
   black Africa   51–2, 55–6, 64–7
   Great Lakes region   31
African Muslims   64
Agadez   52, 56, 61, 68
Agadir   187
age-sex structure   **16**, 17–20, **17**, **18**,
   19, **24**, **25**
   economy and   25–6
   migration and   20–1
AIDS   67
Albania   33, 35–6
Albera, Dionigi   4
Aleppo   150
Alevites   159–60
Alexandretta   150
Alexandria   185, 188
Alexandrine Library   211
Algeria   200, 202, 209, 216, 219
   immigration, asylum and   36, 38,
      46–7, 52
   migratory routes and   52, 55–61,
      63–4, 66–8
'Alliance of Civilisations'   1
Allied commission on Ottoman
      finances   151
Allied powers
   1918–22   144, 150–1
   post-Second World War   142
Amsterdam Treaty   33
Anafi   75, 78
anarchy (*fitna kubra*)   119
Anatolia   141, 142, 144, 150–1, 152,
   160

cities in   79
Anderson, B.   177
Anglo-American Orientalism   93
Ankara University   145
Anna Lindh Euro-Mediterranean
      Foundation for cultural dialogue
      172, 182, 186, 189, 211–12
Annan, Kofi   39
Ansary, Abdou Filali   5
Antalya   151
Antep   151
anthropologists   74, 75–6, 76–9
anti-communism, Greece and   78–9
anti-Israeli operations   127
anti-Judaism, Christian   104
anti-Kemalist revanchism   138, 157
anti-Muslim sentiments   98
Appleyard, Reginald   48
Arab world   68, 81, 127, 178, 221
   Euro-Mediterranean Partnership
      (EMP) and   162–3, 166, 168,
      178, 219
   states   122, 151, 198, 201, 205, 208
Arab-Berber geocultural system   52
Arab-Muslim world   65, 99, 106
   Euro-Mediterranean Partnership
      (EMP) and   164–5, 172–5, 189,
      214, 217
Arafat, Y.   202
Arafatist movement   130
Argyrou, V.   76
Armenia, American mandate for   151
Armenians   142, 144, 150, 152, 153
Aron, R.   223
ASEAN (Association of Southeast
      Asian Nations)   167, 168, 169
Ash'arites   114
Asia Minor   142
Asian clandestines   53
Assiros   79
asylum   41–50
   co-development and   45–8
   Geneva Convention   29, 41, 45

legal clandestine 44–5
rights and immigration control
42–3
'asylum shopping' 43
Ataturk, Mustafa Kemal 140, 152,
179
Athens 75
Aussiedler (ethnic Germans) 32
Australia 43
Austro-Hungarian Empire 73
'axial age' 115
'axis of evil' 203

Baader Meinhof 205
'baby boom' 15
'baby bust' 15, 18
Bakalaki, A. 76, 80, 83
Balearic Islands 36
Bali 106
Balkans 142, 144, 169, 176,
189, 208
Greek identity and 73-6, 79, 81
Baltic States 16
Barak, E. 175
Barcelona 225
Barcelona accords 35, 57–8, 200,
211
Barcelona Process *see* Euro-
Mediterranean Partnership (EMP)
Bati Takliciligi 140
Batum 151
Bauman, Zigmunt 39, 44
Bazunguissa, Rémy 43
Beirut 150
Belgium 222
Benjamin, W. 106
Bensaad, Ali 4
Berlin Wall, fall of 1, 34, 38, 75, 219,
221
Berque, J. 102–3
Bessis, S. 104
Birecik 151
biz (the 'we') 139–41
bizlik ('we-ness') 139
black Africa 51–2, 55–6, 64–7
Black Sea 151
Bond, Martyn 6
borders
closed 35–7

open 34–5, 37–9
safe management of 212
Bordj Moktar 61
Bosnia 36, 90
Boss-Fini law 2002 (Italy) 43
Brindisi 35
Britain 20, 144, 150–1, 199, 203
see also United Kingdom (UK)
Brussels 165, 182, 188
2004 EU summit 58
Buddhism 98, 115
Bulgaria 34, 79
Burckhardt, J. 97
Bush, President G. W. 202, 207
Byzantine Empire 115, 142

Cairo 107, 127
Cairo accords (1969) 129
Caliphs 119–20, 139
Calvino, I. 180
Canada 38
Canary Islands 36, 47
Caribbean 31
Carrier, James 73, 82
Cem, I. 155
Cemal Pasha 150
Central America 31
Central Asia 139, 142
Central Europe 30, 34, 121
Ceuta 30, 47
Chalgham, Abderrahman 59–60
Chéhad, F. 126
Childe, G. 105
China 92, 99
Christianity 68, 125–7, 197, 203
anti-Judaism and 104
collective identity and 89–90, 98
Europe and 157, 209
fundamentalism and 205
Orient and 98
Turkish Conservatism and 142,
144, 146, 152–3
Cilicia 151
'clandestine immigration' 60
Clash of Civilisations (Huntington)
159, 162, 197
'clash of cultures' 217
Clifford, J. 76
co-development 45–8

'code switching'   114
Cold War   37, 75, 81, 96, 162, 168
collective identity   76, 88–112,
     114–15
  clash of civilisations   91–3
  culturalism   93–7
  Islam: malaise in relation to 97–103;
       media coverage of   88–93
  Lebanon's Palestinians and   126–7
  research approaches   103–8
'coming together/differentiation'
     116
Committee for the Defence of
     Ottoman Rights   151
Committee for the Defence of
     Rights of Anatolia and Rumeli
     152
Committee for the Defence of Rights
     of the Eastern Provinces   151
Committee for the Defence of Thrace
     151
Communism   15, 16, 75
communities
  building   165, 191
  secure   165, 173, 178
Comte, Auguste   27, 97
conservatism *see* Turkish conservatism
Constantinople   142
  see also Istanbul
contemporary civilisation   179
Copernicus, N.   105
Council of Europe   216
Council of Ministers of Justice and
     Internal Affairs   42
Couroucli, Maria   4, 80
Creole-speaking societies   81
Crete   9, 77
Crusades   98, 142, 152–3, 153–4,
     160
cultural intimacy   80
culturalism   93–7
CUP cabinet (Turkey)   149
Cyprus   46, 176–7, 192, 203, 212,
     221
Czech Republic 15, 21, 34, 45

Damascus   150
de Maupassant, Guy   91
de Villepin, D.   216

de Wenden, Catherine Wihtol   2, 43,
     45
Decline of the Western World (Spengler)
     92
'deep historical memory'   143–6,
     149–52
'deep policy'   143, 146–7, 152–3, 154
Defence of Rights Committees
     151–2
Demeny, Paul   12
'democracy'   191–2
Democratic Left Party (Turkey)   155
Democratic Party (Turkey)   139
'demographic dividend'   26
demographic transition   11–27
  age structure **16**, 17–20, **17**, **18**, **19**:
       economy and 25–6; migration
       and   20–1
  fertility 13–16, **14**, **16**: migration
       and   20–1
  mortality   16–17
  population trends   12–13, 22–5,
       24, 25
Denmark   15, 33, 61, 188
Dervis, K.   155
'desire for Europe'   30
d'Estaing, President G.   158, 215
Diamantouros, N.   80
'differentiation/coming together'
     116
diglosia   79–81
Direction of Palestinian Affairs
     (Lebanon)   126
Dirkou   61
discordance (*fitna kubra*)   119
disemia   80, 81–2
Douteillet-Paquet, Daphné   45
duality   79–81, 84n
Dublin accords I and II   32–3, 45

East Asia   22, 26
East meets West   73–4
East–West conflict   140
Eastern Europe   15, 30–2, 34, 73
  opening borders   34–5
Eastern Mediterranean   13
Eastern-8   17
  defined   15
Ecevit, B.   155

Egypt   36, 46, 47, 122, 188, 200, 202
11 September 2001   1, 163, 171, 184, 203, 205
11 March 2005   1, 89
Engbersen, Godfried   44
Enlightenment universalism   97
Entente powers   151
Enver Pasha   150
Erasmus exchange programme   216
Erbakan, N.   157
Erdogan, T.   137, 158, 179
Estonia   15
ETA (Basque Homeland and Freedom)   205
ethic of responsibility   186
ethnikofrones   80
EU-25   **17, 18, 24, 25**
  defined   11
Euro-Arab dialogue   223
Euro-Arab diaspora   209
Euro-Mediterranean Parliament   182
Euro-Mediterranean Partnership (EMP)   162–94, 198, 200
  beyond civilisations 173–81: history and common experience 177–81; 'Wider Europe' vs *mare nostrum*   173–6
  in crisis 207–18: Euro-Mediterranean Union 214–17; 'neighbours'   209–14
  deterritorialised region   187–92
  dilemmas and tensions in 167–70, **167**: European Union as 'normative power'   170–1
  Eurocentrism and   166–7
  multilateralism and   182–6
  post-colonial agenda for   181
  reformulating   219–25
Euro-Mediterranean Union   215
Eurocentrism   105, 166–7, 172
Eurodac   31
EuroMed report no 68 (EC, 2003)   180, 212
EuroMediterranean Foundation   172, 182, 186, 189, 211–12
European Commission   46
  Euro-Mediterranean Partnership (EMP) and 169, 174, 184, 220: in crisis   208, 210, 212

European Community (EC)   32–3, 39, 76, 167, 219
  regulations   34, 48
European Council   42, 48, 211, 213
European Economic Community (EEC)   74
European free-trade zone, North Africa and   48
European Parliament   216
'European spirit'   214
European Union   41–3, 57–8
  co-development and   45–8
  demographic transition and 11–12, 21–2
  Euro-Mediterranean Partnership (EMP) and 162, 165–9, 172–6, 181–8, 191–2: in crisis 207–9, 211, 215, 217; reformulating 221–5
  expansion to East   219
  'Greater' Middle East and   200–5
  immigration and   28–9, 33–8
  as 'normative power'   170–1
  Turkish conservatism and   137–8, 153, 156–60
European Union Treaty   42
'Euroscepticism'   155–8, 159
'Eurosupporters'   155
'exceptional partnership'   207
exclusion as rule   31–3
experts (*fuqaha*)   120

Fabre, Thierry   6
Fallaci, O.   98
Fassin, Didier   44
fedayin commandos   127, 128
Felicity Party   155
Ferguson, C. A.   81
Ferrié, J. –N.   106
fertility   13–16, **14, 16**
  migration and   20–1
Finland   15
First World War   144, 149, 152
fitna kubra (discordance)   119
'5 + 5 Dialogue'   46, 50n, 57, 207
Florence, G5 meeting   58
Foreign Relations (journal)   197
Foucault, Michel   44, 114

Foundation for Dialogue between
    Cultures   172, 182, 186, 189,
    211–12
France   58, 68, 150–1, 160
  asylum and   42, 47, 49n
  demographic transition and   15,
    18, 20
  Euro-Mediterranean Partnership
    (EMP) and 178, 186: in crisis
    207, 209, 216; reformulating
    219, 222, 224
  'Greater' Middle East and   199,
    203
  immigration and   30, 32, 36, 38–9
free-trade zones   48, 188, 223
friendly neighbours philosophy   207,
    211–13, 215
fuqaha (experts)   120

G5 meeting in Florence   58
G8 initiative   197–8, 199, 204, 205,
    207
Gardrop Baticiligi   140
Gaza   202, 223
Geertz, C.   76
Gellner, E.   114, 121–2
Geneva Convention on asylum   29,
    41, 45
Geniza   107
Germany   121, 160, 188, 203, 222
  immigration/asylum and   32–4,
    36, 42–3, 45
Ghalioun, B.   117
Gibraltar   35
Gilsenan, M.   106
globalisation   31–2, 69n
  intercontinental links and   52–5
  repressed spatial modes and   55–6
'Gloomy Destiny'   141
Goffman, E.   77, 82
Goiten, S. D.   107
Gokalp, Z.   141
Goody, J.   105
Great Lakes region of Africa   31
'Greater Lebanon'   125
'Greater' Middle East   163, 197–206,
    222, 224
  disparate definitions   200–2
  distinctions   203

European track record   199–200
  G8 initiative   197–8, 199
  Proposal   207
  questions unanswered   204–5
  sticks, carrots and opportunities
    202–3
Greece   15, 31, 36, 167, 185
  Turkish conservatism and   142,
    144, 150–3
Greek identity   73–87
  anthropologists and   75–6, 76–9
  duality and   79–81
  nationalism   74–5
  West 81–3: East and   73–4
Greek Macedonia   79
Gul, A.   1 38
Gulf states   200
Gulf War   219
Gulhane Decree (1839)   143
Guvezna   79

Haifa   150
Hartanis   66
Hastrup, K.   74, 76
Hegel, G.   97, 101, 105, 118
Hellenic Greece   75, 79–80
Helsinki Process   168
Helsinki summit (1999)   159
Henry, Jean-Robert   6
'Herder tyranny'   107
Herzfeld, M.   74, 76, 77, 80–1
'high culture'   121
Hispanics   96
history
  common experience and   177–81
  'deep historical memory'   143–6,
    149–52
  exclusive memories   177–81
  identity crises and   117–21
  Lebanese Palestinians and   126–7
Holland   188
Holy Roman Empire   121
Homs   150
hospitality   77–8
Hourani, A.   97
Hraoui, President Elias   128
human rights   147–9
  delegitimisation of (Turkey)   146–7
  freedoms and (Turkey)   147–9, **148**

immigration control and   42–3
  open borders and   37–9
'human sanctuaries'   43
Hume, D.   114
Hungary   15, 34, 167
Huntington, S. P.   91–3, 96–7, 159,
  197

identity crises and value conflicts
  113–23
  dialectic of   113–17
  front-lines in Sahara   64–7
  history and   117–21
  time zones and   121–3
  see also collective identity; Greek
    identity
Imagined Communities   177
Imamate   120
'Imitation Westernism'   140
immigration   28–40
  control   42–3
  Eastern Europe opening   34–5
  exclusion as rule 31–3: globalisation
    and   31–2
  human rights and open borders
    37–9
  Southern Europe closure   35–7
Imperial Decree of Gulhane (1839)
  143
In Guezzam   61
India   99
Integration   166, 191
'intermediaries'   189–90
International Finance Corporation
  (IFC)   198
International Organisation for
  Migrations (IOM)   48
Invisible Cities (Calvino)   180
Iran   43, 122, 200, 203
  revolution   90
Iraq   43, 150–1, 175, 198–200, 204,
  222
Ireland   15, 33
Irish Republican Army (IRA)
  205
irtica   138
Islam   123, 197, 202, 208–9
  malaise in relation to   97–103
  media coverage of   88–93

Turkish conservatism and   137–9,
  142, 155–9
Islamism   68, 155, 163, 219
isolationism   152–3, 157–8, 159–60
Israel   11, 46, 126, 202
  Euro-Mediterranean Partnership
    (EMP) and   175, 189, 219,
    223–4
Israeli-Arab relations   127, 221
Israeli-Palestinian relations   198, 199,
  201, 202, 221
  'road map to peace'   223
Istanbul   140–1, 142, 150–1, 160
Italy   58, 62, 121
  demographic transition and   15,
    21, 23
  Euro-Mediterranean Partnership
    (EMP) and   188, 222
  immigration/asylum and   31, 33,
    36, 43, 47
  Turkish conservatism and   144,
    151
Ivory Coast   54
Izmir   151

Japan   29, 99
Japan-Arab dialogue   198
Jaspers, K.   115
Jeanneney, Jean-Marcel   38
Jews   150, 175, 203, 221
  anti-Judaism   104
  fundamentalism and   205
'joined destiny' (Lebanese and
  Palestinians)   131
Jordan   15, 46, 122, 188, 200
'Judeo-Christian' expression   104
Julien-Laferrière, François   45
Justice and Development Party (JDP)
  137, 138, 155–7, 159–60
justice and domestic affairs (Valencia
  summit)   184

Kagan, R.   170, 202
kahlouche (swarthy)   66
Kant, Immanuel   37, 39
Karakasidou, A.   79, 80
Kars   151
Kemal Ataturk, Mustafa   140, 152,
  179

Kemalism   138, 141, 152, 157
Kemalist nationalism   139–40, 158
Kenna, Margaret   75, 78–9
Khaddafi, Muammar   48
Khaldoun, Ibn   114
Kili, S.   150–1
Kirkuk   150
Kluckhohn, C.   93
Knesset   202
Kohl, H.   158
Kroeber, A. L.   93, 98–100
Kurdistan   151
Kurds   142, 150, 152–3, 159–60
Kuvva-i Milliye   152
Kuwait   122

Lacarrière, Jacques   77
Laeken   42
Lagos   54
Laroui, A.   99–102
Latin American clandestines   53
Latvia   15
Lausanne Treaty   152
Le Monde   46, 207
Lebanon   15, 16, 46, 150, 200, 224
Lebanon's Palestinians   124–33
  collective identity and   126–7
  nationality   124–6
  post-war illusions   127–9
  present situation of   129–32
Lectures on the Revolution (Peker)   145
legal clandestine asylum-seekers   44–5
Lévi-Strauss, C.   4, 94–6, 98–9
Leviathan, the state as   147
Lewis, B.   92–3, 97, 103, 150
Libya   47–8, 129, 200, 202
  migratory routes and   52, 55–8,
    60–2, 65–8
L'Identité culturelle de l'Islam (von
    Grunebaum)   102
Likud   189, 202
Lisbon   121
Lithuania   15
'local universalisms'   41
LOLF (law on financing public
    administrations)   44
London   121
L'Orientalisme (Said)   73, 103
Lowie, R.   94

Macedonia, Greek   79
Machrek   162, 175
Madama   61
Madrid   121
  bombings   1, 89
  conference   219, 221
Mafia   36, 54, 161
Maghreb   36, 162, 175, 207, 214, 222
  -European links   216
  migratory routes and   51–9, 62–3,
    67–8
  and 'other'   64–7
Makus Talih   141
Mali   47, 55, 60, 61
Malta   46, 176, 190, 203, 212, 221
Maras   151
Marcus, G.   76
Mardin   151
mare nostrum   173–6, 199
Marshall, Thomas   39
Marx, K.   101
Massenet, Michel   38
Mauritania   175
Mazzella, Sylvie   3
Med-10   **16, 18, 24, 25**
  defined   11
MEDA programme   201
media coverage of Islam   88–93
  clash of civilisations   91–3
Mehmed the Conqueror   139–40
Meier, Daniel   5
Melilla   30, 47
Menderes, A.   139
Mercosur   167, 168, 169
Mesopotamia   151
Messianism   163
Mexico   35, 38
Middle East   31, 99, 162–3, 177, 207,
    217, 219
  see also 'Greater Middle East'
Middle East Partnership Initiative (US)
    198
migratory routes *see* Sahara
military regime 1967–74 (Greek)   75,
    78, 84n
Ministry of the Displaced (Lebanon)
    127
Ministry of Foreign Affairs (France)
    216

Ministry of Foreign Affairs (Libya)
    59
Ministry of the Interior (France)   57
'missionary struggle'   152
Mohammed, Prophet   98, 139
Mohammed VI, King   216
Moldavia   36
Mondros treaty   149–51
Morice, Alain   45
Morocco   36, 46–8, 122, 200
    Euro-Mediterranean Partnership
        (EMP) and   163, 188, 207, 216,
        222
    migratory routes and   56, 59–60,
        65–7
mortality   16–17
Mosul   150
Motherland Party   155
Mu'awiya   119
Mudafaa-i Hukuk-u Osmaniye Cemiyeti
    151
'mules'   62–4, 130
multilateralisation   166, 182–6
Muslims   90, 142, 150, 201, 205
    African   64
    anti-Muslim sentiments   98
    Euro-Mediterranean Partnership
        (EMP) and   163, 168, 209, 214,
        215
    identity and   118–20, 122–3, 156–9
    see also Islam
Mustafa Kemal Pasha *see* Ataturk,
    Kemal
mutuality   189

Naba refugee camp   128
Nablus   150
Naples   188, 211
'National Doctrine' parties   157
National Forces (Turkish army)   152
National Movement (Lebanon)   127
nationalism   74–5, 121–3, 139,
    160–1
    nationalist conservatism   141–3
Nationalist Action Party   155
nationality   124–6
'native anthropology'   74, 77
Near East   31
'neighbours'   209–14

EU policy   175
    politics of   224
Neolithic   98
Netherlands   15
New Turkey Party   155
New York   1
Nicolaïdis, Dimitri   6
Nicolaïdis, Kalypso   6
Nietzsche, F.   114
Niger   47, 55, 56, 60–1, 62
Nigeria   54, 56
Noiriel, Gérard   42, 45
non-governmental organisations
    (NGOs)   68, 210
'normative power'   162
North Africa   13, 36, 45, 48, 199,
    204
    cosmopolitanism and   67–9
    migratory routes and   51, 53,
        55–66
    Ottoman territories   144
North America   43
North American Free Trade
    Agreements (NAFTA)   35
North Korea   203
North–South relations   48, 124,
    132
northern Europe   178
Northern-7   18, **19**, 20
    defined   15
Nye, J.   170

Occident   65, 82, 123
    collective identity and   90, 92,
        96–8, 101–6, 108
    Euro-Mediterranean Partnership
        (EMP) and   163, 172, 175, 179,
        180, 219
Occupied Territories   202
Ogien, Albert   45
Organisation for Security and
    Cooperation in Europe (OSCE)
    164, 168
Orient   73, 97–8, 102, 105–7, 179
'Oriental' culture   189
Orientalism   99, 101–3, 108, 225
Orientalism (Said)   73, 103
Oslo accords   128–9, 219, 221
'other'   73, 76, 82, 103

'other'   (*continued*)
  Euro-Mediterranean Partnership
      (EMP) and   172, 174, 191, 208,
      225
    Maghreb and   64–7
    Turkey and *öteki*   139–41
  Ottoman Empire   122, 125, 178
    Greek identity and   73, 76, 79–80,
        82–3
    Turkish conservatism and   139,
        140–5, 149–53, 159
Oualalou, F.   210
Ouargla   66
oulémas (theologians)   89, 120
Ozal, T.   140

Pakistan   43, 122
Palestine   15, 36, 46, 150, 202
  Euro-Mediterranean Partnership
      (EMP) and   163, 177, 219, 223
  see also Israeli-Palestinian relations;
      Lebanon's Palestinians
Palestine Liberation Organisation
    (PLO)   126–7
Paris   121
*Partnership for Progress and a Commom
    Future with the Region of the
    Broader Middle East and North
    Africa* (G8)   197–8
'Paths of Hunger, Paths of Fear'
    (Zolberg)   43
Patten, C.   200, 204, 207
Peker, R.   145–6
Pentagon   163
Perrin, D.   43
Phoenicia   178
pieds noir   199
Piette, A.   106
Pisani, E.   209
Platonism   114
Poland   15, 31, 34, 45, 222
Pompidou, Georges   38
population
  'pyramids'   17, 20
  trends   12–13, 22–5, **24, 25**
Portugal   15, 31, 39, 167
'positive engagement'   203
primitive forces (*açabiya*)   114, 119
Private Enterprise Development
    Facility   198

Prodi, Romano   46, 207, 211–12,
    215
Prophet Mohammed   98, 139
Protestant religion   68
Ptolemy   105
Pythagoras   115

racism   66–7
Radcliffe-Brown, A. E.   94
Réa, Andréa   63
Red Brigades   205
Reform Decree (1856)   143–4
Refugees, High Commission on   43
'regional security partnership'   168
'reinforced cooperation'   208
rejectionism   158
'religious reaction'   138
Renan, E.   97
'repression recruits'   59
Republican People's Party (RPP)   155
research approaches   103–8
Rio Grande   35
Rodinson, M.   103
Roman (Byzantine) Empire   142
Roman Catholicism   68
Romania   31, 34, 36
Roy, O.   103
Rumeli   142
Russia   17, 73, 140, 144, 207, 219
'safe management' of borders   212
Sahara   51–69
  cosmopolitanism in   67–9
  divide   57–8
  globalisation: intercontinental links
      and 52–5; repressed spatial
      modes and   55–6
  as holding zone   59–62
  identity front-lines   64–7
  lines of demarcation 56–7:
      confrontation and 62–4
  zone   48
Said, E.   73, 90–1, 96, 99, 103, 181
Saïda refugee camp   130
salafi characteristics   89
Samsun   151
San Remo conference (1920)   125
Sangatte   30
Sapir, E.   94
'Saracens'   88
Sarkozy, Nicolas   57–8

Sassanide Empire   115
Saudi Arabia   122, 200
Scandinavia   20
Schengen
    accords   30, 32, 34
    region   38, 52, 53
    space   59–62, 209, 214–15
Schengen Information System (SIS)
    31
Schopenhauer, A.   91
Schulze, R.   114
Sea Island, Georgia   197–8
Sebha   56
Second World War   12, 25, 74, 75,
    142–3, 219
'second-hand world'   91
'secondary belongings'   174
'secure communities'   164, 172,
    178
Seljuks   142
'sentinel outposts'   58
Sephardic Jews   189
Serbian militias   90
Serbs   178
Seville   30, 42, 48
    2002 EU summit   58
Sèvres syndrome   137, 141–3,
    159–60
    'deep historical memory'   149–52
    'deep policy'   152–3
    public attitudes   153–5, **153**, **154**
Sèvres, Treaty of   144
sex *see* age-sex structure
sharia   89
Shaw, E. K.   150–1
Shaw, S. J.   150–1
Shiites   119–20, 122, 127
Sicilian Islands   30
Six Day War (June 1967)   126
Skopetea, E.   76, 83
slavery   63–4, 65–7
Slavists   140
Slovakia   15
Slovenia   15
'social engineering'   158
socialism   122
Solena, J.   207
Sophists   114
South America   41
South-East Asia   31

South-Eastern Europe   73–4, 75, 168,
    169
Southern Europe   15, 18–20, 22, 31,
    32
    closing borders   35–7
Southern-4   18, **19**, 20
    defined   15
Soviet Union   16, 73, 103, 181,
    200
Spain   15, 21, 58, 202
    Euro-Mediterranean Partnership
        (EMP) and   163, 168, 185
    immigration/asylum and   31, 36,
        46–7
Spengler, O.   92, 105
Straits of Constantinople   150–1
sub-Saharan Africa   30, 47–8, 51, 52,
    55, 57
Suez Canal   199
Sufism   120
Suleiman the Magnificent   139–40
Sunnis   119–20
Sunset of Dawn (Skopetea)   76
Sweden   15, 186, 188
Switzerland   214
synchronic approach   93–5, 109n
Syria   15, 46, 150–1, 200, 224
    Lebanon and   127, 128, 130
Syrians   178

Taëf accords (1989)   128
Talat Pasha   150
Talib, Ali Ibn Abi   119
Tall e-Zaatar refugee camp   128
Tamanrasset   56, 61, 64, 66
Tampere summit   33, 42
'Tanzimat Mentality' (*Tanzimat Kafasi*)
    140
Tanzimat syndrome   137, 140,
    141–3, 159–60
    'deep historical memory'   143–6
    'deep policy'   146–7
    rights and freedoms   147–9, **148**
'tempo effect'   22
theologians (*oulémas*)   89, 120
'theologocentrism'   103
Thessalonica   30, 42
Thrace   150–1
time zones and identity   121–3
Tin Zouatin   60

Todd, E.   92
total fertility rate (TFR)   13–15, **14**
Toynbee, A.   97, 105
traffic (*trabendo*)   36
Trakya Pasaeli Cemiyeti   151
Triaud, J.-L.   99
Tripoli   59, 66
Tristes Tropiques (Lévi-Strauss)   98
True Path Party   155
Tuareg village   61
Tuaregs   55, 62, 66–7, 68
Tumu   61
Tunis summit (2004)   207
Tunisia   15, 18, 36, 46–7, 67, 200
    Euro-Mediterranean Partnership
        (EMP) and   178, 188, 222
Turanist nationalism   139
Turcosceptic Christian Democratic
        parties   160
Turcoscepticism   158, 159
Turk-Islam Sentezi   139
Turkey   15, 122, 188, 202
    Euro-Mediterranean Partnership
        (EMP) and   175, 179, 188, 212,
        216, 221
    identity and   73, 79, 88
    immigration/asylum and   32, 36,
        46, 47
    see also Turkish conservatism
Turkic empires   139
Turkish conservatism   137–61
    future of   159–61
    Islam and   155–9
    major variants of   138–41
    Sèvres syndrome 141–3: 'deep
        historical memory' 149–52;
        'deep policy' 152–3; public
        attitudes   153–5, **153**, **154**
    Tanzimat syndrome 141–3: 'deep
        historical memory' 143–6; 'deep
        policy' 146–7; rights and
        freedoms   147–9, **148**
'Turkish-Islamic Synthesis'   139
Turkist/Turanist nationalism   139
Tyr refugee camp   130

Ukraine   31
United Kingdom (UK)   15, 18, 42,
        185, 222

immigration and   30, 32–3
    see also Britain
United Nations Educational, Scientific
        and Cultural Organisation
        (UNESCO)   94–5
United Nations Relief and Works
        Agency (UNRWA)   125, 126, 129
United Nations (UN)   15, 22, 29, 176
    Resolution 1559   224
United States of America (USA)   23,
        35, 38, 125
    collective identity and   90, 96, 99
    Euro-Mediterranean Partnership
        (EMP) and 163, 186, 207,
        216–17: reformulating
        219–20, 222–4
    see also 'Greater' Middle East
United States Census Bureau (USCB)
        21, 22–3
Universal Declaration of Human
        Rights (1948)   37, 43
universalism   41, 97
Urfa   151

Valencia summit (2002)   171, 184,
        210–11
value conflicts *see* identity crises and
        value conflicts
Vatin, J.-C.   103
Venice Declaration of the EC   202
Veyne, P.   106
*Vilayat-i Sarkiyye Mudafaa-i Hukuk
        Cemiyeti*   151
Visegrad group   167–8
Vlores   35
Volkgeist   97, 105
von Grunebaum, G.   99–100, 101

Wacquant, Loïc   44
wahhabi characteristics   89
'Wardrobe Westernism'   140
Warsaw   188
'we, the' (*biz*)   139–41
'we-ness' (*bizlik*)   139
Weber, M.   97
West European states   140
Western Europe   16, 26, 42
westernisation   140
    without the West   152–3

'Wider Europe' 163–4, 169, 172
  vs *mare nostrum* 173–6
Wilson, Chris 2
World Trade Center 163
World War One 144, 149, 152
World War Two 12, 25, 74, 75,
  142–3, 219
Wright-Mills, C. 91

Yilmaz, Hakan 5
Yogoslav war 75
Young Ottomans 145
Young Turks 141
Yugoslavia 43, 81, 177

'zero immigration' 33
Zolberg, Aristide 43